THE IMPOSSIBLE HAS HAPPENED

The life and work of Gene Roddenberry Creator of Star Trek

A biography

By Lance Parkin

Aurum
Press

First published in Great Britain in 2016 by Aurum Press, an imprint of The Quarto Group
The Old Brewery
6 Blundell Street
London
N7 9BH
www.QuartoKnows.com

This paperback edition first published in 2017 by Aurum Press.

A catalogue record for this book is available from the British Library.

ISBN 9781781314470

eBook ISBN 9781781314821

2021 2020 2019 2018 2017

10 9 8 7 6 5 4 3 2 1

Typeset in Spectrum by SX Composing DTP, Rayleigh, Essex
Printed and bound by CPI Group (UK) Ltd, Croydon, CR0 4YY

THE IMPOSSIBLE
HAS HAPPENED

LANCE PARKIN is a writer of fiction and non-fiction best known for his Doctor Who work, such as *Cold Fusion*, *Ahistory* and *The Eyeless*. He has worked as a TV storyliner, and written articles for *SFX*, *Star Trek Magazine* and *Doctor Who Magazine*. He is the author and co-author of books such as a guide to the J.J. Abrams series *Alias*, *Dark Matters*, a study of the *His Dark Materials* series by Philip Pullman, and of *Magic Words: The Extraordinary Life of Alan Moore*, a biography of the graphic novelist, also published by Aurum.

The author wishes to thank Amy Absher, Brad Ricca,
Brandy Schillace, Donald Gillikin, Eddie Robson, Edward Nelson,
Jim Cooray Smith, Joe Murray, Lars Pearson, Lisa Nielson,
Mark Clapham, Paul Simpson, Petra Clark, Sam Harrison.

My editor Jennifer Barr and my agent Jessica Papin.
Mark Jones
And Brie and Reuben Parkin.

"Beware of getting too wrapped up in The Wonder Of It All. The quality of a SF tale is usually inversely proportionate to the pretension a writer brings to it."

Gene Roddenberry, from the writer/director
guide for the *Star Trek II* television series

Contents

INTRODUCTION

Gene Roddenberry died on October 24, 1991, a few weeks after the twenty-fifth anniversary of the first broadcast of *Star Trek*. He was only a couple of months past his seventieth birthday, but he had been frail for a long time, and he knew he was dying. His death came at a high water mark for the franchise, when both a hugely popular television series and a very successful series of movies were in production. To celebrate the show's silver anniversary, the TV series *Star Trek: The Next Generation* aired the two-part story "Unification," which brought together Captain Picard and Mr. Spock in a full-scale crossover of the old and new shows. The following month saw the release of *Star Trek VI: The Undiscovered Country*, a movie designed as a capstone for the adventures of Captain Kirk's crew.

"Unification" and *The Undiscovered Country* both included a caption dedicating the project to Roddenberry. Studio publicity stressed that before his death, the creator of *Star*

Trek had seen the rough edits of both the TV episode and the movie, and had liked what he'd seen.

The publicity didn't mention that Roddenberry had long been locked out of the running of both the movie series and *The Next Generation*, and that the notes he'd given the production teams had been all but totally ignored. The studio may not have known that, in fact, he'd returned from viewing *Star Trek VI* and—forty-eight hours before he died—instructed his lawyer to start legal action to have fifteen minutes of material cut from the movie.[1]

Gene Roddenberry, the man, polarized people. William Shatner and Leonard Nimoy, who played Captain Kirk and Mr. Spock, quickly fell out with him over business issues— or as Shatner put it, "He was a chiseler who wanted a cut of outside money his cast earned, demanded to be called master, and prohibited poor Nimoy from using a company pencil."[2] Roddenberry battled substance abuse. He sexually harassed his secretaries, and he didn't just cheat on his wives, he cheated on his mistresses. Despite that, many of his friends, colleagues and family members remained consistently loyal to and protective of him. From the early days of *Star Trek* until today, there have been fans who treat him, his work, and his memory with a reverence usually reserved for the leaders of revolutions.

In 1994, two hefty biographies of Roddenberry were published: *Star Trek Creator* by David Alexander, and *Gene Roddenberry: The Myth and the Man Behind Star Trek* by Joel Engel. The official and unauthorized versions respectively, there are times when they don't seem to be describing the same man. It is possible, as Alexander and Engel demonstrate over and over, to spin the same anecdote to portray Roddenberry as a saint or a monster. One man's "money grubbing" is another man's "fighting for his fair share." An early episode of the original series, "The Enemy Within," sees Kirk split into two personalities—an ineffective, caring type and a scheming, ravenous beast. It's tempting to view Roddenberry as such a Jekyll and Hyde character.

It's clear, though, that Gene Roddenberry was no such thing. His personality was extremely consistent for most of his life; indeed, when he started suffering mood swings a couple of years before his death, those closest to him understood it as a symptom of his failing health. You can refuse to compromise your principles *and* be a boorish, hypocritical jerk.

The fiftieth anniversary marks the point where *Star Trek* has run longer since Gene Roddenberry's death than while he was alive. Six *Star Trek* movies were made in his lifetime; seven have now been made since his death. In terms of television episodes, that milestone was passed nearly twenty years ago. *Star Trek* has lasted so long that we can now watch the series on devices that make Kirk and Picard's computers and personal communication devices look rather clunky.

Three television series—*Star Trek: Deep Space Nine* (1993–9), *Star Trek: Voyager* (1995–2001), and *Star Trek: Enterprise* (2001–5) —have come and gone, as have four movies featuring the *Star Trek: The Next Generation* cast (1994–2002). In 2009, the movie series was relaunched with an (almost) all-new cast playing Kirk, Spock, and company. The three movies—*Star Trek* (2009), *Star Trek Into Darkness* (2013), and *Star Trek Beyond* (2016)—have made a great deal of money at the box office. And 2017 will see a new *Star Trek* television series. While plenty of Sixties shows have been revived, rebooted, or relaunched, on television or for the cinema, it's hard to think of another American TV drama with anything like the enduring appeal of *Star Trek*. It's hard to say which show even comes second.

One candidate is *Mission: Impossible*. The comparison was not flattering for *Star Trek* at first. In many ways, they were sister shows. They were made by the same studio, Desilu—*Star Trek* on sound stages 8 and 9, *Mission: Impossible* on stages 6 and 7; their production offices were both in the "E" building, *Star Trek*'s on the first floor, *Mission: Impossible*'s upstairs on the second. They debuted the same month (September 1966). According to one studio executive *Mission: Impossible* got four times as many viewers.[3] *Star Trek* ended up running for three seasons and seventy-nine episodes, *Mission: Impossible* for seven seasons and 171. There were, at first, more *Mission: Impossible* books, comics, and toys, and the show gained more newspaper and magazine coverage. When *Star Trek* ended, Leonard Nimoy joined the *Mission: Impossible* cast, and it was seen as a considerable promotion. *Mission: Impossible* was a show with a bona fide African-American lead character, a show that dealt directly with contemporary political and social issues without the need to use analogy. *Mission: Impossible*'s afterlife is impressive—most people could hum the theme tune, and remember the rubber masks and the self-destructing tapes. "Your mission, if you choose to accept it" is a catchphrase that's seeped into the popular consciousness. The show was revived for television in the Eighties, and more successfully, of course, as a film series starring Tom Cruise that's now run for twenty years and counting (1996–).

Clearly, though, *Star Trek* has had a more successful afterlife. So why did *Star Trek*, out of all the American TV shows of the Sixties, become such a phenomenon? And where does Gene Roddenberry figure in the answer to that question?

The root of *Star Trek*'s success is that on a week-by-week basis, it delivered some really good episodes of television, ones that many people can rewatch almost endlessly. When they describe the show, *Star Trek* fans occasionally drift into a parallel universe where it was the only show that dared to tackle social issues or other difficult topics, had a multi-racial cast, inspired a devoted fan following, or was revived due to public demand. Gene Roddenberry encouraged people to think *Star Trek* always stood out, but this is clearly untrue.

Every artistic venture that's the work of many hands generates arguments about what the magic ingredients were, and who deserves credit for coming up with them. Gene Roddenberry would portray himself, at times, as the sole creative force on *Star Trek*. But some of the most popular things about *Star Trek* happened despite Roddenberry, not because of him. He was frequently frustrated when directors like Nicholas Meyer, or actors like William Shatner or

Leonard Nimoy, persuaded the studio to adopt their ideas and priorities over Roddenberry's. He actively hated the second movie, *The Wrath of Khan*, seeing many aspects of it as a betrayal of the concept. He firmly believed Patrick Stewart was the wrong man to play Jean-Luc Picard. When he was left to his own devices, Roddenberry's version of *Star Trek* could be drab, pompous, and slow-moving: we see this demonstrated with the original pilot, "The Cage" (1965), *Star Trek: The Motion Picture* (1979), and the first season of *Star Trek: The Next Generation* (1987).[4]

The very least generous assessment of Roddenberry's contribution, though, is that he created the basic framework for *Star Trek*, and then was a key member of the team of writers, directors, actors, artists, and designers, assembled by himself, who brilliantly and efficiently established a memorable future of primary colors, beautiful women, bizarre creatures, and big ideas. *Star Trek* does have an X factor that distinguishes it from similar shows, and a lot of what makes it unique can fairly be described as "Gene Roddenberry's philosophy for the show." This by itself would be an enviable legacy for a writer.

Part of the reason *Star Trek* caught on, surely, is that the show was full of repetition, imitable moments, dialogue repeated so often it became a catchphrase. Fifty years on, it's hard to imagine that there was ever a time when people didn't know what "beaming up" was or that Vulcans have pointy ears and behave logically, no one had heard the words "phaser," "photon torpedo," "tricorder," "tractor beam," "warp engine," or "Klingon." These all had to be introduced to the audience. Each had to be carefully articulated and reinforced to the point that it became familiar rather than bizarre.

Gene Roddenberry would gloss this as representing his keenness to stick to "scientific fact," and to root the series in things astronomers and physicists were talking about. It's not a line that survives contact with the show itself for long—some of the "science" is borderline gibberish. The very first bridge scene of Kirk's first episode manages to include the ship passing through "the barrier at the edge of the galaxy," a discussion of ESP, Kirk ordering "neutralize warp" and "gravitation on automatic," and a man's eyes turning silver because he's been struck by weird lightning. But Roddenberry did ensure that the show stuck to its own rules, that it didn't (on the whole) cheat its audience or pull some magical solution out of its hat.

Every *Star Trek* fan worth their salt can tell you that the precise phrase "beam me up, Scotty" was never used in the original series . . . but the procedure for the transporter followed strict rules, and every episode portrayed it ritualistically. We'd see Captain Kirk get onto the platform with his landing party, he'd issue the command "Energize," the operator (often, but by no means always Mr. Scott) would slide a control, a certain noise would start up, we'd see the shimmering golden "transporter effect." We'd cut to a weird alien landscape, we'd hear the same noise and see the same transporter effect, and the actors would suddenly be standing on that alien planet. Kirk would flip open his communicator and let those remaining on the ship know he'd arrived safely. Then the adventure could start. Kids could play-act this sequence, or write or draw their own stories, using a clear template. Older viewers could identify fellow fans by casually dropping references into their conversations.

Star Trek initially ran for three years. In the end, NBC made the simple decision that a different show could appeal more efficiently to viewers. Roddenberry railed against this, so it's worth looking at what the network put on in its place. The first season of *Star Trek* aired in the 8:30–9:30 Thursday night slot. It was moved to Fridays the following year, and its old slot was taken by *Ironside*, featuring Raymond Burr as a wheelchair-bound detective, which went on to run for eight seasons (and has itself been revived). There's no convincing argument that the network were crazy to make that decision.

In 1969, then, *Star Trek* had come and gone. Gene Roddenberry had an idea for a TV show, it ran for three years, it ended. There were plenty of people who created television shows in the Sixties. Many, in all honesty, created ones with larger audiences and better production values. Network television is extremely competitive, it has few slots for shows, network executives want to find the next big thing and aren't sentimental about cutting their losses. Shows come and go.

So . . . how *did Star Trek* come to rise above the pack?

The show found its audience a couple of years after it was canceled, in "syndication"—when the seventy-nine episodes made between 1966 and 1969 were repeated across America by local television stations, often five days a week in the early evening. Likeminded viewers watching those repeats began coalescing into local fan clubs, which began connecting up to other groups. *Star Trek* fans started showing up to science fiction conventions, and when some SF fans became a little snooty about the new arrivals, *Star Trek* fans began organizing events dedicated solely to celebrating their show. Many of these were huge, attracting five-figure crowds that could overwhelm the organizers and venue owners.

The show, like most shows, had received letters when it was being broadcast from people who enjoyed it, who were inspired by it, who fantasized about meeting the characters, or who just wanted to thank the people who'd made it for cheering them up when they were down. With most shows, correspondence usually died down fairly soon after the show had ended. Roddenberry was aware that syndication had brought a new influx of fan letters, but again this was perfectly normal. By 1972, he had chanced upon the *Star Trek* conventions. He was astonished to find himself being cheered and applauded by thousands of people, to be lauded as the creator of something unique and inspiring.

It was now that Roddenberry did something unprecedented, and that *Star Trek* became the phenomenon we're familiar with. He saw the nascent fandom forming around the show, and deliberately nurtured it by creating the story of the making of *Star Trek*, a narrative just as elaborate as the space saga that encompassed the Romulan War, the

Organian Treaty, and the age of Surak. Roddenberry spun a yarn about the production of the show, the goals he had while making it, and the fights he had with NBC to maintain the integrity of his work. In many places, this myth of the show bears very little resemblance to what actually happened.

Key to the legend was the idea that *Star Trek* was a "failure" on first broadcast. Early fans, egged on by Roddenberry, concluded that the show was just too smart for television, and that the "network executives" were risk-averse ignoramuses who wanted to dumb everything down, or perhaps the method of calculating ratings was fundamentally flawed. Wherever the fault lay, this argument ran, the truth was that *Star Trek* was ahead of its time, dangerous, "too cerebral" for network television, and its fans were therefore particularly insightful people. Unsurprisingly, *Star Trek* fans lapped up this version of events, coming to see the show's cancelation as fundamentally unjust, a wrong that had to be righted.

Star Trek was not a huge success on first broadcast, but the truth of the matter isn't very dramatic. Shown on NBC, it did OK in the ratings, but not spectacularly. It was a show that was relatively expensive to make—while heroic efforts were made to send the *Enterprise* to planets where people replicated periods in Earth history (and so existing props and costumes could be used), every episode also included many optical and model effects. NBC were initially minded to end *Star Trek* at the end of its second season (in spring 1968), but were persuaded to bring it back for one more year, after a letter-writing campaign by fans. Tellingly, Roddenberry was replaced as producer, and a number of key writers left with him. Equally tellingly, everyone involved felt the last season saw a drop in quality. The series ended in June 1969, a month before the first moon landing.

Shows had a natural life cycle and weren't expected to last forever. *Lost in Space* and *Batman* were both huge hits, but only lasted three seasons. *The Man from U.N.C.L.E.* lasted four. Television executives were constantly hunting for the next big thing, just as they do now. Gene Roddenberry didn't think he'd be working on *Star Trek* for the rest of his life, and was coming up with pitches for new shows even as he worked on the series.

Many of the viewers who found the show in syndication were hungry for more. Over the course of seventy-nine episodes, the lore of the show built up. There were a handful of recurring guest characters; there were references back to previous stories. We learned a little more every time we met the Vulcans, Klingons, and Romulans. Like the Sherlock Holmes stories, like Tolkien's Middle Earth, or the pantheons of superheroes of the Marvel and DC universes, the world of *Star Trek* was more than the sum of its parts. Fans soaked up this information, memorized it, filled notebooks with lists, typed up their thoughts, and published fanzines. Their knowledge became almost a form of currency in *Star Trek* fan circles. There was soon enough material to fill any number of books about the episodes, the planets and their inhabitants, the future history, and the technology. Blueprints, star charts, and catalogs of starships were published. *Star Trek* fans were able to buy encyclopedic volumes listing every aspect of the show's fictional universe. There were soon even technical manuals spelling out exactly how to build a phaser, transporter, or warp core.

Star Trek rewarded attentive viewers. A great deal of the background went unexplained in the series. If you watched closely, you could infer, for example, that blue Starfleet uniforms were worn by science and medical people, that the infamous "redshirts" were worn by security men and engineers. Other things were (for a long time, at least) ineffable mysteries. What was James T. Kirk's middle name? What was the precise meaning of the NCC-1701 registration number borne by USS *Enterprise*? While we're on the subject, what did "USS" stand for? Fans could have fun arguing about these, or speculating how a Vulcan man and a human woman could possibly have a child, or why the Federation didn't use cloaking devices like the Romulans did.

More significant, though, a lot of the energy of early *Star Trek* fandom focused on what *hadn't* been shown in the television series. Clearly, there was room for new *Star Trek* stories. A show that could go to any planet, tell tales that were tense thrillers one week, murder mysteries the next, and out-and-out comedies the week after, had the potential to run and run. In reality, while the third season included some striking episodes, many betrayed a sense of diminishing returns. The budget had been cut, and a lot more of the action took place on the *Enterprise* itself. The show was starting to look tired.

The fans engaged more imaginatively with the show than the production team had. They started to consider what might have happened next to the planets the *Enterprise* crew had just freed from tyranny, or to guest characters who'd briefly visited the ship. Distinct strains of fan fiction emerged, reflecting the psyches of early *Star Trek* fans.

There were far deeper issues which the original TV series touched on, but left all but unexplored. Fans were fascinated with, say, Uhura, a beautiful black woman who served as a bridge officer. This was a powerful statement at a point in American history when racial tensions had boiled over. Uhura was clearly an inspiration and role model for black viewers, and for women and girls. But the problem was . . . Uhura never really got to do very much except tell Captain Kirk that hailing frequencies were open. She, like Sulu, never even had a first name.

The way Gene Roddenberry told it, it was a fight even to put an African-American face on screen, and the studio were constantly cutting her lines. There is at least some evidence that in Uhura's case this is true. Roddenberry, though, toured the convention circuit in the Seventies telling fans that, yes, of course Uhura had potential, and her mere presence was a powerful statement that he fought tooth and nail to preserve. It was a line that gained wild applause at conventions. When he had the chance to redress the balance ten years after the TV series ended, as co-writer and producer of *Star Trek: The Motion Picture*, Uhura was given . . . thirty-seven lines in the whole movie. She's not in shot for twelve of them, and six are "Aye, sir."

In the decade between *Star Trek*'s last television show and its revival as a movie, as fans came to explore this world in their fan fiction and essays, a consensus view of *Star Trek* emerged. Initially, the conclusion was that the show was appealing because it was sexy, a little dangerous. This soon broadened into the idea that *Star Trek* was progressive. At a time when prominent idealistic politicians were being gunned down, when civil rights campaigns were exposing structural inequalities and certain groups were seriously advocating a race war, when the US Army was bogged down in Vietnam, and where an atomic war between America and the Soviet Union looked inevitable, *Star Trek* portrayed a tolerant, rational, meritocratic, secular, scientific society. As the civil rights movements of the Sixties passed from current headlines of protests and riots to a folk memory of old battles won and lost, *Star Trek* fans began to present their show as a bellwether of those turbulent times. The series now represented an endgame to the idealism of those movements. In the future blacks, whites, Asians, men and women, Russians, and Americans would all work together for the common aim of exploration and discovery. They would come in peace, without prejudice, and wouldn't impose their views on others. Advanced technology would allow all material needs to be met and, freed from the material needs of the past, a generous, tolerant society would emerge.

This, though, is a far more idealized world than the one depicted in the series itself. The original *Star Trek* television show is optimistic, it's inclusive, but it's not explicitly utopian. We see a few officers on one ship, out on the frontier. Nichelle Nichols, who played Lieutenant Uhura, forcefully reminded the writers that Starfleet was the spiritual successor to NASA, not the US Air Force. Gene Roddenberry's preferred analogy was that his Starfleet was more like the Coast Guard than the Navy, but in practice the *Enterprise* we see is essentially doing the sort of things a US Navy patrol would do in the Pacific in the Fifties and Sixties (Roddenberry had served in the Air Force). The *Star Trek* universe has seen recent wars, and many in the Federation are in the line of fire of rival space powers, pirates, slavers, disease, and natural disasters. The history of Earth between our time and Kirk's encompasses "the Eugenics Wars," the era of the brutal dictator Colonel Green, and atomic holocaust. The Federation may have utopian ideals, but it's not reached the promised land.

There's an attempt to make sure that not every single crew member we see is a white man, but all but two of the bridge crew are, and the show soon expands the roles of Spock and McCoy at the expense of the rest of the cast. Roddenberry said that he'd originally wanted half the crew of the *Enterprise* to be women. The pilot episode had a female second-in-command, played by Majel Barrett, Roddenberry's future wife (and, at the time, one of his mistresses). When the network demanded changes, she was dropped. In the broadcast show, Uhura was the only female bridge officer, and the only other regular female characters were Yeoman Rand (dropped after eight episodes) and Nurse Chapel (Majel Barrett again, in fewer than a third of the episodes). The uniforms in the pilot episode were unisex, with the women wearing trousers. The series, famously, put the women in very short skirts, makeup and elaborate hairstyles. There's little evidence to suggest that the future portrayed in the original series had seen much progress for gender equality.

Many of *Star Trek*'s early fans were women and teenage girls. The few years between the cancelation of the series and its initial success in syndication saw an explosion in the women's liberation movement. *Star Trek* might easily, and with justification, have been condemned as a show in which scantily clad women took on mainly subservient roles, so serving as an example of everything that was wrong with the portrayal of women in television drama. Instead, fans of the show began extrapolating the future of the feminist movement, bringing in readings of the show informed by novelists like Ursula Le Guin. A secular, meritocratic world where women were sexually liberated, and could be scientists and explorers, became a vision of a galaxy where the battles of feminism had been won. In other words, *Star Trek*'s young, thoughtful, creative audience had recast the show as something far more interesting than the television series had ever portrayed.

Gene Roddenberry was a fairly shameless self-mythologizer. In "candid" interviews conducted by close colleagues, even during private conversations with intimate friends, he repeated claims that he must have known weren't true. The creator of *Star Trek* told fans in the Seventies that they were very clever for spotting what he'd done: the show wasn't escapist adventure with a dash of optimism for a future powered by technological progress which occasionally dabbled with light political analogies, it was a vehicle for conveying complex humanist values with an important message for our times, disguised as space opera because that was the only way to get such powerful political messages onto network television.

When he came to create *Star Trek: The Next Generation* in the mid-Eighties, Roddenberry insisted that the show was utopian, that every detail had to support a vision of a future where humanity had solved its problems—not just its technological, but its social problems. Somewhat to the annoyance of some of his other writers, the new *Enterprise* crew never argued among themselves, they gathered around a conference table and agreed on a course of action. The ship had a counselor, who sat at the captain's side on the bridge and offered advice about the psychology of the aliens they encountered. The Klingons were now allies, the crew brought their families along, the women wore trousers, now—and (for a few episodes, at least) some of the men wore miniskirts.

It would be very tempting for a new biography of Gene Roddenberry to try to triangulate between the true visionary and secular saint of David Alexander's authorized biography and the irredeemably flawed human being who only ever had one good idea depicted in Joel Engel's unauthorized account. The "official" version is that Roddenberry's true intent was revealed only when it was freed from the imperatives of network television; the "unauthorized" reading is that *Star Trek* fans took an old show and injected elements that elevated it into something remarkable, and Roddenberry was able to swoop in, say that had been the plan all along, and demand his cut.

But there's another way to look at Gene Roddenberry. As *Star Trek* endured (and his subsequent projects floundered or outright flopped), Roddenberry naturally began to ask himself why this one show had sparked such passion in its fans. It was a question he'd never had the time to consider while he was making the show. Roddenberry listened to the fans, compared *Star Trek* to the other science fiction around it. The answer he formulated was that the appeal of the show was its idealism: it was progressive, it looked to the future, it saw humanity maturing. It had a very simple, very powerful message, one that's surprisingly uncommon in science fiction: the future can be better than the present.

As numerous people, friends and foes, would note, there was a massive discrepancy between the selfless future envisioned by *Star Trek* and the way Eugene Wesley Roddenberry lived his life. He dreamed of a future free of personal jealousy, but needed to jostle to be the alpha male both professionally and privately. He had Dr. McCoy advocate holistic treatments and alternative medicine but he himself popped pills and abused cocaine. He said the future would not be materialistic, but the moment he had enough money, he bought a mansion in Bel Air, as well as a new Rolls Royce with the vanity plate GENE R.

Gene Roddenberry knew he wasn't perfect. His creation, he came to understand, gave him the purpose and platform to be a positive force in the world. Just as the fans in minority groups, the kids who were bullied at school for being nerdy, or who felt different, responded to the tolerant, inclusive, purposeful message of *Star Trek*, so too did its creator. By the mid-Seventies, Gene Roddenberry had started to see how *Star Trek* could redeem *him*.

CHAPTER ONE

EARNING HIS STRIPES

Gene Roddenberry created three television series that were made during his lifetime: *The Lieutenant*, *Star Trek*, and *Star Trek: The Next Generation*. He had ideas for plenty more. Many of these made it to at least some form of pilot episode (*The Wild Blue*, *333 Montgomery*/*Defiance County*, *Police Story*, *The Long Hunt of April Savage*, *Assignment: Earth*, *Genesis II*/ *Planet Earth*, *The Questor Tapes*, *Spectre*, *Star Trek II*); many didn't (*The Man from Lloyds*, *Footbeat*, a show set on a cruise ship, *The Tribunes*). Two (*Andromeda* and *Earth: Final Conflict*) became shows after his death and one (*Lost Universe*) became a comics series. But, as it stands, *The Lieutenant* is the one time we get to see Gene Roddenberry creating and running a television show that isn't *Star Trek*.

Eugene Wesley Roddenberry was named after his father and grandfather respectively. Eugene senior had joined the US Army in 1916 and served in France toward the end of the First World War. He was honorably discharged as a private, promoted to sergeant and moved back to El Paso, Texas, where he met his wife and Gene's mother, Glen Goleman, a committed Southern Baptist. Gene, their eldest child, was born on August 19, 1921. Eugene floated between jobs on the railroad, including a spell as a railroad detective, before making his way to Los Angeles where, in 1922, he became a patrolman for the Los Angeles Police Department, a rank he held for twenty years.

The LA that welcomed the Roddenberry family, which now included Gene's younger siblings Robert and Doris, was rapidly expanding. By 1930, the city's population surpassed one million. It was the height of the Great Depression and the era of Prohibition, but neither appears to have adversely affected the family: Eugene senior was fortunate enough to have regular work and, like many, he largely ignored the alcohol ban. Despite or perhaps because of the hard times, it was also an era of escapism. Genre fiction exploded in print, on the radio, and at the movies. Family friends tell of young Gene devouring copies of *Amazing Stories* and *Astounding Stories*, eagerly watching the Larry "Buster" Crabbe Flash Gordon serials and listening intently each week to *The Shadow*, *The Lone Ranger*, and *Buck Rogers* on the radio. Gene entertained an early interest in poetry, joining a writing club at his high school and continuing to write and study literature when time afforded. At the age of eighteen, he entered Los Angeles City College to study the police curriculum. There he met Stanley Sheldon, the LAPD liaison officer attached to the City College, for whom he would work eleven years later. He also met Eileen Rexroat, his future wife.

While studying at City College, Roddenberry heard about the civilian pilot training program, created to build up the country's bank of pilots in full anticipation that the US would eventually be drawn into the war in Europe. He registered and, shortly after his nineteenth birthday, became a fully licenced pilot. A few weeks after he graduated City College in June 1941, Roddenberry became a cadet in the Army Air Corps. Six months later, the Japanese attacked Pearl Harbor and Roddenberry received orders to head to Kelly Field, Texas, for training. He passed the sifting process and entered advanced training, one of the advantages of which was permission to marry. On June 20, 1942, he and Eileen took their vows before the Kelly Field chaplain.[1] Three months later, now with the rank of second lieutenant, he joined the 394th Squadron stationed in Hawaii to fly B-17 bombers.

While Roddenberry could be gregarious, he was something of an intellectual loner and not popular. Young, very tall (six foot three), and good looking, he often spent nights off the base alone and appears to have taken full advantage of the 2,500 miles distance from his new wife. According to Alexander, many of Roddenberry's squadron mates were unaware he was married at the time. (For her part, back at Kelly Field, Eileen was known to pick up cadets while Gene was on duty.)[2]

Roddenberry estimated that, during the war, he flew eighty-nine missions in total, but the records are not accurate and it was most likely more. He narrowly escaped injury several times, notably when he had to abort takeoff as a result of aircraft malfunction.[3] Not long after, the 394th was rotated back to the US and Gene was reunited with Eileen. He never returned to active duty: his skills were needed on home soil as an aircraft accident investigator with the Office of Flying Safety. He was made captain in April 1944. Meanwhile, he began writing in earnest. He enrolled with the University of Miami but a transfer to New York prevented him completing the course; later he studied at Columbia University and wrote poems, one of which was published in *The New York Times*.

Roddenberry was discharged from the Army in July 1945 and joined Pan American World Airlines as a junior commercial pilot—and two years later came closer to death than at any time during the war. On June 18, 1947, he joined Pan Am Flight 121 for the flight from Karachi to Istanbul. His friend Captain Joe Hart was pilot; Roddenberry was off-duty but willing to help out. Flight 121 had experienced numerous mechanical problems en route to Karachi and these continued. The aircraft lost one engine, putting the other three under strain. When a second engine ignited, setting the wing on fire, Hart told Roddenberry to prepare the passengers for the inevitable crash landing. They were flying in the dark over the Syrian desert, miles from the nearest safe landing site, and running out of time. The aircraft crashed into the sand at 2:00 A.M., splitting in two. Those in the forward section who were not killed on impact were burnt to death by ignited aviation fuel. Seated three rows from the back, Roddenberry escaped serious injury and was able to pull passengers from the wreckage with the help of the two remaining Pan Am employees. Seven crew and seven passengers died, and eleven people needed hospital treatment; eight were relatively unharmed. Gene suffered two broken ribs.[4]

Roddenberry recounted the story many times at conventions in the 1970s. Some of the details sound distinctly far-fetched, but many have been verified. Among the passengers were an Indian royal—the Maharani of Pheleton—and her son, whom he personally rescued. Shortly after dawn, the crash site drew the unwanted attention of desert tribesmen who stripped the aircraft of its valuables. Roddenberry set out alone for civilization, tracing the route of telegraph wires to the nearest town and calling the emergency airfield for help. Or a couple of English passengers swam across a river to a light Roddenberry had spotted. Whatever the precise truth, Roddenberry was commended by Pan Am for his swift action and leadership. Three days after the crash, he wrote to his parents that "the real trick of the matter is that everyone performed wonderfully including the badly injured and proved what fine people average human beings are when confronted by a catastrophe involving life and death."[5]

This near-death experience appears to have prompted a change in Roddenberry's outlook. He returned to New Jersey and was reunited with Eileen. Nine months later, their first daughter, Darleen, was born. Within weeks of her birth, he resigned from Pan Am and relocated the family to California. Roddenberry claimed later that they had moved so he could become a television writer. If this is true, it was an odd decision. California was the home of cinema, not television—the majority of television programs were produced in New York, a short distance from where they had been living. Worse still, the movie industry had contracted, flooding the market with scriptwriters and other production staff. Most likely, the young family relocated to be near Darleen's grandparents, all of whom lived in southern California. With no writing work forthcoming, and after a brief unsuccessful period as a sales manager, Roddenberry applied to join the LAPD in January 1949, following his younger brother Robert in the footsteps of their father. He completed basic training and was posted to traffic duty in downtown Los Angeles.

The next year Roddenberry got his first paid writing job, producing press releases for the LAPD. The Public Affairs Division, as it became, was led by Captain Stanley Sheldon, whom Roddenberry had met at Los Angeles City College, and included Don Ingalls, the future writer-producer of *Fantasy Island* and writer of *Star Trek*'s "The Alternative Factor" and "A Private Little War." It was a troubled time for the LAPD, which was consumed by a corruption scandal. William H. Parker, who had worked with Gene's father, was brought in to professionalize the police force and raise the moral standing of officers. Parker established the Association of Professional Law Enforcers; Roddenberry wrote much of its founding code of practice.

Meanwhile—television. Though still in its infancy, the medium was slowly reaching the masses, particularly after NBC broadcast the 1947 World Series. As audiences grew, the demand for programming increased and new series were created, often drawing on movie serials and radio shows for inspiration. One such series that provides a delicious taste of things to come was the children's Saturday afternoon serial *Space Patrol*, which borrowed heavily from Buster Crabbe's *Flash Gordon* and *Buck Rogers* serials. The hero was Buzz Corry, Commander and Chief of United Planets Space Patrol, a military-exploration unit that policed the space lanes. Children and families went wild and its creator, William Moser, a former Navy pilot, turned *Space Patrol* into a merchandising machine.[6]

Closer to home, and to Roddenberry's personal experience, was *Dragnet*, which made the move from radio to television in December 1951. Featuring stories "drawn from the files of the Los Angeles Police Department," *Dragnet* was an obvious fit for Roddenberry and he started collecting stories from his fellow officers and turning them into treatments for episodes. Roddenberry offered his LAPD colleagues half of his earnings if he was successful. He wasn't.

Roddenberry's break into television came in 1953, quite by chance. Ziv Television Productions wrote to Stanley Sheldon with a request for a technical advisor from the LAPD to support their new show *Mr District Attorney*, which was making the transition from radio. Roddenberry was appointed and immediately took full advantage of the opportunity to pitch his own script, "Defense Plant Gambling," which dealt with the sale of industrial secrets at a large aircraft company. It was credited to "Robert Wesley," the pseudonym Roddenberry used to disguise the fact that he had not sought permission to write alongside his official duties (this was obtained in December 1953). Roddenberry continued to balance writing and police work for three years. In February 1954, he took the sergeant's exam and passed at the first attempt.

Roddenberry later said that he only became a policeman to gain experience so he could sell scripts, but this is hardly plausible. Nor is Roddenberry's oft-repeated story about arresting his preferred literary agent for speeding in order to gain an introduction. Don Ingalls said that he and Gene both took the first agent who would accept them. At other times, Roddenberry said he was "in line" to take over as chief of police.[7] Since he never rose above the rank of sergeant, this seems little more than a daydream on his part.

Roddenberry was transferred to Hollywood division to serve his six months' probation. There he met another probationary sergeant, Wilbur Clingan, who became a firm friend (and would lend his surname to one of *Star Trek*'s most famous creations). Meanwhile, he wrote two more scripts for *Mr District Attorney* in 1954, earning the equivalent of roughly a month and a half's sergeant's salary for each. Toward the end of the year, he wrote the treatment for a science fiction story about two alien agents living undercover in contemporary America.

It eventually became "The Secret Weapon of 117," an episode of the anthology series *Stage 7.* The lead was played by Ricardo Montalban. Roddenberry also pitched "The Transport" for Ziv's *Science Fiction Theater*; the tale features "a device which is television, smellovision, soundvision, all rolled into one"[8] and so bears a similarity to *Star Trek: The Next Generation*'s holodeck. Equally prescient was Ziv's rejection of the story for being too expensive to produce. Nevertheless, Roddenberry landed three more scripts for *Mr District Attorney*, three for Ziv's *Highway Patrol*, and, early in 1956, two screenplays for *I Led Three Lives*, a peculiar series that leeched off popular anti-Communist sentiment. With regular work coming in, and Roddenberry able to pick and choose, he resigned from LAPD in June 1956 to become a full-time writer.

He got a lot of work—multiple episodes of *West Point*, *Boots and Saddles*, *The Detectives*, *Whiplash*, and *The Lawbreakers*. He became the most prolific writer on *Have Gun—Will Travel*, writing two dozen episodes (more than he's credited for on *Star Trek*). Occasionally an interviewer would refer to him as the creator of that show, and—to the annoyance of Herb Meadow and Sam Rolfe, the actual creators—Roddenberry would consistently never correct them. As the titles of the series suggest, Roddenberry was writing Westerns and cop shows, with the occasional foray into series about the military.

By 1963, Gene Roddenberry was an established TV writer. He could afford to buy a family home in Beverly Hills, and was in a position to pitch his own shows.

The Lieutenant ran for one season on NBC from September 1963 to April 1964; its twenty-nine episodes were made, in black and white, by Arena Productions, a television division of MGM run by Norman Felton, whose big hit at the time was *Doctor Kildare*, a show for which Roddenberry had written one episode. The story centers on a newly minted Marine lieutenant, William T. Rice. The lead actor was Gary Lockwood, whose best-known role is as Poole in *2001: A Space Odyssey*, one of two astronauts not in suspended animation on the *Discovery* mission to Jupiter (he's the one who is killed, not the one who goes through the stargate at the end).

Roddenberry wrote the pilot script. Writers Guild rules stated that anyone writing the pilot episode of a TV show was automatically one of the creators of the show, and Roddenberry would have been keen not to share that title with anyone else. He would not be credited as writer again until the last episode, but wrote "The Alien," the fourteenth episode, under his pseudonym Robert Wesley. Watching the series, it's clear that Roddenberry was heavily rewriting other people's work. He was not happy with the quality of the scripts he received, and rarely invited a writer back for a second episode.

Each week saw the Lieutenant faced with a particular problem—in early episodes, that included one of his men taking advantage of their old friendship; being accused of an inappropriate advance towards a woman he tried to help in an alleyway; and being sent undercover to assess whether a drill sergeant was being cruel to recruits. Each issue was tackled with at least a degree of nuance, with plot twists and complications arriving at the end of each act. In most episodes the Lieutenant's character arc was similar; he learned that it's tough being in command, that a degree of imagination is necessary, but it's unwise to go soft on the men under you. If there was an overarching moral, it was one familiar from Roddenberry's other work: that difference should be celebrated, but that progress ultimately depends on differences being put aside for the greater good.

The Lieutenant was repeated at least once on US cable channel TNT in the Nineties, and released on DVD in 2012, but it's an obscure show that would be all but forgotten now if Gene Roddenberry hadn't been involved. Even Roddenberry's authorized biography, written before the repeat run, allocates only two pages to it—and just eleven lines to Roddenberry's contribution, most of the rest being a discussion of Joe D'Agosta's role as casting director (this was D'Agosta's first time in the position he would later hold on *Star Trek*).[9]

Most discussion of *The Lieutenant* has been by *Star Trek* fans, many of whom have only heard of it second hand. Now it's available on DVD, a few fans have started to explore the series, but naturally enough, they've tended to see it through the lens of Roddenberry's better-known show. The star, Gary Lockwood, has a very prominent role as the main guest star in *Star Trek*'s "second pilot," "Where No Man Has Gone Before," but even without him, the majority of episodes include a face familiar from *Star Trek*.

It's something of a parlor game to match the guest cast of *The Lieutenant* to the *Star Trek* episode they would go on to appear in. A quick scan of the cast list demonstrates that *The Lieutenant* hired a number of actors whom Roddenberry and D'Agosta would go on to use in major roles in *Star Trek*—Leonard Nimoy, Nichelle Nichols, Ricardo Montalban, and Walter Koenig among them—and it was often here that Roddenberry worked with them for the first time. Other links are equally easy to spot. The text on the back of the DVD box set points out that the "T" in Lieutenant William T. Rice stands for "Tiberius," the same as James T. Kirk, but astute fans will already have spotted that the name is also echoed in that of *The Next Generation*'s William T. Riker.

Not counting the *Star Trek* connections, there are before-they-were-famous roles for actors such as Bill Bixby, Linda Evans, Dennis Hopper, Rip Torn, Katharine Ross, and Ted Knight. One episode features Madge Cummings, who shortly afterward went on to play Aunt Harriet in the Adam West *Batman* series. The most notable feature of *The Lieutenant*'s cast, though, is that Rice's commanding officer, Captain Rambridge, is played by Robert Vaughn, just before he took on the role that would make him world famous, that of Napoleon Solo in *The Man from U.N.C.L.E.* (1964–8). Vaughan had been nominated for a Best Supporting Actor Oscar for his first major screen role (in 1959's *The Young Philadelphians*) and was one of *The Magnificent Seven* (1960) but he was not a star name in 1963. He had enough clout to be paid the same as Lockwood for

The Lieutenant, despite only being in a scene or two of most episodes. He's charming and makes the most of what are often rather perfunctory lines.

Vaughn seems to have signed onto the show with the promise it was a larger part, and soon asked for his role to be expanded. Studio bosses clearly agreed. A couple of later episodes feature him more heavily; in "The Alien," Vaughn's character takes delivery of a Korean orphan he and his ex-wife planned to adopt before they separated. He struggles to cope, and starts a relationship with a woman with an eye to them marrying so they can adopt the boy (the woman is played by Madlyn Rhue, who would play the *Enterprise* crew member seduced by Khan in the episode "Space Seed"—both her characters, oddly, are keen military historians). It's the episode written by "Robert Wesley," and it relegates Lieutenant Rice to a handful of scenes, while demonstrating Vaughn's abilities at comedy and as a romantic lead. One of a number of reasons *The Lieutenant* wasn't renewed was to free Vaughn up to star in his own series, which would also be produced by Arena Productions. *The Man from U.N.C.L.E.* (1964–8) was to be built around Vaughn, indeed it had the working title *Solo*, after his character.

Roddenberry, forty-two years old, and in charge of his first television show, began wearing suits and sports coats in an effort to look more professional but, as Engel puts it, "many of them were made of primitive synthetic fabrics and the producer sometimes looked more like a cheap pimp than Beau Brummell."[10] Rather less comically,

Engel reports Buzz Kulik, one of the show's directors, as saying of Roddenberry that "he was really out of it, to a great extent, because of his drinking and personal problems." Kulik and his wife overheard a number of loud arguments between Gene and Eileen Roddenberry, with Eileen confiding to Lorraine Kulik that Roddenberry was physically abusive.[11] *The Lieutenant* was budgeted at $117,000 an episode,[12] but would have cost far more without the cooperation of the US Marines. Many exteriors were filmed at Camp Pendleton in San Diego County, and the Corps let the series show off military equipment like helicopters and flamethrowers and loaned real Marines to appear on screen going through drills and exercises. All of this was provided for free. In return, the Corps wanted to be presented in a favorable light, and Roddenberry claimed he was given a long list of topics that he was to avoid. He certainly received detailed notes on each specific script. The price of their involvement was that if the Marines wanted changes, the script had to be rewritten no matter how implausible the notes were. One comment asserted that a scene of a Marine cadet being injured during training had to go, because such a thing could never happen. Roddenberry knew that was nonsense, but amended the script. A lot of episodes feature odd little caveats that would appear to be either a result of notes from the Marines, or included to head off trouble, such as here from "To Set It Right," where Private Cameron, who is black, identifies his colleague Devlin as someone who attacked him when they were at school:

CAMERON:	When someone hits you with a chain, Lieutenant, you know who did it. I was just another nigger that didn't know his place.
RICE:	I told you to knock off that kind of talk, Private.
CAMERON:	Sir, you asked me for fact, I was just quoting what Devlin said to me once.
RICE:	Uh-huh. Has anyone ever said that to you since you joined the Marine Corps, Private?
CAMERON:	No sir. I like the Corps fine. Until a few minutes ago. I even liked Boot Camp, sir. I didn't see one ounce of prejudice there.

As the first episodes were being made, Roddenberry felt confident the show would prove to be a new *Doctor Kildare*—it used the same basic format of a young, idealistic character darting around various roles in an institutional setting, dealing with some serious real-life issues. There was the novelty that it was a show about the role of the military in peacetime, rather than a war story. NBC had high hopes for the show, too, but when they viewed the first episodes they were disappointed, and their nerves weren't steadied when some of the early reviews declared the show was nothing special. It did surprisingly well at first against the stiff competition of *The Jackie Gleason Show* on Saturday night, though, and so was given some leeway.

In *The Lieutenant*, we see some familiar Roddenberry touches and themes, strengths and weaknesses—and the start of a pattern when recruiting leading men. Gary Lockwood was the first lead Roddenberry cast—square-jawed, conventionally attractive, athletic, and slightly older than the character he's playing. Lockwood performs Roddenberry's lines with a straight bat. It's his first show as the lead, and he is notably more confident in the role by the end of the show, but at the start he's far too solemn and stolid. There's evidence Roddenberry wasn't entirely happy with the performance; Lockwood said his producer kept "trying to get the directors to loosen me up; make me smile and do all kinds of boyish things. And it's not my style."[13] This is not to say that Lockwood does a bad job. His is almost certainly a true-to-life depiction of a Marine lieutenant, but he's not quite warm enough. When he smiles in the opening credits, it's presumably meant to be disarming, but it looks rather disconcerting and forced. As *Variety*'s review of the first episode put it, "Lockwood has the looks, a special pensive quality and the basic acting ability . . . but the character he portrays will have to give off more heroic magic."[14]

Roddenberry's leading men are all accomplished character actors, with long and varied careers. Often, though, something in his work seems to bring out a certain stiffness in them, and they end up as a weak point where the solid core of the show should be—that "heroic magic" is missing. It's a charge that could be leveled against Jeffrey Hunter as Pike (the captain of the *Enterprise* in the first *Star Trek* pilot), Robert Lansing as Gary Seven in the "backdoor pilot" "Assignment: Earth" (Roddenberry also cast him as the lead in *The Long Hunt of April Savage*), Robert Foxworth in *The Questor Tapes* (who has the excuse he's playing an android, but Brent Spiner was quickly able to

tease out a great deal more as the very similar charac-
ter Data in *The Next Generation*), and Alex Cord as Dylan
Hunt in *Genesis II*. It's easy to imagine Stephen Macht,
Roddenberry's first choice to play Picard in *The Next
Generation*, following suit.

Looking at the television pilots Roddenberry went on
to make in the Seventies, we might assume that he wanted
shows with bizarre science fiction settings to have a solid,
grounded lead performance. The premise of *Genesis II* is
that someone from our time (give or take) ends up in a
post-apocalyptic future with bizarre new customs. That
character is the audience identification figure, so he has
to play it straight when he's confronted with some new
weirdness, and to be an everyman with integrity and
decency when he's called on to defend the innocent. But this
doesn't give Alec Cord much to work with, and he comes
across as sullen and restricted. Lockwood's performance is
equally hemmed in. Rather than this being a consequence
of the science fiction setting, it seems that, whether he was
writing police shows, Westerns, science fiction, or stories
about military men, Roddenberry wrote his male lead as a
solid, masculine presence—and a little boring.

Seeing Jeffrey Hunter in the first *Star Trek* pilot, or Gary
Lockwood playing either a Marine lieutenant or a Starfleet
officer, it becomes obvious just how much of a contribution
William Shatner makes to the success of *Star Trek*. It's
something of an understatement to say that Shatner's
performance is not naturalistic in places. Many places. It's
clearly a choice, though, with the actor working against

the solid, businesslike nature of a lot of Roddenberry's scripts, finding interesting words to emphasize and odd places to smile or shrug. When he was approached to appear in the second pilot for *Star Trek*, Shatner was shown the first attempt:

> "I saw a lot of wonderful things in it. But I also saw that the people in it were playing it as though 'we're out in space, isn't this serious?' I thought if it was a naval vessel at sea, they'd be relaxed and familiar, not somewhat pedantic and self-important . . . I wanted it to be lighter rather than heavier. So I consciously thought of playing good-pal-the-Captain, who, in time of need, would snap to and become the warrior . . . I guess the way I work as an actor—I say 'I guess' because I don't consciously have a methodology—is to ask 'how entertaining can this be?'"[15]

It's a style of acting that was mocked and widely parodied for a long time, but *Star Trek* is lurid, deliberately bordering on the absurd. Shatner's performance works extremely well with the "pedantic and self-important" material Roddenberry was prone to supply. Kirk, especially early on, shares Lieutenant Rice's unease at being in command. He never lets on in front of his men, but he's troubled. He understands that decisions he makes could result in the deaths of his crew, or provoke wars that will see civilians killed; he understands that his enemies can be justified in their actions, and that there are situations where he must reach decisions quickly and live with the consequences.

Shatner instinctively saw that a solemn, over-serious performance would weigh *Star Trek* down.

Robert Vaughn and William Shatner have similar acting styles, the same sort of commanding presence, but oozing charm, and with a hint that both the actor and character are having more fun than they're allowed to let on. For *Planet Earth*, Roddenberry's second stab at the *Genesis II* concept, Dylan Hunt was recast. John Saxon is a familiar face from Seventies movies, probably best known for playing opposite Bruce Lee in *Enter the Dragon* (1973), and he brings a physicality to the role that's very clearly a homage to Shatner's performance as Kirk. *Planet Earth*'s a lot more entertaining than its forerunner, mainly thanks to its lead actor.

The Lieutenant had a very specific role in the story Gene Roddenberry told his fans about himself. The foundation myth of *Star Trek* was laid out in the 1968 book *The Making of Star Trek*:

[Roddenberry] decided he had to make it appear on the outside like a Trojan horse, the series idea would conceal a few surprises. Roddenberry was determined to break through television's censorship barrier and do tales about important and meaningful things. He was certain television's audience was not the collection of nitwits that networks believed it to be. By using science fiction yarns on far-off planets, he was certain he could disguise the fact he was actually talking about politics, sex, economics, the stupidity of war, and half a hundred other vital subjects usually prohibited in television.[16]

The way Roddenberry told it, *The Lieutenant* proved how hard it was to discuss controversial topics on TV, and as a direct result he drew up *Star Trek*, calculating that the science fiction nature of the show would trick his bosses. It's one of the lines that fans have heard many times, one of the things they "know": that *Star Trek* is a clever, allegorical show that grasps controversial topics that nothing else on television could touch.

It's not, though, an argument that holds up very well in the face of the evidence. The allegories in *Star Trek* are hardly impenetrable. However dim the network overseers were, they probably spotted that the aliens in "Let This Be Your Last Battlefield," whose faces are black on one side and white on the other, and who have been locked in a war between those who are black on the right side and those who are black on the left, is a commentary on race prejudice. There aren't all that many "political" episodes of *Star Trek*, if we use the word to mean ones that deal with difficult, specific contemporary issues.

If we want to see Roddenberry's true original intent, we could refer to the pitch document, a fifteen-page description of the premise, characters, and selling points of the show which he wrote in March 1964. The document includes twenty-five brief summaries of potential stories. About half are recognizable as stories which ended up being made, and a *Star Trek* fan could identify many of these by their working titles ("The Next Cage," "The Day Charlie Became God," "President Capone," "The Mirror") and others by the summary: ("a planet which duplicates famous Humans, and then forces them into gladiatorial combat," "some 'hanky-panky' occurs when escorting a cargo ship of women to a deep space colony").

What we see in the pitch document is a mixed bag which includes a number of stories that might be termed "philosophical," or that present moral dilemmas. "The Perfect World" is a prototype of "The Return of the Archons," which asks how a society might maintain order without becoming authoritarian. It's an important question, but an eternal one. "A Question of Cannibalism" has the crew visiting a colony planet and learning that the "cow like creatures raised on the ranches there are actually intelligent beings." "Charlie X" is about how terrible it would be if one man's wishes came true. "The Radiant One" features a beautiful woman whose embrace is irresistible but deadly (it may have been the basis of the broadcast episode "That Which Survives"). These aren't stories ripped from newspapers in 1964 and given a science fiction makeover, they're all stories the Ancient Greeks told. The question at the heart of the episode "Reason"—"can a robot be capable of emotional feeling?"—is one that fascinated Roddenberry, and he would go on to revisit it many times, but it's not one of the hot-button civil rights issues of the Sixties.

There are, generously, two "timely political" stories proposed in the pitch document. In "The Pet Shop" the ship visits a world where "women are the masters, and men are women's pets." The concept of "Kongo" is essentially the same, but it's set on an antebellum world where blacks keep whites as slaves. Again, while women's rights and race relations were political issues in the Sixties, these are more general stories about worms turning. The message is no deeper than "you wouldn't like it if things were the other way around, would you?"

Other proposed stories seem to be simple adventure/survival yarns with no allegorical or satirical content. "To Skin a Tyrannosaurus" would have seen a crewman forced to survive on a primeval world with only a sling and a club. In "Camelot Revisited," the crew would have found themselves "engaged in lance and sword play to preserve their own skins." Perhaps the pitch document itself was a Trojan horse, and Roddenberry secretly planned to deal with far more controversial topics, but this isn't what happened when *Star Trek* made it to the air.

Watching *The Lieutenant*, then watching *Star Trek*, the conclusion is inescapable: the average broadcast episode of *The Lieutenant* is far stronger stuff when it's tackling timely, controversial topics than the average episode of *Star Trek*.

"Balance of Terror," the first *Star Trek* episode to feature the Romulans, "addresses the issue of prejudice." A new character, Lieutenant Stiles, displays hostility toward Romulans and explains he lost relatives in the last war with them, a century ago. When it's revealed that Romulans look like Vulcans, Stiles immediately accuses Spock of being a Romulan spy, leading to exchanges like:

KIRK: Well, here's one thing you can be sure of, Mister. Leave any bigotry in your quarters. There's no room for it on the bridge. Do I make myself clear?

STILES: You do, sir.

It's a subplot, and one that's dealt with quickly and neatly—there are a couple more incidents where Stiles is suspicious of Spock and receives reprimands, but at the end of the episode, Spock risks his life to save Stiles, and Stiles is shamed into being won over:

STILES: I'm alive, sir. But I wouldn't be. Mr. Spock pulled me out of the phaser room. He saved my life. He risked his life after I—

SPOCK: I saved a trained navigator so he could return to duty. I am capable of no other feelings in such matters.

It's a message about the dangers of intolerance, but an extremely broad one. The story is as simple as can be: a character overcomes his prejudice against a whole group by seeing an individual from that group acting in a way that surprises him.

In terms of the narrative conventions of the show, it's essentially false drama. Even the least savvy viewers would know it was extremely unlikely the regular character Mr. Spock was really a Romulan spy, and would be rooting for him, not Stiles, a character we've never seen before and won't see again. In "Balance of Terror," the main plot says something quite interesting about the nobility of the enemy, and how military men share many values and concerns, regardless of which side they're on—the Romulan captain has come to see a kindred spirit in Kirk, and he dies with a line oft-quoted by fans: "I regret that we meet in this way. You and I are of a kind. In a different reality, I could have called you friend." It's a good episode, an extremely entertaining hour of television, and the main plot sees some great writing and performances . . . but "Balance of Terror" is not a deep treatise on the roots and consequences of prejudice, the likes of which American TV had never seen before.

In *The Lieutenant*, "Mother Enemy" has a similar main plot to the subplot of "Balance of Terror"—a Marine (played by the future Mr. Chekov, Walter Koenig) who wants to progress to officer training faces prejudice from his colleagues when it's learned that his mother is a prominent member of an American Communist group. In "To Set It Right" a "Negro" Marine starts a fight with a fellow Marine from his home town who he knows to be a racist. Both stories are the main plot of the episode, and the problems are explored from a variety of angles. The two Marines who face prejudice are themselves aggressive and less than honest with the Lieutenant when questioned. Lieutenant Rice is forced to face his own prejudices and limitations, and to reconcile his own standards with the demands of military regulations. He misjudges situations and makes mistakes as he goes. In "To Set it Right," he admits he's never known any "Negroes" his own age, and later struggles a little with terminology when he talks to Norma Bartlett, Private Cameron's fiancée, played by Nichelle Nichols.

RICE: I didn't mean this as an intrusion, Miss Bartlett. I'm having a few problems with your fiancé myself. I thought you might be able to help. They concern Private Cameron's . . . ethnic background.

BARTLETT: You mean he's a Negro?

RICE: Yes, ma'am. I, ah, I've been trying to reach him, to talk to him. I haven't had much luck. He seems to be going on the assumption that because he's Negro and, well, I'm . . . Caucasian . . .

BARTLETT: Lieutenant, if the words "white" and "black" come easier, why not use them? They're perfectly handy, acceptable references. If you'll stumble around embarrassed it's just going to make both of us uncomfortable.

It isn't at all clear what the resolution will be in either case, and while the end of "To Set it Right" is similar to that of "Balance of Terror"—the black Marine and the racist learn to get along when they have to cooperate to survive a climbing exercise—the end of the episode where they share a joke about the black soldier not needing to wear camouflage face paint on a night exercise feels far more like the start of an uneasy truce than a declaration that this is the way to end all racism. The conclusion of "Mother Enemy" is quite subtle—the Lieutenant decides the Marine whose mother is a Communist isn't ready to be an officer, because of the young man's conduct in the episode, not because of his mother's political beliefs. Both he and his captain are sure it's the best decision, but regret it. There's no place in either episode for poetic justice, and Lieutenant Rice can't rely on sentimental notions of "fairness" or giving his men "the benefit of the doubt." It does matter that "Negro" and "Communist" are real things, while "Romulans" and "Vulcans" aren't, as it places the narrative far closer to home, and forces the audience members to position themselves in the debate and not to treat it as an abstract discussion.

Was *The Lieutenant* canceled because it was too controversial, as Roddenberry implied?

At some point, the Marines withdrew their cooperation. Suddenly, the show was denied free access to locations, hardware, and real Marines to appear in location footage. This could only have added to the expense and detracted from the authenticity. Gene Roddenberry said this happened because the Marines objected to a particular script. The problem is that at different times, he made this claim about a number of stories. At times he agreed with Norman Felton that it was "To Set It Right" that was the culprit, and also claimed the episode had never been broadcast.[17] But he said elsewhere that it was the network, not the Marines, who objected, and that the active steps he took led to the episode being shown:

"My problem was not the Marine Corps, here, it was NBC, who turned down the show flat. The studio, MGM, said,

'You'll spend a hundred and seventeen thousand dollars which you won't be able to recover, and we take this very seriously.' . . . I had only one thing I could do, I went out to [the] NAACP, and an organization named CORE, and they lowered the boom on NBC. They said, 'Prejudice is prejudice, whatever the color.' And so we were able to show the show."[18]

What's the truth of it? First, that Roddenberry liked to exaggerate in stories, particularly when the stories were about himself and allowed him to be portrayed as heroic in the face of insurmountable institutional opposition. "To Set It Right" was made, and although sources vary on whether it was ever shown, the fact is that it *was* broadcast, on February 22, 1964, exactly as scheduled. Roddenberry's quote blurs the tenses, but a close reading would suggest NBC objected at an early stage and told MGM they wouldn't pay for it, that MGM quite reasonably didn't want to make an episode they couldn't sell, but then NBC relented, then the episode was made and broadcast. We have no records of how hard fought a battle it was, or who fought it, or if the script was changed to allay the network's concerns. Roddenberry would have been involved, and his own perception of those events and personal emotional investment in them could well have been radically different than the perception of whichever NBC executive was worried.

So did the Marines have a problem with the episode? Roddenberry says in the quote above that they didn't, and the rock climbing sequences and some of the location work certainly appear to involve their cooperation. The end result is that a show depicting racial prejudice in the armed forces was written, approved by the Marines, made by the studio and shown on network television.

Elsewhere, Roddenberry claimed it was "Mother Enemy" that was the problem: "the Marine Corps got mad at us finally because we insisted on doing this script, based on a true story, where a young Sergeant was up for officer candidate school and he was denied because his mother was in the Communist Party. They didn't want us to do that, but we insisted on doing it."[19]

"Mother Enemy" was the twenty-seventh episode of twenty-nine shown, being broadcast on April 4, and final confirmation that *The Lieutenant* wasn't going to be renewed came in mid-March. If the Marines had withdrawn their cooperation that late, it would barely have mattered, as the show was already ending. It's entirely possible "Mother Enemy" was in production when the show was formally canceled, and so Roddenberry associated the episode with the show's cancelation. There's no evidence that the story content had anything to do with the show not being renewed.

There was certainly never the assumption that the show would be renewed—the possibility was always that it would not. On March 12, 1964, Roddenberry wrote a letter to fellow producer Quinn Martin saying, "it does appear more and more like *The Lieutenant* will be picked up for a new season."[20] There were several factors that tipped the balance against it. Roddenberry had lost Robert Vaughn to *The Man from U.N.C.L.E. The Lieutenant* would be more expensive without the cooperation of the Marines. The national mood had changed—President Kennedy had been assassinated (Roddenberry recalls they'd been filming a funeral scene when news reached the set, most likely the one seen in the sixteenth episode, "Gone the Sun"). The war in Vietnam was escalating, and while the mass anti-war movement of later years was yet to develop, a show about the Marines would have to address any number of divisive issues, and run the risk of being caught out by real-life events.

In the end, the main reason *The Lieutenant* wasn't renewed was that competition for primetime slots was fierce and the show didn't make much of a mark. There was a lack of press coverage. It's tempting to think that the controversy over "To Set It Right" was stoked a little, perhaps even by Roddenberry himself, to get some publicity for the show, and to make *The Lieutenant* seem "edgy." It was the twenty-first episode, with eight still to air. If the first season had picked up viewers and positive publicity at that point, the powers that be might have been persuaded to keep it on the air.

The following season, *The Lieutenant*'s early evening slot on NBC was taken up by *Flipper*, *Kentucky Jones* (produced by Buzz Kulik, about a widower who adopted a Chinese orphan), and *The Famous Adventures of Mr. Magoo*, in which the near-sighted cartoon character re-enacted great works of literature.

Roddenberry said in his letter to Quinn Martin that he had been assured that even if *The Lieutenant* was canceled, he would be put in charge of developing a new series. The *Star Trek* pitch document was dated March 11, 1964, and the letter to Martin was dated March 12. Roddenberry had finished working on *The Lieutenant* by April, and had been commissioned to write the *Star Trek* pilot by May. At the time, it looked like another door was opening as soon as the first had closed. Getting *Star Trek* onto television would prove a far more lengthy and convoluted process.

While *Star Trek* didn't debut until September 1966, Roddenberry wrote the first pilot episode straight after working on *The Lieutenant*. Watching "The Cage" in that context, there are some striking parallels and holdovers. Many of the preoccupations of the earlier show end up troubling Captain Pike of the *Enterprise*. The pilot starts three weeks after Pike has lost members of his crew on a mission, and the ship's doctor catches him brooding about it in his quarters in an exchange that could have come from the mouths of Lieutenant Rice and Captain Rambridge.

BOYCE: Chris, you set standards for yourself no one could meet. You treat everyone on board like a human being except yourself, and now you're tired and you—

PIKE: You bet I'm tired. You bet. I'm tired of being responsible for two hundred and three lives. I'm tired of deciding which mission is too risky and which isn't, and who's going on the landing party and who doesn't, and who lives and who dies. Boy, I've had it, Phil.

BOYCE: To the point of finally taking my advice, a rest leave?

PIKE: To the point of considering resigning.

It's a tone that carries through into the first season of the broadcast series, with the weight of the world now on Kirk's shoulders. The early episodes of *Star Trek* include a lot of material that's similar to *The Lieutenant*—the ship's captain having to maintain discipline, and struggling with the loneliness of command, and having to resolve issues where friendship or other personal matters interfere with regulations or his duty. Although a few women serve on the *Enterprise*, the early episodes in particular have a very masculine feel to them. The role of the women in "Mudd's Women," for example, is straight out of a Western—they're mail order brides for lonely miners.

The Lieutenant has essentially been seen only as a footnote in *Star Trek* history, mainly appearing in actors' anecdotes, which usually take the form "I first met Gene Roddenberry when I was in one episode of…" Walter Koenig does himself a serious disservice in his autobiography *Warped Factors* by reducing his angry, twitchy performance in "Mother Enemy" to one sentence ("During this same period I had the principal guest role on an episode of *The Lieutenant*, a TV series created and produced by Gene Roddenberry").[21]

The Lieutenant ran for just one season, so it was seen as a failure. When he talked about it, Gene Roddenberry needed to distance himself from it to position *Star Trek* as an antidote to old-fashioned shows. He had to frame *The Lieutenant* as typical of all the things he *wasn't* able to do on television at the time. *The Lieutenant* is not some great undiscovered classic of a show, but neither is it a disaster. Though made with the approval of the Marines, and portraying them in a broadly positive light, it certainly doesn't whitewash them. There are rich pickings for anyone who wants to study the depiction of militarism in American popular culture immediately before the Vietnam War, or race, or gender. "To Set it Right" deals with issues of racism in a way that's surprisingly nuanced and interesting to watch, and nothing like as cringeworthy or preachy as we might reasonably expect it to be.

Lee Erwin was the writer of both "To Set it Right" and the *Star Trek* episode "Whom Gods Destroy," and it's absurd to suggest that his *Star Trek* episode, in which a group of weird alien lunatics literally take over their asylum, somehow managed to convey complex topical issues that *The Lieutenant* couldn't get away with. Then again, unlike *The Lieutenant*, *Star Trek* thrives after half a century, and it's not hyperbole to say that a billion more people have seen "Whom Gods Destroy" than "To Set It Right." To get its message across, a show has to be on air.

CHAPTER TWO

SHOW ME SOME MORE OF THIS EARTH THING CALLED KISSING

Ask most members of the television audience to complete the following sentence and they could probably come up with a plausible working answer:

> "*Star Trek* has gained quite a reputation for . . ."

There are many possible responses, positive and negative, serious or flippant, that might deal with any number of topics, from the production values of the show to the deep philosophy behind it. But the first time that sentence appeared in print was on page 360 of the 1968 book *The Making of Star Trek*, credited to Stephen E. Whitfield and Gene Roddenberry, and it ran:

> "*Star Trek* has gained quite a reputation for using 'revealing' costumes in its shows."

Star Trek was considered a "sexy" show from very early on. Its costume designer, William Ware Theiss, had gone so far as to develop the "Theiss Theory of Titillation," which he defined in *The Making of Star Trek* as "the degree to which a costume is considered sexy is directly dependent upon how accident-prone it appears to be."[1] In other words, he frequently constructed costumes from rather flimsy material and draped them over the female guest stars in a way that made it seem they were about to fall off. "A basic part of Bill's theory requires the use of nudity on unexpected places, such as baring the outside of the leg, from the thigh to the hipbone. This is a rather sexless area, but it is also one that is normally covered."[2]

A good early example was Sherry Jackson's costume for "What Are Little Girls Made Of?," the seventh episode to be broadcast. Jackson played an android, Andrea, and wore a one-piece ensemble that combined a halter top with tight trousers. A strip of fabric, one blue, one olive-brown, covered each breast, but very little else on her top half. Her arms, back, shoulder, cleavage, ribs, and hips were all bare. The outfit was kept carefully in place with tape. It was a striking look, the publicity department were sure to take many photographs of Jackson, and newspapers and magazines were more than happy to run them. When Roddenberry took two episodes of *Star Trek* to Tricon, a major science fiction convention in Cleveland held the week before the show's television premiere, he brought a couple of models with him to show off the costumes, including Sherry Jackson's ensemble.[3] This set a pattern for many subsequent episodes. Even people who didn't watch *Star Trek* knew it was a show with weird creatures and scantily clad women.

The earliest episodes of *Star Trek* were made over fifty years ago. Social mores change. It's astonishing to discover that in 1971, when Gene Roddenberry wrote and produced his first movie, *Pretty Maids All in a Row*, MGM ran a national "Miss Pretty Maid" beauty contest to publicize it. The poster declares "Hey, you in the hot pants! If you're 18 to 25 years old and look good in hot pants, you're eligible. *Very eligible.*" The winners of the regional heats would receive "a new hot pants outfit designed by Dimitri of Italy," the grand prize was "an all-expenses-paid trip to Hollywood and an evening on the town with Rock Hudson." The gender politics of the film itself are bizarre to modern eyes. The lead character is a middle-aged high school counselor who sleeps with his students and advises a colleague to do the same. Roger Vadim, the director, saw the willingness of a Hollywood studio to make such a movie as "a sign of something very healthy—that society is changing."[4]

Star Trek and—in a process of guilt-by-association—its creator purport to be predicting what society will look like centuries from now. Instead, when we watch *Star Trek*, it screams the Sixties at us. *Star Trek: The Next Generation* is older now than the original series was when *The Next Generation* was first shown. There are places where it, too, looks far more like what it is, a product of the late 1980s, than the window into the twenty-fourth century it's meant to be.

The attitudes are, in many places, worse fashion victims than the hairstyles and eyeshadow.

The original show's gender politics might be the perfect example. Take one of the more visible aspects of the show: the fact that the Starfleet uniforms for women include a miniskirt. Yes, of course, a woman should be free to choose to wear what she likes, and some women want to wear short skirts. The Starfleet uniform is a popular choice for women cosplayers, those people at science fiction conventions who dress up as characters from the show, all of whom have chosen and lovingly reconstructed the costume. Grace Lee Whitney, who played Janice Rand, the yeoman assigned to Captain Kirk in early episodes of the series, genuinely loved the uniform: "People often ask me at conventions if I liked the mini-skirted uniforms the women wore on the show. My answer: Absolutely! I wanted to show off my assets, and Bill Theiss's uniform creations certainly did that (of course my moral values are much different today than they were back then!)"[5] She even occasionally took credit for the look, and noted that Nichelle Nichols would carefully pull her hemline up when she sat down, to show even more leg.

Whitney was annoyed that *Star Trek: The Motion Picture* had a unisex uniform and she wasn't allowed to wear makeup. She felt director Robert Wise "was deliberately sabotaging me. I felt he did not want me to look glamorous, as I did in the original show . . . It seemed he wanted me to look plain and old—and it just about killed me. I was so horribly upset, practically suicidal, throughout the picture."[6]

But James T. Kirk's *Enterprise* is not some post-patriarchy where women are wearing what they want because they've been freed from the male gaze. Rather the opposite. One of the visual clichés of the show is that when a beautiful woman is introduced, we hold on a soft-focus shot of her for a few seconds while some seductive music plays. The camera angles are such that we can usually infer that we're seeing what Captain Kirk is seeing.

Centuries in the future, there may be women serving in Starfleet, but there are limits to their opportunities. In the second-season episode "Who Mourns for Adonais?" McCoy laments of a female officer, "She's a woman. All woman. One day she'll find the right man and off she'll go, out of the service." (Later in the episode, the character McCoy is discussing is sexually assaulted by an alien posing as the god Apollo.) The very last episode, "Turnabout Intruder," features a female Starfleet officer who swaps bodies with Kirk because she's bitter the "world of starship captains doesn't admit women."

Expecting a more enlightened approach on Sixties American network television is not a pipe dream only possible with decades of hindsight and multiple waves of feminism between us and them. We can say this with confidence, because in the pilot episode of *Star Trek* itself, "The Cage," written and filmed in the second half of 1964, male and female crew members of the *Enterprise* wore the same uniforms, with thick tops, trousers, and ankle boots. There were two women bridge officers, including the second-in-command. The story represents a cerebral attempt to explore problems with the concept of an "ideal" relationship between a man and a woman.

"The Cage" didn't feature Captain Kirk. While Leonard Nimoy played Mr. Spock in the pilot, a different character, a woman called Number One, took both his rank as first officer, and his emotionless personality. She was played by Majel Barrett, who would later marry Gene Roddenberry. Pike has a female yeoman, J.M. Colt. Female crew members are clearly the exception rather than the rule, and Colt is new to the job. When Colt is out of earshot, the captain confides, rather undiplomatically, to Number One, "I can't get used to having a woman on the bridge. No offence, Lieutenant. You're different, of course."

The episode's story revolves around the captain's "fantasy woman." Lured to a distant planet by a distress signal, he is captured by aliens who can read his thoughts and place images in his mind. He experiences a series of perfect illusions—he rescues a damsel in distress; he enjoys a picnic with his wife in a beautiful park (the only glimpse of Earth's future we are given in the whole of the original TV show); then—the one everyone remembers—he is treated to a dance from a green alien slave girl. All three women are avatars of the same woman, Vina, who implores him: "You can have whatever dream you want. I can become anything, any woman you've ever imagined. You can have anything you want in the whole universe. Let me please you."

Pike rejects all these scenarios, so the aliens capture Number One and Yeoman Colt and offer them to Pike, telling him, "Number One has the superior mind and would produce highly intelligent children. Although she seems to lack emotion, this is largely a pretense. She has often had fantasies involving you . . . (Turning to Colt) The factors in her favor are youth and strength, plus unusually strong female drives."

It's Captain Pike's story, and one of the main purposes of a pilot episode is to see the lead character in action. His captivity is literally a series of male fantasies. Women are exotic creatures, presented to a man for him to select a breeding partner. That said, Pike never seems about to give in to any of the temptations on offer. We focus on the alien slave girl's dance for two minutes, we're told "They actually like being taken advantage of"— an extra sequence, where Vina was whipped by a slaver, was filmed but edited out. Then Pike stands and leaves, disgusted by what he and we have seen.

And this strange mix of the lascivious and the enlightened is characteristic of *Star Trek*. It's taking the phrase "women are more than just sex objects" and applying it over-literally: women *are* sex objects, but they're other stuff, too. Right at the start of the series, we're seeing an attitude that will always be part of the show's DNA, and it comes straight from its creator. Gene Roddenberry made this attempt to square the circle in 1976:

"You cannot write in science fiction . . . without realizing that sexual equality is as basic as any other kind of equality. This does not mean that in future pictures I will ever stop

> using women as sex objects, as I will not, but to be fair we
> have always used and will be continuing to use males as sex
> objects, too. As a matter of fact, when I was younger and
> much more agile, I've been used as a sex object myself; I
> think it's great fun."[7]

The second half of this comment is the more striking, and is the line that gets the laugh, but the first half is at least as important. *Star Trek* and its creator *are* committed to equality. Roddenberry repeated the following anecdote many times:

> "I had insisted on half women on board. The network came
> to me and said, 'You can't have half women. Our people
> say it will make it look like a ship with all sorts of mad sexual
> things going on—half men and half women.' So we argued
> about it like a poker game and they finally said, 'Okay. We'll
> settle for one-third women.' I figured one-third women could
> take care of the males anyway."

It was a frequent refrain from Roddenberry that anything regressive in the show was imposed on him by the "television executives," a nameless, faceless set of adversaries who were seemingly intent on ruining everything by imposing antediluvian "standards" across the industry. The way he told it, he fought a series of heroic running battles to keep up the quality of the show. This was a strategic decision on his part, based on an early conversation which he very much took to heart:

"I'm sure that many remember me as a difficult, touchy person. In many cases, they're right. Some of this I did purposely. I had a meeting with a studio executive who said 'Gene, I'm going to give you some advice. You're beginning to get the nickname of "Crazy Gene" around the studio because you're calling up and saying how much does it cost to paint a woman green, stuff like that. The only way you can make the show what you want it to be is to take advantage of the fact that you are sort of a crazy person. Actually you are fairly easy to get along with, but you've got to create the image of yourself as a battler, a fighter, a person who is liable to toss an executive out of your office if he comes up with an impossible request.'"[8]

For most of the Seventies and Eighties fans seemed more invested in the content of the *Star Trek* universe and in the actors than what was going on behind the scenes. Relatively little research into the production of the show was done. The main source for information about the behind-the-scenes battles during the making of the show came from Gene Roddenberry himself. His account was that the network rejected the pilot episode because they thought it was "too cerebral." The bosses particularly didn't like the idea of a female first officer or "the guy with the ears"—Mr. Spock. They did see enough potential to take the unprecedented step of ordering a second pilot, but demanded a number of substantial changes. Roddenberry had the choice of fighting to keep Leonard Nimoy as Spock or Majel Barrett as Number One, and—it's a punchline he and Majel Barrett-Roddenberry would both end up using at conventions—he "kept the Vulcan and married the woman because he didn't think Leonard Nimoy would have it the other way around."

The version of events Roddenberry told interviewers and packed convention halls in the Seventies had the full benefit of hindsight, and flattered the fans as well as himself. The crazy network executives didn't like Mr. Spock, and he ended up the most popular character! The second-in-command of the *Enterprise* could have been a woman all along, if only the executives were a little more forward-thinking! He was trying to create a vision of the future where the human race had progressed, but his bosses were stuck in the past! They thought the show was too smart, what they really meant was that they thought their audiences were too dumb! Right from the beginning, I was fighting an uphill battle to maintain the integrity of *Star Trek*!

Clearly, there's a kernel of truth in all of this. There were things you couldn't show or say on television in the Sixties. The networks needed their shows to maintain a mass audience and this meant they worried about offending people (and, more importantly, scaring away advertisers). Many writers and producers wanted to push the boundaries, while the network bosses would tend toward toning material down and playing it safe. The shows emerged from the tension between those two forces.

For the last twenty years or so, *Star Trek* has attracted more scholarship and archival research than any other American

TV show—although still nothing like the granular, ultra-comprehensive work *Doctor Who* fans have long been doing in Britain—and as a result many of the studio memos and other pieces of correspondence have been unearthed. Other people who were involved in the making of *Star Trek* have written books or been interviewed for magazines or DVD features, and we have new perspectives on events. It's clear now that there are a number of salient facts Gene Roddenberry omitted from his version.

First of all, there's the obvious one: NBC were not hostile to *Star Trek*, they ended up making three seasons of it. The entire point of commissioning pilots, rather than whole seasons, is to test a concept in action and see what can be improved. The $630,000 spent on the pilot included—unlike a Western or cop show—the cost of building sets, props, and costumes which it would be hard to use for any other purpose, and so NBC clearly had a financial and artistic investment in making *Star Trek* work. Roddenberry told fans it was "unprecedented" for a show to be granted a second pilot, but he must have known that was nonsense—it was uncommon, but plenty of shows did, including *All in the Family*, *Lost in Space*, and *Gilligan's Island*.

Herb Solow and Robert Justman, respectively executive in charge of production and producer on the original series, published their own behind-the-scenes account, the book *Inside Star Trek: The Real Story*, in 1996. They say there that the executives had no particular philosophical objection to a woman first officer, they just didn't like Majel Barrett in the role. Roddenberry had been having an affair with Barrett for several years by this point. Not all of the executives knew this, although some did. There was dissatisfaction with her performance both from those who knew about the relationship and those who didn't. A couple of individuals in the know were worried about the consequences for the show if the two split acrimoniously, or if it became public knowledge that the executive producer was having an extra-marital affair with its female lead. *Inside Star Trek* concludes that Roddenberry might have concocted the story because he didn't have the heart to tell Barrett the studio didn't like her acting.

Once they'd seen the pilot in February 1965, NBC made it clear they wanted changes and ordered three new scripts to assess the potential of the series. These were delivered in May. Roddenberry wrote one, and extensively rewrote the other two. The first, "Mudd's Women," was a comedy story written by Stephen Kandel about a galactic conman. It was mostly set on the ship, so it would be cheap to make. It wasn't seen as a good pilot episode, but reading the script would have served to demonstrate that *Star Trek* could change pace if needed. "The Omega Glory" was a script by Roddenberry featuring two alien tribes with ideologies very similar to American democracy and Soviet Communism. Robert Justman hated it. The story was eventually made at the end of the second season.

The studio were concerned that *Star Trek* would be an expensive show to make, and while it sounds counterintuitive, it therefore made sense that they should produce the most elaborate script, "Where No Man Has Gone Before" by Samuel A. Peeples, as the second pilot. The story saw the *Enterprise* pass through an energy barrier, and two of the crew (one of them played by Gary Lockwood) become beings with godlike powers. It required elaborate model-work and optical effects. The challenge was to make it on a tight budget, and Roddenberry and his team did just that. Helped by the fact that they could use sets and costumes from the first pilot, and a shorter running time, the second pilot cost a little over half as much as "The Cage": $354,974.

"Where No Man Has Gone Before" is a halfway house between the first pilot and the regular series. Viewed now, it's interesting to see what's missing—Scotty and Sulu are there, Dr. McCoy and Uhura aren't. Spock is restrained, but still emotional, and becomes visibly annoyed when he loses a chess game to his captain. The captain has a new yeoman, but it's not Janice Rand, as it would be in the regular series. The biggest change, of course, was that the *Enterprise* had a new captain. William Shatner was third choice to play Captain Kirk, after Jack Lord and Lloyd Bridges. Shatner has noted wryly that, as the pilot was rejected for being "too cerebral" and the network were concerned about the budget, "I suspect Roddenberry thought I was the perfect choice for the lead role in a show because I wasn't too intelligent for the audience, and he didn't have to pay me a lot of money."[9]

What about "equality"? The crew still wear a unisex uniform, gold or blue thick sweaters and black trousers. There's a prominent female guest role—Sally Kellerman as Dr. Elizabeth Dehner—but she's killed off during the episode. So what can we deduce about Gene Roddenberry's attitude?

Here is the description of J.M. Colt, the yeoman who appears in the first pilot. It's written by Roddenberry for the March 1964 pitch document, so early on in the process that the captain was not yet called Pike, but had his original name, Robert April. It wasn't intended that the public would ever read this, and it has not been interfered with by even a single television executive:

> The Captain's Yeoman. Except for problems in naval parlance, J.M. Colt would be called a yeo-woman. With a strip-queen figure even a uniform cannot hide, Colt serves as Captain's secretary, reporter, bookkeeper— and with surprising efficiency. She undoubtedly dreams of serving Robert April with equal efficiency in personal departments.

Colt's replacement as yeoman in the second pilot, Smith— played by the model Andrea Dromm—was herself replaced, of course, when the show went to series, by Grace Lee Whitney's Yeoman Rand. Janice Rand was obviously intended to be a major character. The initial publicity for *Star Trek* billed Whitney as the female lead. The cover of her 1998 autobiography, *The Longest Trek: My Tour of the Galaxy*, uses a picture from a photo shoot done before the phaser props were ready (they're carrying electric torches instead and pretending they're futuristic guns) and she's dressed in the "original" uniform, not the minidress. Whitney was thirty-six when she played Rand—she was born in 1930, the year before William Shatner and Leonard Nimoy. The idea was that she was Kirk's equal, that there would be a degree of sexual tension, but that they were professionals. Roddenberry told Whitney it would be "like Kitty and Matt on *Gunsmoke*. It could not be consummated. It had to be love from afar, an unrequited love between the captain and me."[10]

What ended up on screen was a character who was twenty-four, and by far Kirk and Spock's junior in terms of rank and experience. Her role was to serve, to be rescued, to be the victim in "The Enemy Within," when the "bestial" Kirk tries to have his way with her, and in "Miri," when she is tied up and taunted by a gang of children.

Rand was dropped after eight episodes, and it happened so quickly that her scripted appearance in the next episode, "Dagger of the Mind," was rewritten for another actress. Officially, Roddenberry and his team felt that Dr. McCoy was a better character, and that the "unrequited love" angle with Rand not only wasn't working out, it made it hard for Kirk to play romantic stories with other women. The show was running over budget, and of all the regular characters, Rand was felt to be the least essential.[11]

Grace Lee Whitney had a drinking problem, and William Shatner alleged in his book *Star Trek Memories* (1993) that this affected her work, saying: "Grace's condition had worsened to the point where her scenes were consciously being given to other characters or completely written out of episodes."[12] She vehemently denied this, and while she admitted she was on diet pills and amphetamines to control her weight, she said, "I never drank on set, nor would I have allowed alcohol to interfere with my performance . . . it wasn't my drinking that caused me to lose the part on *Star Trek*. It was losing the part on *Star Trek* that really sent my drinking off the scale!"[13]

In her autobiography, Whitney revealed that, after a wrap party for "Miri," a man she refers to only as "the Executive" got her alone and, with both of them very drunk, told her he wanted to make sure Rand had more to do on the show. He forced her to undress, then perform oral sex on him. She went from there to Leonard Nimoy's house. Nimoy was her best friend in the cast, a recovering alcoholic himself, and he would continue to support her. Attitudes to sexual assault were very different at the time. She lacked a term for what had happened, as she didn't consider it "rape." Whitney told Nimoy the name of her attacker (and Nimoy knew him) but apparently never named him to anyone else, even when offered "a considerable sum of money by a major New York publisher":

> "I refused to do that . . . there were two reasons I refused to name him: one, I am a recovering alcoholic, and in order to keep my sobriety . . . I must make amends to all persons I have harmed—even those who have hurt me. I must not harm others. So I refused to hurt this man or his reputation. And two, I was afraid of him and what he might do to me."[14]

There has been some speculation online about the identity of this "executive," with some—inevitably perhaps—suggesting it was Gene Roddenberry himself. Whitney implies that "the Executive" was still alive when *Star Trek Memories* was published in 1993, and Roddenberry died in 1991.[15] Shatner's book refers to the attacker as a "network executive" and Roddenberry was certainly not that. In her autobiography, Whitney conceded that Roddenberry made advances towards her, but what she says and the tone in which she says it contrasts starkly with the way she talks about her attacker:

> "Did Gene make passes at me? You better believe he did! Passes, innuendoes, double-entendres, the whole nine yards. But I wanted to keep our relationship on a professional basis and I was basically moral at the time (it wasn't until after I got written out of *Star Trek* that my sexaholism went off the scale). Who knows? Maybe if Gene had gotten me in the sack, I might have done all three seasons of *Star Trek* instead of only half a season!"[16]

Whitney long thought she'd been fired at the request of "the Executive." The assault was on a Friday night, August 26, 1966,[17] and she was informed that her contract would not be extended the following Tuesday, August 30.[18] Many years later she came to accept evidence that the decision had been made before the assault—we have a memo talking about reducing her role that dates from August 12, 1966.[19] She doesn't make the connection, but "the Executive" may have preyed on her when he did precisely because he knew this was his last opportunity, as she would be getting fired the following week. There's no evidence that anyone but Nimoy knew about the assault at the time.

In August, Roddenberry had brought Gene L. Coon onboard as a line producer, to help with the day-to-day running of the show. The two Genes had worked together on *The Lieutenant*, and Coon brought a fresh eye to *Star Trek* that would lead to changes that fundamentally strengthened the show. One of the most significant was the elevation of McCoy to a more central role. Bob Justman and Roddenberry both accepted the logic of reducing Rand's part, but the original plan seems to have been for her to reappear as an occasional guest star. On October 28, Roddenberry wrote a memo to Coon suggesting they look for an opportunity to reintroduce her. Writers including Harlan Ellison and David Gerrold included the character in their scripts, but Rand never returned to the original show.

As Shatner puts it in *Star Trek Memories*, for Whitney being fired from *Star Trek* "marked the beginning of a personal slide that would become so deep and horrendous as to ultimately include a harsh, skid-row existence and prostitution."[20] Whitney claimed that in the Seventies, when Roddenberry was planning to revive the show, he told her,

"Grace, I've never made such a big mistake in my life as allowing NBC and Paramount to write you out. If I'd only seen my way clear, I could have kept you aboard. You would be the only person, really, who knew the inside story of Captain Kirk, and you could have been waiting for him when he came back from the escapades. We would have had a whole new focus for the show and for the character . . . I'm going to put you in the next series."[21]

It's worth noting that this may be an example of Roddenberry telling someone what they wanted to hear. Rand does not feature in the plans for the *Star Trek II* television series, which reached an extremely advanced stage. As it was, Grace Lee Whitney returned as Rand for blink-and-you-miss-them cameos in the *Star Trek* movies. The most substantial saw her as communications officer on Captain Sulu's USS *Excelsior* in *Star Trek VI* (1991), and she returned to the same station for "Flashback," a 1996 episode of *Star Trek: Voyager* set during the same timeframe as that movie.

Once Janice Rand was written out, the most prominent regular female role on the original series was, of course, that of Lieutenant Uhura, played by Nichelle Nichols. She, though, soon decided to quit at the end of the first season. She had been offered a part on Broadway, and was not enjoying her experience on the show. Nichols attended an event in New York where Martin Luther King Jnr was speaking. She met Dr. King afterwards, and was astonished to learn he was a *Star Trek* fan. He told her that she was an important role model to young black women. She returned to Hollywood, and told Roddenberry what had happened:

> "I don't know if you know what Gene looked like, but he
> was a big guy and was like 6'3" with that hawk nose and a
> great sense of humor and this brilliant mind and a futurist
> and—whatever great things you heard about him are just
> a small part of what that man was. I looked down at him
> sitting behind his desk when I told him the story and I finally
> shut up, and a huge tear is rolling down his cheek. And he
> said, 'Thank God someone understands what I am trying to
> achieve.'"[22]

If Nichols had left—and she has said she'd got as far as handing Roddenberry a letter of resignation—the show's only female "regular" cast member would have been Majel Barrett's Christine Chapel, a character who'd only appeared three times in the first season. Herb Solow claimed of Roddenberry that "the only performers he would stand up for were the actresses with whom he'd had a previous relationship: Majel Barrett, Nichelle Nichols, and Grace Lee Whitney."[23] In her autobiography, though, Whitney flatly denied sleeping with Roddenberry: "Sorry, Herb—you and Bob wrote a great book, but you got this one wrong. It doesn't matter how you define the word 'personal,' it is simply not true . . . I never had a romantic relationship with Gene Roddenberry before *Star Trek*, during *Star Trek* or after *Star Trek*."[24] Nor did he show any great interest in building up Uhura's role. Many years later, his secretary Susan Sackett suggested that "throughout his lifetime, he was never quite able to see women in a completely objective manner, and he brought a lot of excess baggage and hang-ups from his generation."[25] Chapel appeared in more episodes from the second season, but for the most part, *Star Trek* settled into a pattern of a "girl of the week"—episodes would see a parade of female Starfleet officers in the regulation miniskirt, or an alien space babe. Every actress was gorgeous, most could act, many of them were strikingly good. They played strong characters, and often demonstrated a gift for comedy and a real screen presence . . . and after one episode, they would vanish without trace. The pattern is set by Janice Rand's "replacement" in "Dagger of the Mind," Marianna Hill as Starfleet psychiatrist Dr. Helen Noel.

Roddenberry fought battles with television executives over these characters, but only over what they wore. *Star Trek* costume designer William Ware Theiss would go on to work with Roddenberry on many projects. They clearly enjoyed playing with network's often bizarre restrictions.

Roddenberry had a favorite example of the ludicrous rules he was expected to follow. In *The Making of Star Trek* he states that "the navel is also taboo . . . you are not supposed to show it or call undue attention to it."[26] Decades later, Roddenberry would still be telling conventions that he and Theiss conspired to design the skimpiest possible outfit that still managed to cover the belly button. The best candidate for the *Star Trek* costume that does this would seem to be the one worn by Lois Jewell as Drusilla the slave girl in "Bread and Circuses," who wears a brown outfit consisting of two triangles of material that converge at her navel. On his later project *Genesis II*, Roddenberry and

Theiss had a mutant woman bare her midriff to reveal . . . two belly buttons, as an in-joke.

Another possibility, though, is that Roddenberry made up the story. It is true that a number of otherwise skimpy outfits on *Star Trek* have odd high waists, or strips or drapes of material that conveniently cover up the navel. But it's also true that in every season there are at least a couple of examples where they're exposed—the dancing girls in "Shore Leave"; Khan's followers in "Space Seed"; the bellydancer in "Wolf in the Fold"; the "evil" Uhura in "Mirror, Mirror" (and the other women seen in the episode); Droxine in "The Cloud Minders"; several of the "hippie" women in "The Way to Eden." It's possible Roddenberry received a memo asking him to make the costumes less revealing, and that this memo mentioned the navel . . . but no such memo has ever been found in any of the various archives scoured over the years by fans researching the show. Tania Lemani, who played the bellydancer in "The Wolf in the Fold," remembers that "in those days you were not supposed to show your belly button on TV,"[27] but the fact she was playing a bellydancer in the first place demonstrates that this wasn't a strict, puritanical regime. The evidence would seem to be that shows were supposed to avoid showing too much skin, but were allowed to get away with a degree of mild naughtiness, and that by the late Sixties, the "ban on belly buttons" was honored more in the breach.

And if we take a step back, then this adds up to a consistent picture: Gene Roddenberry was clearly committed to stretching the boundaries of "what you could show" when it came to women on television, but this didn't involve him fighting to get a story that featured subversive gender politics on air, or to champion giving the women in the cast larger and more varied roles. Instead he was campaigning to liberate actresses from their clothes. He talked about wanting to establish that the *Enterprise* crew was split roughly equally along gender lines—but the women were secretaries who looked like strippers and wanted to sleep with their boss.

There is a very odd paradox at the heart of *Star Trek*, or at least it's easy to find many examples where the show wants to have its cake and eat it when it comes to women and sexuality. We can trace this back to its creator. Sex was very important to Gene Roddenberry.

Roddenberry wrote about sex, he talked about sex in interviews and lectures, and he created characters who espoused thinly veiled versions of his attitudes to sex. It's clear that he saw American society in the 1960s as particularly "hung up" on sex, that the human race was (to quote an alien space babe in *Star Trek: The Motion Picture*) "a sexually immature species," and that this was one of the issues which would need to be worked on before the bright future of *Star Trek* could be attained. Roddenberry's scripts in the Seventies went even further in exploring sexuality: "Planet Earth" depicted a matriarchal future society, and *Pretty Maids All in a Row* was a sex comedy.

Moreover, Gene Roddenberry practiced what he preached.

The official record looks rather straightforward. He married twice, both marriages lasting more than twenty years. He'd married Eileen-Anita Rexroat on June 20, 1942, when he was twenty and she was eighteen. They had two daughters, Darleen (born 1948) and Dawn (born 1953). They divorced in 1969, and he quickly married Majel Barrett. They had a son together, Eugene Wesley Roddenberry Jnr (born in 1974, he's been known as "Rod" since childhood). Roddenberry remained married to Majel until his death in 1991.

In his private life Roddenberry's attitudes to sexuality and gender could be extraordinarily self-interested and often rather regressive, even by the standards of the time. His official biography itself has to concede that "Gene had always lived by his own code of marriage ethics, a set of standards that did not have sexual fidelity near the top of the list or, perhaps, even on the list."[28] By the early Fifties, working at the LAPD, it was an open secret that he had a string of affairs with secretaries.

When he started working in television, Roddenberry had flings with actresses. Many women clearly found him very charming, and it's the women in his life who seem the least conflicted and most generous in their praise.

His plans did not always come to fruition. Of his choice of model Andrea Dromm to play the yeoman in the second pilot, Herb Solow says, "It was a non-part. But during the casting process, director Jimmy Goldstone overheard Gene say, 'I'm hiring her because I want to score with her.' It was not only a non-part, I'm sure it was a non-score as well."[29]

He met Majel Barrett (her stage name; she'd been born Majel Leigh Hudec) in 1961, and becoming lovers "sort of developed after we'd become friends."[30] Majel had no doubt at all that Gene was telling her the truth when he said his marriage to Eileen was loveless and the two of them were staying together for the sake of the children. She also didn't think he'd ever leave his wife. While they didn't flaunt their relationship, and not everyone working at the studio knew, they made little attempt to hide it and attended parties as a couple.

In 1964, Roddenberry also had a relationship with Nichelle Nichols. According to Nichols the affair was over before she was cast in *Star Trek*, and—while there was some speculation on set—no one else on the show except Barrett had any idea it had ever happened until decades later. Nichols wrote about the relationship in her autobiography, *Beyond Uhura*, which was published after Roddenberry's death. After appearing on *The Lieutenant*, she and Roddenberry started with a few lunch dates, then began a relationship that lasted "several months," apparently over the spring and summer of 1964. It had quickly "become uncomfortably intense for both of us." She knew "his divorce wasn't yet final" (this seems somewhat overstating the state of play: while the marriage had clearly been an unhappy one for some time, it wasn't formally ended until July 1969). Nichols says they at least discussed getting married—she was far less "idealistic" than he was, seeing huge problems for both of them in an "interracial" relationship.

Roddenberry then surprised her with a trip to meet Majel Barrett—and they surprised him in turn, as the two knew each other. Both being young actresses, they'd met at an audition. The two women had a polite conversation. Roddenberry said, according to Nichols, "I couldn't go on behind either one of your backs. I love you both too much. I didn't know any other way to bring—to tell—the two women that I love that I'm in love with two women,"[31] Nichols realized Barrett "was dedicated to Gene above all else," and stepped aside—although not before reminding Roddenberry that, since he was married, he actually had three women in his life.

Roddenberry was working on the pitch and pilot episode for *Star Trek* throughout 1964, and he told Nichols "there will be something important in it for you."[32] She was cast in neither pilot, but Roddenberry put in good words for her elsewhere. Nichols has remained extremely loyal to her ex-lover, saying, "His appetite for life was insatiable. He was one of the most interesting people I've ever known, and throughout the years I have always been proud to call him my friend."[33]

Unlike the vast majority of the original regular cast of *Star Trek*, Majel Barrett never wrote her autobiography. So, while her relationship with Roddenberry came up in the questions she was asked in interviews and at conventions, she never presented a full account of her own story. A constant presence in Roddenberry's life since 1961, she was his mistress when he came up with *Star Trek* and pitched it to the network, and he cast her in "the Spock role" for the pilot, and then as Christine Chapel in the broadcast series. They would marry in 1969, very soon after he divorced Eileen—possibly even before his divorce came through. She is the mother of his son. She appeared in small roles in many of his subsequent projects, and had a recurring guest role as Lwaxana Troi, mother of regular character Deanna Troi, in *Star Trek: The Next Generation*.

While opinion of Roddenberry divides his colleagues and acquaintances between those who loved him and those who loathed him, Majel Barrett has proved far harder to draw a bead on. People agree she seemed taller and more striking in real life than she did on screen (officially she was five foot nine). No one argues that she was devoted to Roddenberry, passionately in his corner, or that she was central to the lasting success of *Star Trek* because she cultivated the fans, got them on side. Some portrayals have her almost as a Borgia dowager, the dark power behind the throne; according to others she was empty-headed and oddly oblivious to the world. She once told an interviewer, "I don't think. I really don't. I'm not an intelligent person. I'm very shallow. I like being shallow. I like fun and laughter." When the interviewer suggested that was exactly the sort of thing someone cunning would say if they were trying to mask their intelligence, Barrett changed the subject to hat ribbons.[34] Those who loved Gene often use Majel as a scapegoat. Those who found him dishonest and manipulative hold up his relationship with his wife as evidence.

"There may be times when I feel like dipping my wick, and I do so. When it's right. When it feels good people may say 'oh, that Gene Roddenberry, he's no good. He's an unfaithful husband.' I say unfaithful to what—?"

"Majel, surely?"

"No, not at all. People aren't concerned in their deepest selves about Majel. They're concerned about themselves, their rules and so on. They mean I am unfaithful to the ideal, their ideal, of marriage . . . Majel and I have our own agreement."[35]

Within a few years of marrying Barrett, Roddenberry had begun a long-term affair with his secretary, Susan Sackett. In 2002, Hawk Publishing released *Inside Trek: My Secret Life with Star Trek Creator Gene Roddenberry*, Sackett's 220-page account of their relationship. She started work as his secretary on his fifty-third birthday, August 19, 1974. Gene's son Rod was five months old. Roddenberry soon persuaded her to skinny-dip in his pool, and within a year was making more overt sexual advances: "Teasingly he asked if I would engage in a certain sex act—delicately put, it's the one Monica and Bill enjoyed so much in the 1990s. Today this would be grounds for an harassment suit, but in those days this sort of thing generally went unchallenged."[36]

Later they would smoke pot together and consummate the relationship, which continued until Roddenberry's death. Whatever "arrangement" Gene had with his wife, whenever Sackett stayed overnight at his place, she "usually slept fitfully, fearful that Majel might burst in and find us there."[37]

For a number of years, Roddenberry had been working on an original *Star Trek* novel, "The God Thing." He only ever wrote sixty-eight pages of it, but Sackett had read what there was of the manuscript. One evening, Roddenberry showed up at her house with a child's paddling pool, twelve pints of baby oil and some foaming milk bath, and she guessed he had a very specific fantasy in mind, based on "The God Thing": "there was a scene in which several female sirens tantalized Captain Kirk while they engaged in a weightless free-for-all, rolling in oil, their bodies glistening in what began as a sensual gymnastic event for Kirk and turned into a deadly contest for his life."[38]

Things didn't quite go to plan. "There was hardly enough oil to cover the bottom of the pool, and it didn't mix well with the foaming milk bath. We tried to slide around in it and pretend we were weightless, writing space cadets or something, but it was really quite messy. Also the floor was hard, so it wasn't very comfortable."[39]

In the only novel Roddenberry did complete, the novelization of *Star Trek: The Motion Picture* (1979), there are more references to men getting erections than are strictly necessary to tell the story:

> "Hello, Jim." As always, her lips seemed to caress his name as she spoke it.
>
> He could almost catch the scent of her body fragrance, and he could feel the slight pressure of his genitals responding to those memories.[40]

By the Eighties, other people Roddenberry worked along-side would become either uncomfortable with or merely amused by his obsession with sexualizing his work. As he prepared *Star Trek: The Next Generation*, he noted that Deanna Troi's race the Betazoids "engage in almost constant sexual activity"; in the series, we learn that they have nudist wedding ceremonies. Herb Wright, co-producer of the first season of *The Next Generation*, says that when they started discussing one of the new alien races, "He spent twenty-five minutes explaining to me all the sexual positions the Ferengi could go through. I finally said, 'Gene, this is a family show, on at 7:00 on Saturdays.' He finally said, 'Okay, you're right.'"[41]

Roddenberry did use *Star Trek* to engage more thought-fully on the subject of sexual relationships and societal attitudes. Typically, the male lead character of an American TV show in the Sixties was a young heterosexual man who "gets the girl"—in a serial, a string of girls. Captain Kirk was famously good at conforming to this model, with a guest star falling for his charms most weeks. Action-adventure shows of the time rarely delved into the personal lives of their characters, and nothing Kirk or his crew get up to really suggests that the future society of *Star Trek* has wildly different social mores than 1960s America.

Christine Chapel had a fiancé in "What Are Little Girls Made Of?" and a crush on Spock by "Amok Time." Very little else was said on the subject, and there was nothing to suggest that marriage took any other form than one man and one woman bonding for life, and having children. An episode was planned, but never made, in which it would be established that McCoy had a daughter, Joanna, but that they were estranged since he'd divorced her mother.[42] Not until the movies—and then in one which Gene Roddenberry had little to do with—did we meet a character whose parents we knew weren't married when he was born. There were, to be fair, a number of "interracial" marriages—although in *Star Trek* terms, that came from marrying a Vulcan, an energy being or an android, rather than a human being of a different race.

Roddenberry did, though, imagine the nature of marriage changing. He took for granted that it would cease being a religious ceremony. A wedding service in *Star Trek*'s first-season episode "Balance of Terror" begins to the strains of "Here Comes the Bride," but Kirk hits a secular, inclusionary note . . .

KIRK: Since the days of the first wooden vessels,
all shipmasters have had one happy privilege.
That of uniting two people in the bonds of matrimony.
We are gathered here today with you, Angela Martine,
and you, Robert Tomlinson, in the sight of your
fellows, in accordance with our laws and our many
beliefs so that you may pledge your—

. . . before the ceremony is interrupted by a Romulan attack. The view of matrimony espoused by Kirk was not a radical one in the 1960s, when many Americans had started to see marriage less as a religious sacrament and more as a civil contract. There's no evidence that the network blinked an eye at the wording of the ceremony.

At the end of his life, Roddenberry was asked when, in his vision of the future, two people would marry. He replied:

> "I think they don't, in a perfect world. I don't think there's that kind of mutual possession. Marriage in the form that it is now cannot possibly continue into the future. That is why we have so little of it in *Star Trek* . . . my idea was to portray a world in which people are developed enough as humans to be sufficient unto themselves, and in which they have a wonderful world of human alien contact to explore. They don't remain single, from my point of view, in order to satisfy some romantic need on the part of the audience."[43]

After the original run of the show was completed, Roddenberry started to think through a more detailed and radical model for its future society. The novelization of *Star Trek: The Motion Picture* contained a number of interesting gems, particularly early on. Some fans had speculated that Kirk and Spock were in a homosexual relationship. Roddenberry had Kirk himself rule out the possibility that he and Spock were lovers, but with a degree of open-mindedness and humor:

> "Although I have no moral or other objections to physical love in any of its many Earthly, alien and mixed forms, I have always found my best gratification in that creature *woman*.

Also, I would dislike being thought of as so foolish that I would select a love partner who came into heat only once every seven years."[44]

We can see that there has been a sexual revolution on Earth. Marriage can now be a short-term contract—Kirk and a woman called Lori Ciana have recently "lived the basic and simple one-year arrangement together."[45] People can be coached on sexual technique—we learn that Jim Kirk was named after "my mother's first love instructor."[46] Spock and Kirk's relationship is complex and best expressed using the Vulcan word *t'hy'la*, glossed in the following terms: "The human concept of friend is most nearly duplicated in Vulcan thought by the term *t'hy'la*, which can also mean brother and lover."

Roddenberry's attitude did evolve over the years. He was careful that *Star Trek: The Next Generation* should watch its pronouns—famously, when Picard took over from Kirk, the opening narration changed from "Where No *Man* Has Gone Before" to "Where No *One* Has Gone Before." After Roddenberry's death, Susan Sackett

"began to notice that there was an increasing tendency on the part of the writers to masculinize the series . . . during the early seasons of TNG I was constantly on the lookout for gender-discriminating terminology . . . I monitored scripts for things like "crewman," which would always be changed to "crew member," and sentences like "my men are working on it," which could easily be changed to "my staff (or crew) are working on it." These were subtle, but (I felt) important contributions toward updating the 60s mentality of the original series."[47]

One of the most subtle and interesting developments was Roddenberry's idea that Riker and Troi would share "a sort of prototype relationship, a friendship between the opposite sexes carried to its fullest capacity."[48] In *Gene Roddenberry: The Last Conversation* (1994), a book that collects an extended interview/discussion between a dying Roddenberry and writer Yvonne Fern, he explained the concept: "They are friends, first and foremost, and then they have this sexual component. And they can choose to utilize that component—act on it or not. But it's not a romance."

Needing a word for this, he coined the Betazoid term *imzadi*, meaning "beloved." Fern tells him that she thinks it comes across as a far more conventional relationship, and Roddenberry seems resigned to it being written that way. In the final *Next Generation* movie, *Nemesis*, Riker and Troi, now middle-aged, get married in a ceremony that looks like a generic modern-day American wedding. Why did Riker wait so long to make an honest woman of his *imzadi*? Sadly, it's probably not a reference to "Manhunt," a second-season episode where Roddenberry's wife played Troi's mother as she hit "the Phase":

TROI: My mother is beginning a physiological phase. It's one that all Betazoid women must deal with as they enter mid-life.

RIKER: Yes, it's something Troi warned me about when we first started to see each other. A Betazoid woman, when she goes through this phase, quadruples her sex drive.

TROI: Or more.

RIKER: Or more? You never told me that.

It's not hard to argue that, in the original series, McCoy proved a better character than Janice Rand. If you had to choose whether *Star Trek* should continue with Number One or with Spock, you'd be mad not to pick Spock. Nor is it hard to see why Nichelle Nichols might have been frustrated with her role as Uhura. But the same thing happens with *Star Trek: The Next Generation*. Of the three women with central roles in the pilot, two are gone by the start of the second season, and the third has been marginalized. Each time, you can justify the decision, but it's a consistent pattern: male characters are given more and more to do, but what start out as strong, central female characters disappear. Gene Roddenberry finds it hard to write for women as anything other than objects of male desire. As early as "The Cage," his conscience is nagging at him about this, but he never listens to it for long. From the vantage point of the twenty-first century, Gene Roddenberry looks distinctly old-fashioned when he talks about women and sexuality more generally. At his worst, he represents some of the most unpleasant behavior of the past rather than the best of the future.

CHAPTER THREE

CREATED BY . . .

Gene Roddenberry is the creator of *Star Trek*. A caption comes up at the start of every episode saying it is "created by Gene Roddenberry." The back cover copy of Roddenberry's novelization of *Star Trek: The Motion Picture* runs:

> THE GREAT BIRD OF THE GALAXY WRITES A *STAR TREK* NOVEL!
>
> The writer-producer who created Mr. Spock and all the other *Star Trek* characters—who invented the Starship *Enterprise*, who gave the show its look, its ideals—puts it all together again here in his first *Star Trek* novel![1]

When some *Star Trek* aficionados talk about Roddenberry, we get an inkling of how religions must start. The following comes from the dustjacket of *Gene Roddenberry: The Last Conversation*:

As Gene receded from life, Yvonne's increasingly solitary task was to convey the richness, the insight, the radiance they saw in each other and in humanity. This beautiful book, written as a philosophical dialogue, is a last confessional call upon centuries of earlier attempts to codify our understanding of human experience and what lies beyond . . . As we read and reread this stunning work, we are moved a little closer to the luminous future that Gene Roddenberry knew was already within us.[2]

"The Great Bird of the Galaxy" had been Roddenberry's nickname on set. Coined by co-producer Robert Justman in a very early production memo, it was worked into the script of the first episode to be broadcast, "The Man Trap," when Sulu thanks Rand with a lighthearted "May the Great Bird of the Galaxy bless your planet." Roddenberry enjoyed the nickname and it gained currency within early Star Trek fandom.

It is ironic that Robert Justman should have come up with a name that so aggrandized Roddenberry, as he would go on to co-write with Herb Solow the book that makes the most compelling case for shifting credit for Star Trek's success away from its creator. As the subtitle of Inside Star Trek: The Real Story, implies, Solow and Justman made the case that there was a "false story" out there that needed addressing. While on the publicity round for the book, Solow elaborated:

"Well one of the myths is that—and I can readily understand how this occurred in the first place and then grew and grew and was magnified—is that one man did the whole thing. One man had the idea, wrote the scripts, directed, produced, cast all the actors, designed the sets, did the costumes and the hair and everything else, and that just isn't true. We had a complement of about a hundred and twenty-five enormously talented men and women who contributed greatly to the success of *Star Trek*."[3]

There were definitely times where Gene Roddenberry would agree with this sentiment. As he said himself, on September 4, 1985, at the unveiling of his star on Hollywood Boulevard: "When they say on a show 'Created by' anyone, like 'Created by Gene Roddenberry,' that is not true. I laid out a pathway, and then the only thing I will take credit for is I surrounded myself by very bright people who came up with all those wonderful things. And then you can appear very smart."

But on more numerous occasions he would say things like: "I am as near to an absolute monarch as is possible in this industry. I have complete control over what my show says and does. Much, much more freedom. And far more direct responsibility for what goes out there to the audience. *I* am *Star Trek*."[4]

This is nonsense. Fern brought up the line in an interview a couple of years later:

"Yes, he did feel he was the center of the *Star Trek* universe. No question about it. He said to me over and over again, 'I am *Star Trek*,' which as Herb pointed out, if he had said that while they were making it, they probably would have stoned him to death. But, 'I am *Star Trek*' is something he said over and over again. Now I know from other people that he did appreciate the work that other people did, but he didn't publicly acknowledge it, which is a mistake on his part and it leads to the conclusion that he tended to be the be all and end all of *Star Trek*, and he wasn't."

Roddenberry had made the "absolute monarch" claim at the end of his life, several years after his removal from the day-to-day running of *Star Trek: The Next Generation*. As for the movies, here's what Nicholas Meyer, the writer/director of *Star Trek VI*, which was in production as Fern was in conversation with Roddenberry, had to say about the creator's role:

"Roddenberry's deal on the *Star Trek* movies called for him to receive a credit . . . and, I assume, a salary and profit participation, but it did not include actual involvement in making the movies after *Star Trek: The Motion Picture*. Nonetheless, there had evolved the tradition of kissing the ring . . . It was not, as I say, my finest hour. Roddenberry was old and in ill health, soon to die. The fact I was tired and unwilling to revisit the screenplay when it was almost time to start shooting was of less moment than my conviction that what was in the script was correct. I left the meeting and returned to work, leaving others to mop up the damage I had done."[5]

There may be shows that are so successful and important to their studio or network that their executive producers are able, for a time, to operate as absolute monarchs. Even so, they won't always get their first-choice actor for a particular role, there will always be circumstances beyond their control, they are always accountable to the people running the studio and the network. And, a lot of the time, the things that work are the happy accidents, the guest or bit-part player who steals the scene, the solution that the director and actors had to semi-improvise because of technical difficulties on the day.

It's important to note that there is nothing inherently wrong with an executive producer taking the credit for using someone else's idea. Deciding on the best of the available options among the many ideas pitched to him is an executive producer's job and is itself a difficult, creative act. A writer might come up with a great script but he's working within the framework the executive producer has established. Before the writer writes that script, the producer has chosen it over the other potential scripts and weighed up factors the writer might know very little about, like actor availability, other scripts in the works, technical challenges, and how much money remains from the season budget. Roddenberry assembled his team, picked the actors, writers, and production staff, and managed their conflicting demands.

No one would seek to deny Roddenberry his credit. The distinction is that, as Solow put it, "Gene had a blind spot about recognizing the contribution of others."[6] This wasn't simply an abstract desire of his to be seen as the "creator" of the show. Roddenberry routinely rewrote every script early on. There was the legitimate practical problem that, with any new show, writers struggle to capture the right tone, or to write dialogue that sounds like the sort of things the regular characters would say. This was clearly more of a problem for *Star Trek* than it would be for a generic Western or cop show. There wasn't much science fiction on television, so few people had experience writing scripts in the genre. Avid fans of SF had to understand they were writing for a specific show, and not producing short stories for magazines like *Galaxy* or *Analog*.

There was, though, a mercenary reason: Roddenberry's contract paid him between $750 and $3000 for working on someone else's script, depending on the level of rewrites. It incentivized him to work on every single script that came in. Solow likened it to "putting the fox in charge of the henhouse; it was Gene, himself, deciding what stories and scripts needed rewriting."[7]

One of the constant accusations in the case against Roddenberry is that throughout *Star Trek*'s run, and afterwards, he sought to ensure he received a cut from any aspect of the show that was capable of generating money. Certainly he could be quite calculating about this. His attorney, Leonard Maizlish, a constant presence in Roddenberry's life for the duration of his writing career—and particularly at the end—looked out for his client in ways that many found rather disreputable. In December 1966, when Maizlish tried to take a cut of Leonard Nimoy's fee for the album *Mr. Spock's Music from Outer Space*, it marked the start of a long-simmering feud between Nimoy and Roddenberry. Another notorious example was his insertion of a clause into the contract of the composer of the theme music, Alexander Courage, which allowed Roddenberry to write lyrics for the theme. Roddenberry did so, never intending to use them on the show. Why? Because a royalty was due every time the *Star Trek* theme was played, and if the song had lyrics, the lyricist split the money 50/50 with the composer.

In a similar vein, he was listed with Stephen E. Whitfield as co-author of *The Making of Star Trek*. Roddenberry was extensively interviewed, supplied a great deal of background material, and afforded Whitfield every access to the production, but he didn't write a word for the book, or apparently read it before publication. He did, though, receive 50 percent of the advance and royalties.

Maizlish was also involved in the setting up of Lincoln Enterprises, a deliberately murky process. Roddenberry was trying to conceal this activity (and revenue) from his then wife, as he didn't want to split the company's assets in the event of their divorce. Lincoln Enterprises had initially been created by Roddenberry and Majel Barrett as a service paid for by the studio to answer fan mail for the series. Roddenberry enlisted the help of *Star Trek* fan Bjo Trimble, and she diligently did what she could both to send autographed photos of the cast and shield the actors from some of the more enthusiastic audience members. Someone at Lincoln Enterprises was canny enough to collate a list of names and addresses, and the company soon evolved into a mail order business which sold *Star Trek* memorabilia.[8]

The company issued catalogs offering a series of exclusive items, including "Flight Deck Certificates" signed by Gene Roddenberry and "Captain Kirk"—whose signature varies, but is usually identified by amateur internet graphologists as belonging to Majel Barrett. The two most popular lines were scripts and film trims. Roddenberry simply had the studio print up more copies of each script than he needed for the production, snuck the surplus copies home and sold them to fans for $5.50 plus postage a time—about $35 in today's money. It was strictly against Writers Guild rules to sell scripts without compensating the writer. Many years down the line, Lincoln Enterprises reached arrangements with the studio and the writers involved and they continued to sell scripts on a more legitimate basis.

For $1, fans could buy a "film trim," a strip of eight frames from footage that had been shot but not used in the series. The subject matter included characters, test shots, model work, and images of the sets. These could be projected onto a screen using a slide projector, and were hugely sought after in the early days—it was a chance to own an actual slice of *Star Trek*. There was only one possible place Lincoln Enterprises could have acquired the film. Solow and Justman relate that when it occurred to an editor working on the third season that he could save money by using old footage of the *Enterprise* flying through space, he went down to the studio vault and was surprised to discover it was completely empty. The security guard said that a while before, "Mr. Roddenberry and his friend, that girl from *Star Trek*, Mabel something" had backed a truck up to the door and told the guard the studio was throwing the film away.[9]

Film is fragile, and many of the frames sold by Lincoln Enterprises have inevitably been lost, or become scratched or faded in the last fifty years. Some fans collected huge numbers of them at the time, however, and these hoards have tended to survive. There are a number of internet projects dedicated to digitally scanning and sharing the frames, which often give valuable clues to the production process, filming dates, scenes that were shot but edited out, or angles on sets, props and costumes that we don't see in the finished episodes.

While the show was in production, interviews and *The Making of Star Trek* pushed the idea of Roddenberry as the head of a large, vibrant creative team. It was after its cancelation that his reputation as a lone visionary took root. This part of the process was very public. In the words of a 1994 court case:

From 1970 to the mid-1980s, Gene criss-crossed the United States, giving lectures (sometimes as many as 40–50 a year) at college campuses and other places about *Star Trek*. He explained the *Star Trek* philosophy as one of "infinite diversity in infinite combinations" . . . Gene traveled throughout the country, very often with Majel, participating in hundreds of

Star Trek conventions. They would give speeches, answer questions, mingle with fans, sign autographs and judge costume contests. He read and answered fan mail. He signed autographs. He gave hundreds of newspaper, radio and television interviews.[10]

After *Star Trek* was canceled, many of the people involved behind the scenes frankly ended up with better careers than Gene Roddenberry did. They had moved on, and were too busy making new television shows or movies to attend the conventions. The fans of the series were thoughtful and engaged, and many had committed *The Making of Star Trek* to memory (the book was in its nineteenth printing by 1977), but they naturally were more keen on getting the autographs of the stars of the show, the actors they recognized, than the script supervisors, co-executive producers, and so on.

Gene Roddenberry's name appeared on the opening credits—and the title sequence for the original series didn't include a full cast list as it did for *Star Trek: The Next Generation* and the later shows. For the first season, the names of William Shatner, Leonard Nimoy, and Gene Roddenberry were the only ones to appear, in that order.

Later, there was a slight reorganization. The captions now ran "*Star Trek* created by Gene Roddenberry / Starring William Shatner / Also starring Leonard Nimoy as Mr. Spock / and DeForest Kelley as Dr. McCoy." Every other regular was bunched up on "featuring" cards at the end, for the simple reason that not every member of the "regular" cast was there every week: Uhura is in sixty-six of the seventy-nine episodes, Scotty is in sixty-four, Sulu fifty-two. Chekov doesn't join until the second season and is in thirty-six, Christine Chapel is in twenty-five, Janice Rand in eight. When fans list the "regular cast," they rarely include John Winston's Lieutenant Kyle, who appears in eleven episodes of the TV series and in *The Wrath of Khan*. The character was also in the animated series, voiced by James Doohan. Kyle's was a small role, but he's seen at the helm and operating the transporter, and he was significant enough to be given an evil twin in the episode "Mirror, Mirror." His exclusion from the list of "regulars" is almost certainly because he was never part of the convention circuit in the Seventies—as *The New York Times* put it:

> But despite all that, and a cameo in the film *Star Trek II: The Wrath of Khan*, the show means little to him. "I liked the cast and crew," said Mr. Winston, 78, a London-born actor. "But there was nothing to build on with that character. What could you have done with three or four lines? I got paid for it, and I forgot about it."[11]

Conventions lured fans to come to them by offering impressive guests. William Shatner has confessed:

> "I turned down the first few invitations because I thought it wasn't dignified. Actors don't go to conventions. That's for mobs! Actors act! Leonard felt differently; he didn't take the whole thing quite so seriously. Even before the conventions

began, he was making personal appearances at state fairs around the country."[12]

Most of the other cast members, though, enjoyed the appreciation and interest fans showed in them. They were also paid appearance fees (albeit extremely modest ones at first). Writers like D.C. (Dorothy) Fontana and David Gerrold attended the cons, and were popular guests, but Roddenberry was the big draw, the behind-the-scenes guru. The Great Bird of the Galaxy. William Shatner says, "What I've never got used to, and what I've never come close to experiencing outside of a *Star Trek* convention, is the palpable wave of love that invariably roars forward from these audiences, crashing down and washing over whatever 'featured speaker' is lucky enough to drown under its wake."[13]

Roddenberry loved the adulation, a huge hall packed with people listening intently to his every pronouncement. Meanwhile, in the dealers' room, Majel Barrett could be found at the Lincoln Enterprises table, and many convention goers report being impressed by her ability to remember them from a previous convention, and her approachability. The Roddenberrys made for an impressive double act, and they spent a decade getting *Star Trek* fans firmly on their side.

Roddenberry continually pushed his name forward. The cover of Susan Sackett's book *Letters to Star Trek* (1977) featured a prominent credit for its "Special Introduction by Gene Roddenberry," but is most remarkable for a painted cover where Roddenberry (smiling and holding a pencil) is front and center, with Kirk, Spock, and the *Enterprise* behind him. Whoever approved the cover had concluded that Roddenberry was the major draw for the sort of people who would buy a book of letters sent to the *Star Trek* production office.

In the Seventies and early Eighties, *Star Trek* remained a cult. Many of the people who'd made the show back in the day were aware that there were conventions but knew very little about what was said there, and they weren't scouring the pages of *Starlog* or the fanzines. *Star Trek* routinely started receiving more mainstream coverage around its twentieth anniversary. Fans themselves started digging deeper into the history of the show. It became abundantly clear by the end of the Eighties that whatever role Gene Roddenberry had once played, and whatever the studio publicity was claiming, he was no longer in charge of the franchise. A reassessment of his role was long overdue.

A number of people have sought to identify those besides Roddenberry who deserve significant credit for *Star Trek*'s success. We can break that success down into four "eras": the original series, the revival of the show's fortunes, the movies, and *Star Trek: The Next Generation*. We will see how the success of the *Star Trek* movie franchise in the Eighties, for example, is almost entirely *despite* Gene Roddenberry, and that credit is due to Harve Bennett, Nicholas Meyer, and Leonard Nimoy.

Solow and Justman's book is an attempt to redress the balance with respect to the original series. As Solow has said:

"if you reduce it down, it comes down to five basic people, and I talk about that in the book. The five people without whom *Star Trek* just would not have gone . . . I don't think it would have gone past the early development stage. Those are the ones, I think, the public should, or the *Star Trek* fans should, know about and realize their great contributions."[14]

In that joint interview, Fern identifies the "five people" as: Solow and Bob Justman themselves, for turning Roddenberry's proposal into a show NBC bought and which Desilu could make on a weekly basis; Matt Jeffries, who designed the model of the *Enterprise* as well as the sets and props; William Ware Theiss, the costume designer; and Gene L. Coon. The book doesn't claim that these are the *only* five people responsible for the success of *Star Trek*—for example, D.C. Fontana and Leonard Nimoy are praised effusively. But it does demonstrate just how large the team on *Star Trek* was.

Coon, the last name on that list, died in 1973 at the age of forty-nine. William Shatner's *Star Trek Memories* dedicates a whole chapter to him, one called "The Unsung Hero." Shatner describes him as "a man who was directly responsible for the lion's share of the creative contributions that served towards making Roddenberry's *good* science fiction show into a frequently *great* one."[15] In his 1973 survey of the series, *The World of Star Trek*, published just a few months before Coon's death, David Gerrold couldn't resist remarking that the show did so well because "it had good Genes."[16] In the twenty years between that book and

Star Trek Memories, though, Gene L. Coon almost completely disappeared from accounts of the creation of *Star Trek*.

Coon was appointed producer in August 1966, and is first credited on the episode "Miri." That was the tenth episode to be filmed as part of the regular series (not counting the two pilots).[17] In practice there's no one episode where Coon joined the show, as many different episodes were "in production" at any given time.

Coon came onboard just before the series started broadcasting. He took stock of the episodes made to that point, built on what was working and cut away what wasn't. It's notable that one of the first decisions made on his watch had been to lose Janice Rand, and to use McCoy more, particularly as a foil to Mr. Spock.

Coon quickly made his mark, writing or co-writing five episodes for the second half of the debut season: "Arena," "A Taste of Armageddon" (with Robert Hamner), "Space Seed" (with Carey Wilber), "The Devil in the Dark," and "Errand of Mercy." Every one is a solid, memorable hour of television, with elements of suspense, and a strikingly good, very simple idea at the heart of it. "Arena" is the one in which Kirk has to defeat "the Gorn," a giant lizard man, in unarmed single combat. In "The Devil in the Dark" a lava creature is killing miners, with the twist that it's doing so to protect its young. Each story has a formidable, even monstrous villain, one with a code of honor but also a core of brutality. "Space Seed" introduces Ricardo Montalban as Khan, and "Errand of Mercy" is the first time we see the Klingons. It would be Coon's scripts, not the series bible written by Roddenberry, that would introduce, name, or clarify some of the core concepts of *Star Trek*: he names Starfleet, tells us that Kirk and his crew are from the United Federation of Planets, introduces the Prime Directive that bans interference with the development of other cultures. Structurally, the first batch of stories tended to start small and gradually ratchet up the threat until there's a massive showdown in the final act. Now, following Coon's example, *Star Trek* would get to the action much faster.

One thing his own scripts don't demonstrate very well is that Coon was keen to include a lot more humor in the series. Throughout his career, when a Gene Roddenberry script tries a joke, it can feel reminiscent of the scene in *Star Trek IV* where Spock intones the definition of the word as "a story with a humorous climax." Roddenberry often crafts a line that's an odd, forced deadpan. Something we're clearly meant to laugh at, rather than something that's actually funny. Left to his own devices, Roddenberry wants *Star Trek* to be serious and to be taken seriously, so he creates something that's rather po-faced. Coon understood the concept of comic relief—that you often heighten the drama by introducing moments of comedy. More to the point, he understood that television audiences want a degree of warmth from their heroes and need to see them smile from time to time.

William Shatner reveled in the change, and instinctively understood that he wasn't being asked to remove or to tone down the furrowed brows and earnest delivery of the early episodes, but to *also* to throw in smirks and playfulness. "Arena" is a great example. The second half of the episode concentrates on scenes involving Kirk by himself on an alien world, trying to dodge the Gorn while fashioning weapons and traps from the plants and rocks. With no one else in the scene, and little dialogue, Shatner essentially starts playing off himself, working in moments of triumph and tragedy, and when things go wrong, often playing it with "comic" reactions of the "oh . . . c'mon, give me a break" kind.

We'd expect any series to have made a few course corrections after half a season, and before Coon was on the show, it had already produced a few very strong episodes. But suddenly the show hit a winning streak.

Star Trek was broadcast for the first time on September 8, 1966. The production team had picked one of their least favorite episodes to launch with. "The Man Trap" was chosen because it was a straightforward monster story, with a large role for Dr. McCoy. For many years, the myth was that *Star Trek* was an underdog—that the network weren't all that keen, that the ratings were low. It's the version of events that Gene Roddenberry told fans in the Seventies and, if you're inclined to believe it, it sounds convincing: the network needed two pilots before they were persuaded; the show was canceled after "only" three seasons; its immense success later proves that if only NBC had shown a little more faith, they'd have seen the quality of the show at the time and publicized it more. In this version of events, of course, Roddenberry is painting a picture of himself as the lone defender of the faith in the wilderness, not the absolute monarch of a magnificent kingdom. The fact is that he was neither of these things.

Star Trek did always exist in a precarious state. It was an expensive show to make, and its ratings never quite justified the price. To understand why it was nearly canceled during its second season, and why it was actually canceled at the end of the third, we need to understand who was paying for it.

There were four parties with a stake in the profits of *Star Trek*. Desilu, the Norway Corporation, and NBC each had a 26⅔ percent stake, with William Shatner owning the other 20 percent.[18] While the original series was being produced, and for fifteen years afterwards, this was purely academic, as there were no profits. It does, though, identify the important players in the production.

When you watch the first and second seasons of *Star Trek*, the caption at the end declares it's a "Desilu Production in association with Norway Corporation." Very astute American viewers might recognize "Desilu" from the end of *Mission: Impossible* or *Mannix*, but they're most likely to have seen it at the end of *I Love Lucy* or *The Lucy Show*. Desilu was comedian Lucille Ball's production company, which she originally set up with her (on- and off-screen) husband, Desi Arnaz—it's not hard to see how the studio got its name. By 1966, Desi and Lucy had divorced, and while she remained an extremely popular performer, and in firm control of Desilu (she *did* have a claim on being the absolute monarch there), the studio was in something of a decline. *Mission: Impossible* and *Star Trek* were conscious attempts to diversify its productions.

Desilu, then, was the "studio." Physically, *Star Trek* and *Mission: Impossible* were filmed in Hollywood, at the company's sound stages on Gower Avenue. It was a relatively small site, a rectangle boxed in by Gower Avenue, Melrose Avenue, the Beth Olam cemetery and the enormous Paramount Studios lot (an accident of geography that would have profound consequences for the destiny of *Star Trek*). It is located at the far end of the Hollywood Walk of Fame.

The Norway Corporation was not some formidable Scandinavian multinational with diverse global business interests that somehow happened to include making *Star Trek* but no other television show. It was a corporation set up by Gene Roddenberry once *Star Trek* was given the green light. Roddenberry was the sole owner and employee. A 1992 court established that "Norway was merely the vehicle in the alter ego of Roddenberry and that he ran it for his purposes and that basically no one else was interested in it, and that it was not a separate independent corporation." It was set up for tax and legal reasons as a place for Roddenberry to bank the checks he got for *Star Trek*. When he died, the corporation passed into the control of his widow. The "Norway Corporation" was Gene Roddenberry.

The "network" in *Star Trek*'s case was NBC, the National Broadcasting Company, based in New York but with offices in Hollywood. Desilu sold *Star Trek* to NBC for an agreed fee per episode. For NBC, it was slightly more complicated. They made their money purely by selling advertising and sponsorship deals. They had a series of calculations to make: they had to arrange their shows on the schedules to maximize their audiences; they had to work out how much to spend marketing each show; and they had to decide if a brand new show would do better than a current one. They were in competition with the other two networks, ABC and CBS.

NBC was in a cut-throat world of dynamic scheduling and marketing decisions. They set their advertising rates in advance, based on projected ratings. They were under constant pressure to keep down costs, build audiences, and weed out underperforming shows.

When we hear Gene Roddenberry talk about "studio executives" and "network executives," then, these are two different sets of overseers, from Desilu and NBC respectively. The "network" wanted to build a mass audience and for *Star Trek* to remain fresh and appealing. The "studio" wanted to keep the network happy so that they would continue to buy *Star Trek*, but they weren't worried, directly, about ratings, advertisers, or scheduling. For the studio, there was one overriding imperative: they had to keep making *Star Trek* for less than NBC had agreed to pay for it. If not, they would effectively be paying NBC to show *Star Trek*.

Roddenberry would have understood the distinction between the studio and the network, of course. We can take it that when he talked to *Star Trek* fans about "television executives," he was simplifying a little to make for a more pithy anecdote. That said, while Roddenberry worked in Hollywood for over thirty years, and seems to have socialized mainly with people in the industry, he never mastered the art of studio politics. He never seemed to understand that the organizations handing over millions of dollars to make his shows were made up of individuals with their own careers, needs, targets, agendas, and bosses. In times of trouble, Roddenberry's instinct was always to defend his own position, rather than work with others. He would be "Crazy Gene," as he'd concluded that digging his heels in was how he would get his way.

As executive in charge of production, Herb Solow worked for Desilu. The chain of command was simple: Solow was Roddenberry's boss and reported to Lucille Ball, the head of the studio. Solow says of Roddenberry:

> As he grew and grew in stature, what he would do is take out the frustrations of not being in total control by picking scapegoats, so he would treat NBC as someone who was against him, for instance, which just wasn't the truth. NBC was trying to be supportive, but if there was a problem, Gene would turn it around and blame NBC, at times blame Desilu. That was the modus operandi for him in those later years while doing the first series.[19]

Star Trek had a specific problem, and it wasn't that "the ratings were low"—it was that the show was expensive to make, and performed slightly under NBC's target audience figures. The networks promised advertisers that a show would reach a particular number of viewers. If the show underperformed, the network had to pay back some of the money advertisers had given them (or give them free advertising of at least the same value, which amounted to the same thing).

The first episode won its ratings timeslot, against relatively weak opposition. Although in the following weeks it fell to second in its slot, it settled down to a point where it was doing better than most of the new shows. The network committed to a full season in November, but the ratings started to fall a little further. By January, it was third in its timeslot some weeks.

In March 1967, NBC signed up for a second season of *Star Trek*, ordering sixteen episodes, with the option of picking up another ten, which would add up to a full season of twenty-six. This was perfectly normal—established hits were picked up for a full season, but the networks reserved the right to pull the plug on most shows.

The second season started production only a few weeks after the first had been completed. It debuted on September 15, 1967 with the episode "Amok Time"—the one where Spock's burning need to mate compels him to return to his home planet. It's the first time we see the planet Vulcan, or any Vulcan character except Spock, and the first time we see the "Vulcan salute" or hear Spock say "Live long and prosper." One of the most memorable episodes of *Star Trek*, featuring its breakout character, it's extraordinarily important to the *Star Trek* mythology, and has always been a huge fan favorite. And it bombed in the ratings.[20]

You'll find a number of sneering references to "Gomer Pyle" in early *Star Trek* fanzines and newsletters. *Gomer Pyle* was an extremely popular sitcom, a spinoff from *The Andy Griffiths Show* about a naive man who signs up to the Marine Corps. Like the lead character, it was vaguely moronic but good-natured. In *Star Trek* fan discourse, "Gomer Pyle" became shorthand for the very worst of lowest common denominator network television. Gene Roddenberry got in on the act in a speech he delivered in the seventies (it appears on the 1976 album *Inside Star Trek*):

> "To get a prime time show—network show—on the air and to keep it there, you must attract and hold a minimum of eighteen million people every week. You have to do that in order to move people away from *Gomer Pyle*, *Bonanza*, *Beverly Hillbillies* and so on. And we tried to do this with entertainment, action, adventure, conflict and so on. But once we got on the air, and within the limits of those accident ratio limits, *we did not accept the myth that the television audience has an infantile mind.* We had an idea, and we had a premise, and we still believe that."[21]

The reason for the ire is that *Gomer Pyle* was the show on opposite the second season of *Star Trek*, and more than twice as many people watched the sitcom. *Star Trek*'s second-season premiere was in the bottom twenty shows for the week. The following month, rumors started that the show would be moved—a sign that the network were not confident about its prospects.

There was already a major source of nervousness among the production team: *Star Trek* was under new management. On July 27, 1967, [22] Gulf+Western, who owned Paramount, bought Desilu from Lucille Ball for $17m. Rumor had it that the only reason for the acquisition was that Paramount wanted to expand their studio lot and Desilu's property on Gower Avenue was right next door. So it was a mild inconvenience to Paramount's expansion plans that Desilu had four network TV shows in production: *Star Trek*, *Mission: Impossible*, *Mannix*, and *The Lucy Show*.

Another blow was that, towards the end of the second season, and having produced about half the episodes of the original series. Gene L. Coon had decided to move on. He was in the midst of an expensive divorce—he'd reconnected with his childhood sweetheart when he learned she had moved to Hollywood and become an actress and model. Coon was in demand as a script writer, and working on *Star Trek* meant long days and an increasing number of disputes with Gene Roddenberry, who thought the show was becoming too comedic. Roddenberry particularly hated "The Trouble with Tribbles," David Gerrold's script about little furry aliens who bred at an exponential rate (he warmed to it eventually).

Coon stepped aside as producer in early September.[23] There was no lasting rift, as there would be at other times when Roddenberry fell out with someone. Coon would continue to write for *Star Trek* under the pseudonym Lee Cronin, and before his early death, would work with Roddenberry again five years later on a new series, *The Questor Tapes*.

With ratings low, NBC were hesitating to commit to the future of the series. They wouldn't even guarantee to pick up the last ten episodes of the second season. It was a very nervous time on the set, but the network finally committed to ordering the remaining episodes on the very last day specified in their contract: October 18, 1967. The decision on a third season would be made in the New Year.

Now the *studio* was having second thoughts about making more *Star Trek*. Herb Solow remained in place, but there were new layers of studio executives above him. They were not traditional television or movie men and they were looking at program-making purely as a business proposition. *Star Trek*'s balance sheet contained a harsh truth: thanks to cost overruns, NBC were buying each episode for less than it cost Desilu to make. If they made ten more episodes, the studio would lose money ten more times. If *Star Trek* came back for the third season, then as things stood, the studio would continue to lose money for another year.

It sounded like a compelling reason to pull the plug. There was, however, a counterargument: as it stood, there would be too few episodes for *Star Trek* to go into syndication. If the series was canceled now, the show would never make another cent. If *Star Trek* ran at least until the end of a third season, preferably a fourth, then the studio would eventually be able to sell it to new markets, and gain some income from that. Solow was able to persuade the new studio executives that the numbers said they needed to make at least another season of *Star Trek*.

To say Solow was proved right is, of course, something of an understatement. Exactly how much *Star Trek* has made for the studio is incalculable. The chairman of Paramount is on record as saying "if somebody had a figure, it would be made-up because there's just no way of actually saying that this is how much it made."[24] But it runs into ten figures. To be fair to the executives, not one person was predicting that in 1967. All Solow was suggesting was that if the show went into syndication it might mitigate the losses.

Gene Roddenberry certainly wasn't predicting a long and prosperous future for *Star Trek*. Back in April 1965, while waiting to hear whether NBC liked the first pilot, he had worked on a pitch for a different show, *Assignment: Earth*. In November 1967, sensing the writing was on the wall for *Star Trek*, he dusted off that script and rewrote it as a *Star Trek* script, one which sidelines the regular cast in a flagrant attempt to set up a spinoff series about an alien investigator and his kooky sidekick in modern-day America. The plan was doomed from the start—Robert Lansing, the ostensible leading man, had told Roddenberry he wasn't going to commit to a regular TV role. Roddenberry then compounded the problem by becoming obsessed with the hemline of guest actress Teri Garr. His constant refrain that her skirt wasn't short enough led to arguments with William Ware Theiss on set, and a walkout from Garr, who hated the experience so much that she continues to refuse to be involved with *Star Trek* in any capacity, including discussing it in interviews. This was not the most promising foundation for a successful series.

By now, a few loyal fans of the show were semi-regular guests on the *Star Trek* set. Two of the most prominent were Bjo and John Trimble, organizers of the Cleveland convention where episodes of *Star Trek* were first shown publicly. They'd met Gene Roddenberry then and accepted an invite to come and see the set. By the second season, they were regular visitors and the cast knew them by sight, while Bjo was helping Roddenberry run Lincoln Enterprises. "John and I were visiting the shooting of 'The Deadly Years' when The Word came down—cancelation was certain at the end of the second season. This episode being shot was, in fact, one of the last *Star Trek* episodes to be aired before cancelation!"[25]

The Trimbles sent out an urgent letter to various *Star Trek* fan club organizers dated December 1, 1967. The plan called for each person who received a letter to urge ten more to send in a letter of their own. Bjo Trimble's experiences answering fan mail for the show had given her priceless insight into the sort of tone that worked and the sort that didn't, and she urged people to be thoughtful and concise, rather than call the network idiots and issue threats. She explained that fans should send letters to NBC, rather than the studio, and they should be sent in anonymous-looking envelopes, ensuring that the letters were opened. NBC were inundated, and their standing policy of replying personally to each letter meant the diversion of considerable resources. The campaign peaked in February.

On March 1, 1968, the following announcement was

made at the end of the episode "The Omega Glory" (and repeated the following week): "And now an announcement of interest to all viewers of *Star Trek*. We are pleased to tell you that *Star Trek* will continue to be seen on NBC Television. We know you will be looking forward to seeing the weekly adventures in space on *Star Trek*."

As far as anyone knows, an on-air announcement that a show had been renewed was truly without precedent. It may well have been designed to stop the flood of letters to the network—if so, it backfired, because for the next month, NBC were swamped with "thank you" notes from grateful *Star Trek* fans. The fact the fans rallied, sent in letters and saved the show is the essential founding myth of *Star Trek*. The nasty television executives had been defeated by a massive grassroot activist movement, rallying under the slogan *STAR TREK* LIVES.

There are three highly contentious issues around the campaign. How many letters were actually received? Was this a grassroot movement, or was it an operation run by Gene Roddenberry? And would *Star Trek* have been canceled without the letter-writing campaign? Herb Solow is best placed to put on record the studio's conclusions about the affair:

"The unfortunate part about it was it was blown out of proportion because of a letter that Gene Roddenberry wrote to Isaac Asimov, when he talked of the fact that a million letters were sent to NBC and that, of course, wasn't the fact at all . . . I located the man at NBC back in 1967 who was responsible for answering all the fan mail. So what we learned was that 'one million letters' was really twelve thousand letters. But twelve thousand was huge. It was the largest outpouring of mail NBC had ever received. But again, it was an orchestrated event. The executives at NBC became aware that it was orchestrated and kind of resented the embarrassment. So it helped to get *Star Trek* renewed from year two to year three, but when year three came along, *Star Trek* found itself in a terrible time period with very little promotion behind it, so you have to say the letter writing campaign helped and hurt at the same time."[26]

How many letters? A million, or twelve thousand? *TV Guide* at the time quoted an NBC vice president's figure of "100,000," although *The World of Star Trek* says *TV Guide* gave a figure of "200,000."[27] A newspaper report of March 17, 1968 stated a number of Spock-like precision, saying the network received 114,667 letters between December and March, with 52,151 in February.[28] NBC said in a Mailcall pamphlet, an internal report on fanmail, that the figures were 115,893 and 52,358.[29] Bjo Trimble says, "NBC admitted, unofficially, that over one million letters had crossed their desks. Within a year NBC was to announce during an interview on the mail campaign that only 500,000 had come in, and ten years later, NBC claimed that only 50,000 letters had been received!"[30] She's also noted that each item of correspondence counted as "one letter," even if it contained a petition with dozens of names on it. The figure of "a million" took hold in *Star Trek* fan circles, being repeated in, for example, the book *The World of Star Trek*. As Solow says, it looks as if that number originally came from Gene Roddenberry. In the end, it doesn't matter that much: a four-figure number would have been an impressive demonstration of audience loyalty.

Was Roddenberry involved? Oh, yes. John and Bjo Trimble mounted a Herculean effort, and ran a smart campaign. They corralled a group of avid *Star Trek* fans, they supplied a template letter that made its points passionately and was well-reasoned, and they told campaigners the best address to send their letter to. Bjo Trimble is a model for fan activism and inclusion. Very few people now could rally as many to click "Like" as she inspired to handwrite a letter, put it in an envelope, then pay for a stamp and post it. But by her own account, she checked with Roddenberry before proceeding.[31] She says that when they sent out a call for action, one of the sources for addresses was the fan mail sent to the show which "Gene helped us obtain from the fan mail service that Paramount contracted with." This, of course, was Lincoln Enterprises, which Trimble helped Roddenberry run.[32] Roddenberry paid to print up the *STAR TREK* LIVES and I GROK SPOCK car stickers that ended up on the back of every limousine in the NBC executive parking lot in New York, after a fan, Wanda Kendall, smuggled herself past security.[33] He supplied scripts and film trims to be auctioned off to raise money for the initial postage costs (it was when he saw them going for $20–$50 a time that he realized Lincoln Enterprises should be selling them).[34]

Would *Star Trek* have been canceled without the campaign? We know that it was possible the network wouldn't renew the show, and that people working on *Star Trek* were pessimistic. Then again, we know that there was at least a possibility that the show would survive, because Gene Roddenberry thought a letter-writing campaign might help. We know that the campaign didn't reverse a decision that had already been made to cancel the show—NBC hadn't made up their minds. We know that by February, NBC had firmed up their plans for the fall schedule, and *Star Trek* was on it. It would be churlish to think that the campaign wasn't a factor in the network's decision. Boiling down nearly fifty years of debate, the answer would seem to be this: the network was debating whether to renew, and the campaign was a factor that helped lead them to decide they should order the third season. It wasn't the only factor, but it *might* have been the decisive one.

It was a Pyrrhic victory. Herb Solow left Paramount soon after *Star Trek* was renewed, unhappy with the business culture there. NBC lowered their ratings estimates. The cost of buying a minute of commercials during the show fell from $36,000 to $30,000, and the price NBC were willing to pay Paramount fell accordingly. *Star Trek* would have to become a much cheaper show to survive, with the episode budget dropping from $200,000 in the first season to $180,000 in the third. However, the actors' contracts guaranteed big pay rises if the show made it to a third season. Squeezed from both sides, the show's location filming and elaborate effects would have to be cut back, and the guest cast limited.

With Herb Solow gone, Roddenberry had lost his key ally in the management team. Buoyed with the success of the letter-writing campaign, believing it gave him leverage, he issued an ultimatum: he would leave *Star Trek* unless it got a Monday 7:30 P.M. timeslot. NBC scheduled it for Fridays at 10:00 P.M. His bluff had been called. Roddenberry was moved aside to a position as executive producer, with Fred Freiberger brought in to his old role running the show. Roddenberry essentially sat in his new office on the other side of the Desilu lot and sulked throughout the third season. "I was really forced to break off from the show, and I could see it was going to die and I spent that year trying to develop new projects for the following season. Later, I also found out that there would be no fourth season, no matter what."[35]

Leonard Nimoy utterly hated the season three debut, "Spock's Brain," and from this point started agitating with the studio to improve the quality of the scripts. His quiet, forceful campaign to maintain the integrity of his character left a lasting, positive impression on many at the studio. D.C. Fontana left her script consultant role, and was replaced by Arthur Singer, who Bjo Trimble characterized as being "famous for choosing senselessly violent scripts."[36] Fontana didn't think Singer understood the series—she reports that on a set tour, she had to explain to him what the transporter did. She objected to rewrites on "The Enterprise Incident" that had Spock seducing a (female) Romulan commander in what she thought was a far too conventional way. The final straw that led to her cutting her ties with the show was when she was told that McCoy was the same age as Kirk, so wasn't old enough to have a grownup daughter, the focus of the episode she was writing, "Joanna." She felt the new team were ignoring key facts established in the series to that point.

Fans have usually seen the third season as a travesty. This overstates the problems. The budget cuts did lead to a lot of quite similar stories where a handful of aliens arrive on the *Enterprise* and disrupt the smooth running of the ship. But most shows start to repeat themselves sooner or later—the third seasons of *Batman* and *The Man from U.N.C.L.E.* were just as guilty of "seen it before" plot-lines, absurd gimmicks, and increasingly odd guest stars. There are some very well-regarded individual episodes in *Star Trek*'s third season, like "The Tholian Web," "The Empath," and "The Enterprise Incident." As far as he could, Roddenberry washed his hands of the third season, but was happy to take credit for the "interracial kiss" between Kirk and Uhura in the episode "Plato's Stepchildren." Even some of the stinkers—"Spock's Brain" and "The Way to Eden"—have their moments. The lack of money also forced the production team into some imaginative design work, like the stark black backdrops of "The Empath" and the surreal studio-bound Wild West of "Spectre of the Gun." The third season is really not all that bad.

Gene Roddenberry was done with *Star Trek*. In 1970, Paramount offered him the option to buy their 26⅔ percent stake in the series for $100,000 (some reports say $150,000), which would have given him control of the property. He didn't have the money, but wouldn't have paid it if he had, believing it to be a preposterous amount. We have a legal record of the value he placed on *Star Trek* at the time: in 1969, he offered his share in the rights to the series as part of his divorce settlement with Eileen, valuing them at $1,000. He would make the same offer again in 1972. Thanks to inflation, that meant the value of the rights had fallen in real terms.[37] She turned down the offer because she thought it overvalued *Star Trek*. To put this into perspective, the alimony agreement they reached was that Gene would pay Eileen $2,000 a month.

After seventy-nine episodes, *Star Trek* was finished.

CHAPTER FOUR

SYNDICATION AS VINDICATION

So that was that: *Star Trek* was over.

The studio salvaged all they wanted from the show, which was Leonard Nimoy. Without missing a beat, the actor moved from playing Spock in the third season of *Star Trek* to Paris in the fourth season of *Mission: Impossible*. The rest of the cast and crew started looking for their next jobs, and most were entirely pragmatic about it—the writing had been on the wall for months.

The standard accounts of the history of *Star Trek* portray the Seventies as a decade-long struggle. Gene Roddenberry tirelessly led the fans through the wilderness, and eventually the rest of the world caught up with a show which was ahead of its time. Stories need villains who can throw obstacles in the way of our hero, and in this case it's the Philistine "television executives." Bob Justman explains,

> Gene set about making NBC the heavy, the villain with regard to everything: schedule, ratings, programs practices (censor), publicity, etc., thus playing to the fans. He felt that the fans were more important than the network. He cast himself as the god and NBC as some demonic force from the other side.[1]

The more generous fans forgave "the suits" for not being smart enough to see the profound message of *Star Trek*, but thought that surely they were being perverse and malevolent when they claimed there was no appetite for more adventures with Kirk and Spock. These were the monsters who'd tried to dumb down *Star Trek* when it was being broadcast, and let it be canceled. Those suits were proved wrong when the show's popularity exploded after its cancelation. The story had a happy ending, culminating with 1979's *Star Trek: The Motion Picture*, for which Gene Roddenberry was triumphantly reinstalled.

It's a nice story, and no doubt that's exactly how it felt in the Seventies for those at the forefront of the fanzine and convention scene, the letter writers and authors of fan fiction. Gene Roddenberry regularly stood in front of crowds of fans giving a version of events that matched this account, and he would receive huge cheers.

However, most of the story is demonstrably untrue. What happened to *Star Trek* next came about without any involvement from Gene Roddenberry, to the point where he was barely aware at first that it was happening.

It's easy to lose sight of the fact that television used to

be ephemeral. *Star Trek* fans have been able to put copies of all seventy-nine episodes on their shelf for thirty years, upgrading from VHS, to DVD, to Blu-Ray. Even the idea of a boxset is beginning to look antiquated, as Netflix, Hulu, Amazon, and other streaming video services expand their catalogs. Viewers can press a few buttons now and watch the beginning of "Charlie X," one of the first *Star Trek* episodes to be shown in 1966, and it's almost quaint when Kirk asks the captain of a small cargo ship: "Is there anything we can do for you, Captain? Medical supplies, provisions? . . . We have a large supply of entertainment tapes."

The earliest fanzines often included very simple lists of episodes, plot summaries, and similar aides-mémoire, with fans scrambling to make notes or—in rare cases— jam the microphone of a tape recorder against their television's speaker. For the average *Star Trek* fan, a library of "entertainment tapes" containing every episode would have seemed an impossibly futuristic, immensely desirable prospect in 1966. It wasn't entirely without precedent in the real world, even then—military bases and larger ships had film libraries, and these could even include television series. The busiest room in many early conventions was the screening room, where episodes rented from the studio were projected onto a big screen. For the vast majority of viewers when *Star Trek* was first shown, though, a television episode was broadcast, possibly repeated once, then it was gone.

The studios sought ways to eke out as much money as possible from the television shows they made, but in the late Sixties almost all their revenue was derived from the original network broadcast and the first repeat. Money came from direct sponsorship of a show, and from the sale of advertisements. New episodes attracted the most interest from sponsors, and the highest advertising rates. Over the summer, people tended to go out more in the evenings, and networks would show repeat runs of returning shows—it was cheap to do, and the episodes were still relatively fresh. In an era before home VCRs, even avid viewers would miss the odd episode or two of their favorite show (early fanzine contributors would often relive the trauma of a family outing denying them the chance to see a particular *Star Trek* episode). The more general viewer might come to a show later in its run, or not be so committed as to tune in religiously every week. It meant that a lot of people who liked a show caught some episodes for the first time when they were repeated. The first repeats tended to do well—when *Star Trek* went into reruns after the end of the first season in April 1967, it won its timeslot.[2]

After that, studios saw any revenue as a bonus, as money for old rope. Contracts for television drama typically reflected this. Many actors and members of the crew would get a single payment based on the number of days they'd worked on an episode. The lead actors, the writer, director, producers, and a few others would typically be paid for the first showing and the first repeat. In theory, these key personnel were entitled to a cut of the profits from a show. In practice, the studios usually found inventive ways to assert that the show hadn't quite yet made its production costs back. This mentality—and pay scheme—explains why Roddenberry, Shatner, Nimoy, and everyone else involved with *Star Trek* thought the series was dead once it wasn't renewed for a fourth season. They had, they thought, received their last check for the series. William Shatner had a 20 percent profit participation, and Roddenberry had around 30 percent—but this appeared worthless, as Paramount calculated the show was between $3m and $5m away from recouping its production costs, stating in 1969 they "believed it would never show a profit."[3] The studio were proved wrong, but not until fifteen years later. *Star Trek* finally went into the black in 1984, and regular profit payments began for those entitled to them. In 1969, though, none of the cast or crew had anything to gain by promoting it. Indeed, if they became too closely associated with *Star Trek*, it might limit their future opportunities. Whether they had enjoyed working on *Star Trek* or not, whether they'd liked the final product or not, was irrelevant. They were all keen to move on.

The entire cast struggled with this. James Doohan, for example, found himself in an invidious position. He hadn't been paid much for being on *Star Trek*—$850 an episode for the first season, and that was a better deal than most of the regular cast—but he'd become identified with the role to the point that casting directors routinely joked about his lack of a Scottish accent.

In the early days of television, no one imagined much of an afterlife for shows beyond that first repeat showing.

Times were changing, though, and Leonard Nimoy believed he had cut a particularly smart and forward-looking deal because he would be paid up to the fifth repeat.

The studios did have two markets for their old TV shows. The first was that American shows were sold abroad. While Hollywood movie studios were starting to look to the international potential of their product, little effort had been made by the television industry. There was rarely very much money in foreign sales—TV channels usually bought series in bulk as a cheap way to fill their schedules. It's worth remembering that while color television was on the horizon, most countries had not yet adopted it. Even in the UK, the first time viewers saw *Star Trek* (or, for that matter, Adam West's *Batman*, *Scooby-Doo*, *The Flintstones*, and *The Monkees*), they'd have seen it in black and white. There were shows made in Britain with an eye on the American market—*The Avengers* being by far the most successful— but the American studios were content with their huge domestic market, and the vast amount of control they had over it.

There was a secondary domestic market. Before cable, Americans watched television on local stations that were either independently run, or "network affiliates" which showed national broadcasts from ABC, CBS or NBC in the morning, the evening news, and then prime time (starting at 7.30, later 8.00, in the evening). They made their own programs, usually local interest, but filled up their schedules by buying old shows from the studios and repeating them. This was called "syndication." Shows were bought as job lots in "syndication packages," and the received wisdom was that a series had to run for 100 episodes (four seasons) before there was enough to syndicate. This was never a hard and fast rule, and *Star Trek*'s tally of seventy-nine episodes was close enough. If you worked out how much each station paid for an individual episode, it was a tiny amount of money—but by selling a hundred episodes at a time to hundreds of small stations, it all added up.

Local stations "stripped" the show—showed it every weekday evening in the same timeslot. If a series had run for 100 episodes, a local station would have shown them all in five or six months. With *Star Trek*, it took sixteen weeks to get through the three seasons, and then many stations would just start again at the beginning. Stations could be quite careless, airing episodes out of order, or not showing the advertised episode. They would often ruthlessly edit the episodes down to fill the timeslot, or drop particular episodes if they'd ever had complaints about them. Local events—most often sports—would take priority over *Star Trek*. Two families in the same large city might sit down and watch *Star Trek* on the same evening, but they'd be watching different episodes at different times.

The nature of the process meant that some stations picked *Star Trek* up quickly while others were slower off the mark. Syndicated reruns of the show began in Boston, Cleveland, Detroit, and New York in the autumn of 1969 (the last episode, "Turnabout Intruder," had been shown in June). More and more local stations discovered that a well-made, colorful show did fantastically well when it was scheduled to run against the networks' early evening news programs. By February 1970, Paramount were running trade ads boasting that *Star Trek* was being shown by sixty-one stations, and outlining the improved audience share achieved by those showing it in New York, Chicago, Los Angeles, Providence, Minneapolis, Las Vegas, and Salem.[4] In March 1972, it was reported that "about 125 stations" ran it in the US.[5] By the time *The World of Star Trek* was written (it was first published in May 1973), the tally was up to 143 markets.[6]

There was for many years a conspiracy theory among fans that the audience for *Star Trek*'s original run had always been huge, and had only appeared low because of the way the ratings were collated. With the methods used to collect the ratings skewed towards families, the argument ran, the system rewarded shows aimed at the lowest common denominator and failed to register the legions of smart single people, people living alone, or college kids watching cerebral stuff like *Star Trek*. The show had therefore been popular all along and the networks were just too old-fashioned and foolish to see it. The idea was held as gospel throughout the Seventies and repeated by former cast and crew on the show. It fitted Gene Roddenberry's narrative perfectly. Majel Barrett summed it up: "We found out that the people who were actually watching us during the third season were the young marrieds, the intellectuals, scientists, astronauts, those kinds of people. So, while we never had huge ratings, we had absolutely incredible demographics: eighteen to forty with above-average intellect."[7]

The Roddenberrys probably thought that was correct. They were certainly willing to repeat it under oath. After Gene Roddenberry's death, a document prepared by Majel Barrett's legal team asserted: "It had low ratings and was a financial disaster . . . The series was finally cancelled in 1969, after finishing third in its time slot for each of its three seasons . . . *Star Trek* was considered a failure."[8]

More recent scholarship shows that this wasn't the case. Commercial television is set up, dispiriting though it is to point this out, to deliver audiences to advertisers. The system used by Nielsen was central to the networks' planning (although they drew data from other sources) and was a carefully designed, constantly refined statistical model capable of producing astonishingly precise information. Then, as now, the networks wanted to have shows that appealed to all sorts of different demographics. It was hugely in their interests be able to go to advertisers and tell them which shows people with disposable income liked. Not every advertiser wanted only to reach families. Many would have been keen to know about shows that attracted a loyal, attentive audience. As Michael Kmet at the blog Star Trek Fact Check puts it:

> renewing the series might have made sense because of the overall younger demographic it appealed to, which even in the late 1960s was becoming more important to advertisers. Paul Klein, the vice president of research for NBC, told

Television Magazine in 1967 that "a quality audience—lots of young adult buyers—provides a high level that may make it worth holding onto a program despite low over-all [sic] ratings." He went on to tell the magazine that "'quality audiences' are what helped both *Mission Impossible* and *Star Trek* survive another season." In a later *TV Guide* interview, Klein specifically mentioned *Star Trek* again, telling the magazine that the series was renewed in spite of weak ratings, "because it delivers a quality, saleable audience . . . [in particular] upper-income, better-educated males."[9]

The network knew who was watching when it made its decision to cancel *Star Trek*. The fact of the matter is that neither was the show's performance catastrophically bad, nor was it secretly being watched by millions of viewers the networks couldn't detect. It just didn't do particularly well. If it had been cheaper to make, the ratings it was getting would almost certainly have meant it was renewed, but it was the second most expensive drama on television. There were many at Paramount glad to see the back of it, as it had lost them a lot of money. Syndication simply suited *Star Trek* better than being networked on NBC. Ironically, it made it utterly impossible to calculate how many people were watching.

Two things about syndication in particular allowed *Star Trek* to blossom. The first was that it was shown a lot more often. Casual viewers now put the show on in the background, and became aware of its iconography: Spock's ears, the phasers, photon torpedoes and transporters,

Kirk's opening monologue, the catchphrases. *Star Trek* became a familiar part of the TV landscape. At the same time, because each episode went where no man had gone before, it didn't look as samey as a lot of television. As William Shatner said: "We were in many situations that were not the standard police story of 'get the bad guy.' There were variations. I think that was a large reason for *Star Trek*'s popularity."[10]

Fans could now rewatch their favorite stories, or start watching an episode and realize "this is the one where . . ." If they missed an episode, they didn't have to wait very long before it came around again. The hodgepodge of local stations mapped almost perfectly onto the hodgepodge of local *Star Trek* groups, and the fan community quickly realized that it was far easier to lobby a small, local station than a group of New York network executives. *Star Trek* was a big deal for the local stations, whereas for NBC it had just been another show. Rather than see fans as an annoyance, local stations tended to quickly embrace and recruit a set of articulate, passionate viewers.

Of course, when a local station bought a syndication package it was a far less troublesome, risky and expensive process than when Desilu were making it for NBC. No one at local stations in Boston or Cleveland had to approve a budget overrun to cover some new optical effect, juggle the egos of the cast and writers, or argue whether a particular line or costume was suitable. With the show canceled, there was none of the pressure or anxiety that had come to characterize *Star Trek* when it was in production.

Harve Bennett, a television producer in the Seventies who would go on to oversee the *Star Trek* movie franchise, sounded a note of caution:

> In those days, in order to succeed with a series, you had to deliver twenty million people. *Star Trek* never did that so it got canceled. But it delivered fifteen, fourteen, ten. Well, that was enough to support it in syndication during the Seventies. You could find your favorite *Star Trek* on every channel off network. Great. All the same people who loved it stayed with it.[11]

Many new fans started watching *Star Trek* when it was shown in syndication, but Bennett's broad point—that the show now looked bigger because the pond it was in was smaller—is clearly correct. Almost everyone with a television could watch NBC, but the reach of the stations that showed *Star Trek* in syndication was much more patchy. The potential audience was far smaller, far fewer televisions were on at five than were on at nine. While *Star Trek* became "more popular" in syndication, it doesn't mean that suddenly vastly more people were watching every time it was on. It means that cumulatively, over the next few years, a vast number of people would end up seeing *Star Trek*.

The way it was shown uniquely suited *Star Trek* and, while most shows withered away after cancelation, *Star Trek* flourished. Whatever the total audience tally, syndication sustained a set of viewers who were extremely engaged and supportive of the show and allowed this audience to be heard by the stations showing it.

The second change syndication brought was far more significant, but has tended to be underplayed by people studying the phenomenal rise of *Star Trek*: it was shown much earlier in the evening than it had been when it was first broadcast. NBC had scheduled the first two seasons at 8:30 P.M. (the first season was shown on Thursdays, the second on Fridays), and for its third season, *Star Trek* was shoved to 10:00 P.M. The timeslots were inconvenient for anyone wanting to go out in the evening (particularly when it moved to Fridays), but crucially, it was simply on too late for younger potential viewers. In syndication, the show was typically put on at 5:00 P.M. or 6:00 P.M. (some stations had it as early as 4:00 P.M., others as late as 7:00 P.M.). For the first time, very young kids got the chance to see *Star Trek*.

Older *Star Trek* fans were clearly important. It was they who started organizing clubs and conventions and publishing fanzines. It's worth noting that even these "older" *Star Trek* fans tended to be young. Looking at photographs of early conventions, it's striking that the vast majority of the attendees are teenagers or in their very early twenties. Few of the prominent fans—the fanzine editors, or members of the "Committee" who organized the first conventions—were all that old. Bjo Trimble, author of the *Star Trek Concordance*, was a "veteran"—thirty-six when the original run of *Star Trek* ended. Two of the co-authors of *Star Trek Lives!*, a book by fans about the

Star Trek phenomenon, were twenty-seven, and the eldest, Joan Winston, was thirty-eight. Allan Asherman, like Winston one of the "Committee," was twenty-two. Gene Roddenberry, James Doohan, and DeForest Kelley, who all turned fifty in 1970 or 1971, look so much older than anyone else in the room. The Roddenberrys were keen to emphasize the seriousness and intelligence of the show, but when they talked of older viewers, they were referring to the fact it was popular with undergraduates—a 1972 article stated that "every campus" was full of *Star Trek* fans. Of course parents and professors watched—but the organized fans were in their late teens or twenties. David Gerrold could say in 1973 that "generally Trekkies are adolescent or post-adolescent girls."[12]

This indicates that NBC did miss at least one trick. The demographic data was telling them *Star Trek* scored well with "upper-income, better-educated males," and this might conform to the stereotypical image of "Trekkies" as nerdy guys. Bjo Trimble was told that the network had tried to conduct a demographic survey of *Star Trek* fans, based on the data they could glean from the protest letters during the 1967/8 campaign, but even using computer analysis couldn't tell "what kind of people were watching it."[13] The evidence would seem to suggest that *Star Trek* resonated most with young *women*. If NBC had seen that, they might have been able to market and schedule the series more effectively.

With *Star Trek* being shown in syndication much earlier it was reaching even younger people than the teenyboppers. *Star Trek* was now something the whole family could watch and it was often on during the family meal. Very young children responded to the broad characters, the colorful sets, and the monsters. Their parents could find levels to the show that their younger children would miss, and that included the political allegory, but—like Adam West's *Batman*—it also meant the camp performances, the scantily clad women, not taking things that sounded pompous at face value. Fans have tended to cringe at the idea of children loving *Star Trek*—it cuts against the idea that the show was popular because it was edgy and political and by implication makes those who take *Star Trek* seriously appear "childish." But saying that a lot of people liked the sillier aspects of *Star Trek* is not a criticism. Far from it: it demonstrates that *Star Trek* appealed to all sorts of people for a wide variety of reasons, including ones the makers of the show didn't intend, or perhaps even acknowledge or fully understand.

There's very little evidence that Gene Roddenberry had ever thought about tailoring anything for children who were watching the show—he introduced the younger character of Chekov at the start of the second season because he worried that the cast looked middle-aged to a lot of viewers, but he didn't do it to appeal to the under-tens. He was making a serious primetime show for an adult audience, as he had with *The Lieutenant*. He made every effort to distance himself from *Lost in Space*, the contemporary show most obviously "like" *Star Trek*. His constant concern when he was making *Star Trek* had been that it was drifting away from being serious and weighty.

Roddenberry said he saw *Star Trek* as a way of dressing up weighty thoughts and subjects, almost as if the primary colors and alien belly dancers were the sugar coating for some bitter medicine. In syndication, this flipped around— it became a fun action show which demonstrated, if you were inclined to look, some interesting sprinkles of social commentary or political analogy. As soon as it was out of Roddenberry's control, it became something far more fun, and more local. When he pitched it, Roddenberry had compared *Star Trek* to *Gulliver's Travels*; in syndication, it suffered the same fate as Swift's novel—the satirical bite was lost and audiences tended to concentrate on the absurd spectacle, on what we might term the visual effects. Viewers began to shape *Star Trek* and find things in it that resonated for them.

There's an interesting period of about three years or so, starting with the cancelation of *Star Trek* in the first half of 1969 and building to the first major convention in January 1972, which saw an explosion in grassroot fan activity, and about three years after that where this consolidated into a national fan movement. It was here that the foundations were laid for the future of *Star Trek*. The transition from middle-ranking network show to perennial smash hit in syndication was possibly the most important moment in the history of *Star Trek*. In those crucial early years, Gene Roddenberry wasn't around all that much. First of all, he was keen to make the move from television to cinema.

On June 7, 1968, as *Star Trek*'s third season was barely underway, Roddenberry sent a letter to *Tarzan* producer

Sy Weintraub proposing a revamp of the movie series. Since *Tarzan the Ape Man* (1932), starring Johnny Weissmuller, there had been a new Tarzan movie virtually every year, with four changes of lead actor. After thirty-five years, the franchise was struggling to keep up with modern tastes. *Tarzan and the Valley of Gold* (1966) had been a relaunch for the series, with a new actor, Mike Henry, in the lead, and an original story by science fiction author Fritz Leiber. His novel, the first sequel authorized by the estate of *Tarzan* creator Edgar Rice Burroughs, was published simultaneously. The movie saw a suave Tarzan in a James Bond-style caper fighting an international criminal mastermind in modern-day Mexico. Two movies in the same vein followed, but audiences weren't keen.

Roddenberry proposed a rethink that concentrated more on the character's alter ego, Lord Greystoke (in the original books Tarzan was orphaned in the African jungle, his father being an English aristocrat). His version was to be set in the late nineteenth century. Roddenberry didn't include elements like Jane and Cheetah, and was keen to make Tarzan a smart, resourceful man, the genius of the Edgar Rice Burroughs books. The pitch was successful and Roddenberry was commissioned to write a script. His story had a science fiction element to it—a weapon that could fire a beam of heat was found in the jungle, the technology of the ancient Egyptian gods. The script was completed, but the project went no further, reportedly because of concerns about the budget. That year's *Tarzan and the Jungle Boy* (1968) would prove to be the last of the series.[14]

In August 1968, around the time he was working on Tarzan, Roddenberry moved out of the family home—he'd made the announcement he was finally leaving Eileen two weeks earlier, at his daughter Darleen's wedding. The separation had been inevitable for a long time, and Gene moved in with Majel Barrett. The divorce came the following year after a financial settlement was reached in a three-day session in early July 1969, involving the couple's lawyers and accountants.

> Gene and Eileen negotiated over their community property, including Norway Corporation, a loan-out corporation which owned all rights to *Star Trek*. Gene offered to sell his interest in *Star Trek* to Eileen for $1,000, but she turned down the offer. Finally, Eileen agreed that Gene would receive her interest in Norway—including the right to royalties and rerun fees from *Star Trek*; in exchange, Eileen retained only her right to a "one half interest in future profit participation income from *Star Trek* to which the parties are entitled," and received, among other things, most of the couple's jewelry and substantial alimony payments.[15]

Eileen took custody of their younger daughter, Dawn, who was fifteen at the time. Dawn remained close to her father and would live with him for a spell. Their elder daughter, Darleen, was five years older, and had already moved out. Two decades later, the wording of the financial settlement would become the heart of a bitter legal dispute between the couple (and after his death, between Eileen and Majel

Barrett). For now, Gene and Eileen went their separate ways, selling the family home and splitting the proceeds.

Herb Solow, Roddenberry's former boss on *Star Trek*, had moved on from Paramount and was now Vice President of Worldwide Television and Motion Picture Production at MGM. He remained friends with Roddenberry and continued to socialize with him. Knowing Roddenberry needed a break, he sent him on an expenses-paid trip to Japan, "scouting locations" for MGM. As Gene told *People* magazine in 1987:

> "After I had been there a number of weeks, I discovered I missed Majel a lot. Now, an American bachelor on an MGM expense account in Japan . . . this can be heaven! But I found myself with these pretty little girls in silk kimonos. . ."
>
> ". . . and out of them," inserts Majel.
>
> "I found myself talking to them about Majel. One night I realized what I was doing. I paid the girl, went back to my hotel and called up Majel to ask her if she would do me the honor of becoming my wife."[16]

Roddenberry married Majel in Japan on August 6, in a Shinto ceremony. Neither was religious, but they thought it would be disrespectful to get married in Japan in a Western-style service. It also gave them an opportunity to dress up—their wedding photo shows Majel in an elaborate kimono and headdress, and Gene far from being outdone in traditional Japanese attire. When they returned to the States, shortly afterwards, it turned out that Gene's divorce hadn't technically been settled—the final judgement wouldn't be entered until Christmas Eve that year. To make the marriage official, Gene and Majel had a low-key civil ceremony in the US on December 29, 1969. They would always celebrate August 6 as their wedding anniversary.[17]

Herb Solow continued to help Roddenberry, assigning him to script and produce Roger Vadim's first American movie, a job which paid Roddenberry $100,000, a great deal of money. Vadim had made a huge number of films in France and Italy, and was best known in America for *And God Created Woman* (1956), starring Brigitte Bardot, and *Barbarella* (1968), starring Jane Fonda. His movies were scandalous in France for their depiction of sexuality, and so were downright notorious in the United States. Vadim was equally famous for his relationships with his leading actresses. He had a child with Catherine Deneuve, had been married to Bardot, and at the time he worked with Roddenberry he was estranged from Fonda.

Anyone who only knew Gene Roddenberry from his CV might have seen him as a natural fit if Vadim was trying to make another *Barbarella*-style science fiction film, but that wasn't the plan. MGM believed that American audiences were ready for a European-style sex comedy, and Vadim wanted to adapt Francis Pollini's 1969 novel *Pretty Maids All in a Row*, set in an American high school where Tiger McDrew, a middle-aged school counselor, is sleeping with the female students . . . and then murdering them. With that in mind, it's a little uncharitable to suggest Solow might have seen something of Roddenberry in the character, but when Roddenberry develops Tiger, he becomes more like him—Tiger gains a military background, and a tendency to justify his actions by talking in broad terms about social change. Roddenberry makes the protagonist someone who can go home to a wife he loves, who forgives him his tendency to "dip his wick." He's clearly an identification figure—within limits—for the writer.

Roddenberry's influence stretched as far as the cast. James Doohan (Scotty) and William Campbell (who'd featured in *Star Trek* as the immortal Trelane and the Klingon Koloth) played a pair of policemen. Dawn Roddenberry was an extra on the movie (she's credited as "Girl #1"). Rock Hudson—forty-six, and a little past his prime, but still a bankable star—was cast as Tiger McDrew. Roddy McDowall and Telly Savalas were cast as the principal and the detective investigating the murders. Angie Dickinson played a teacher who was the object of desire for a male student, Ponce de Leon Harper (John David Carson).

The source material is not all that promising. The novel switches between scenes where Ponce de Leon lusts after his teacher, graphic descriptions of Tiger having sex with different schoolgirls (and occasionally his wife)—a typical line being "Her mouth glided, all the while, her tongue was sliding, caressing her Tiger's hot, huge formidable—the whole while"[18]—and scenes of the rather literally named detective Surcher as he looks for clues to the murders. Roddenberry sticks to the broad structure of the book, but imposes much more interesting character arcs, and adds a suspenseful—if rather incoherent—ending where Ponce confronts Tiger. It's not entirely clear if it's meant to be a twist that Tiger's the murderer, and in both the book and movie there's no great moment where he's unmasked—different characters gradually realize at different times. The movie hurdles the low bar of being funnier and better crafted than the book, and the cast play it as fairly broad farce. When Miss Smith, one of Ponce's teachers, learns he's having "problems with erections," she decides she'll flirt with him to help him out, not realizing that the problem is he's permanently aroused. The school counselor advises her to sleep with him and she does.

Roddenberry started off with high hopes. He didn't like the book, but told one correspondent at the time that *Pretty Maids All in a Row* "started here as a sex comedy but which I hoped to rewrite so that it also has some meaning and some statement about the world around us today. Specifically, it concerns high schools and my opinion of the way we run high schools is pretty low."[19] In the movie—like the book—the police assume that one of the "Negro" students is responsible (though the book makes more of the fact the school has recently been desegregated). The final film includes a scene that's not in the book, and in which we hear a tape of Tiger saying:

> "In a typical high school it would be difficult to invent a system more destructive of a child's natural creativity. Only in the most backward penal institutions does one discover equally oppressive rules of silence, restriction of movement,

constant examination of behavior. A world in which one must
learn to work, eat, exercise and sometimes even defecate by
the clock."

It's extremely easy to imagine Roddenberry declaring the
same thing, word for word, in an interview or as part of
a lecture, and it's hardly woven seamlessly into the film.
That, though, is about it for his "statement." There is a
dash of satirical social commentary, in a subplot that
clearly appealed to Vadim, who went out of his way to
mention it in a *Playboy* interview: "Despite the multiple
murders, *Pretty Maids* is more satire than serious drama. The
only apparent concern of the community regarding the
murders is whether they'll force the cancelation of next
week's football game. Our point: How little importance is
placed on human lives today."[20]

There is, of course, the problem that this is a movie
about high school students lining up to have sex with their
teachers. The book hits a consistently seedy note. The
movie is more confused. As with a number of Roddenberry
projects, there's a weird single-entendre feeling to it. The
movie tries very hard not to think about morality, and
sets out to establish that it's set in a sort of heightened,
sunny, carefree world . . . but it's one punctuated by murders of schoolgirls. In a *Sight & Sound* poll in 2013, Quentin
Tarantino listed *Pretty Maids All in a Row* as one of his twelve
"greatest movies of all time."[21] He's an aficionado of "grind-
house" cinema, the exploitation films that offered 1970s
cinemagoers the sort of sex and violence you couldn't see

on TV, and this movie was something of a forerunner of those. If he'd made the movie, Tarantino might just have been able to square the circle, convince the audience that it was being postmodern and playful. Neither Vadim nor Roddenberry is the right man for that job, and *Pretty Maids All in a Row* is, inescapably, a movie about sexual violence against young women, pitched as a comedy.

The movie received a fair amount of pre-publicity and attention, which centered around the "Pretty Maids," the schoolgirls Tiger seduced, played by eight young actresses of various "types" and ethnicities: Joy Bang, Gretchen Burrell, Joanna Cameron, Aimée Eccles, June Fairchild, Margaret Markov, Diane Sherry, and Brenda Sykes.

Roger Vadim's interview for the April 1971 edition of *Playboy* was illustrated with nude shots of the "Maids" specially taken by the magazine. He didn't mention Roddenberry there, or in his book *Memoirs of the Devil* (1975), where he described how the traditional Hollywood system was in such decline that "there was not a single other film being made in any of the six main Los Angeles studios" when he was there,[22] and he was astonished how many departments he had to deal with, and how vast they all were: "Only in Russia have I seen such a cancerous bureaucracy . . . I regretted having to take up a budget of three and a half million dollars for a film that should not have cost more than eight hundred thousand."[23]

By this point, one of the Maids had objected to the way the nude scenes were being shot. As this was one of the first Hollywood movies to feature nudity, her contract didn't specify that she had to take part in those scenes. Vadim was annoyed, feeling that she and her agent had known the nature of the role, but the studio president James Aubrey intervened personally, understanding that they shouldn't force her to film the scenes against her will.[24] The actress has never been publicly identified, but Diane Sherry is the only one of the Maids who doesn't appear nude in the movie or the *Playboy* shoot, and later publicity photos feature the other seven maids, but not her. She would go on to play Lana Lang, Clark Kent's schoolboy crush, in a few scenes of *Superman: The Movie* (1978). When Vadim told Rock Hudson that *he* was expected to appear full frontal, things were settled far more quickly, with Hudson replying: "If you want to take a look at my dick, that's fine by me, but I'll be darned if I'll flash it for all the fucking world to see!"[25]

Roddenberry's main task was to keep Vadim under control, but they fell out and Roddenberry left the set until the movie was filmed, telling a friend "there is nothing worse than writing something you hope is pretty witty and having the director not quite pull it off."[26] Roddenberry was drinking heavily at the time. A couple of years previously, on his return to the States after a fishing trip, customs had impounded the extensive array of pills they'd found in his bag—diet pills, sleeping pills, barbiturates (Seconal, the drug that killed Judy Garland), an antidepressant (Cytomel), and a tranquilizer (Equinil). These were all legally prescribed, but were common recreational drugs at the time.

Once filming was complete, the studio weren't happy with Vadim's first cut of the movie. Roddenberry was able to salvage something usable in a re-edit, but no one labored under any illusion that they'd produced great work. Vadim described it as "entertaining without being ambitious. The reviews were fairly good in Los Angeles, dreadful in New York and excellent in other cities. On the whole it was a success."[27] It was not a movie that helped anyone's career—it was John David Carson's first and last starring role; Roger Vadim never worked for an American studio again; it was one of Rock Hudson's last movie roles before he made the move to television. Many of the "Maids" went on to careers in the sort of exploitation movies Quentin Tarantino admires, but none became stars. Amusingly, and presumably entirely by coincidence, Vadim's *Playboy* essay ends with a line that's almost an echo of Roddenberry's sentiment about the human race still being in its childhood:

> "The American fear of sex is gradually diminishing—in motion pictures, in periodicals, on the stage, in private life. That's one of the most refreshing developments I've noticed on my current visit. By going through this experience, perhaps one day Americans will finally become adults."[28]

Roddenberry's loss of control of *Pretty Maids All in a Row* all but killed his chances of moving from television to cinema. Before its release, he placed all the blame squarely on Vadim, saying, "I wrote it as a comedy but I'm afraid that much of the American quality of the comedy was not understood by the director."[29] When he heard that the movie had made its money back, he briefly thought it might lead to other work. He wanted to write a movie about the police and racial politics, and researched it by riding along with the police. He was "worried over the polarization of the police into a sort of 'minority group complex' along with the polarization of blacks and browns into more and more violent directions."[30] It wasn't to be, and by the beginning of 1972 Gene Roddenberry's attempt to move from television to cinema was in tatters.

CHAPTER FIVE

GENE RODDENBERRY'S
LOST UNIVERSES

The first major *Star Trek* convention took place in New York over the weekend of January 21–23, 1972. The "Committee," the group of fans who'd organized it, expected about five hundred people to attend the Statler Hilton Hotel. Attendees would pay $2.50 to see Gene Roddenberry, Isaac Asimov, Majel Barrett, Hal Clement, and D.C. Fontana. There was a dealers' room, where *Star Trek* merchandise would be sold, and NASA sent a large display of replica real-life spacecraft. The most avid group of *Star Trek* fans in the country had underestimated the appeal of the show. Over the weekend there were around 3,300 paying guests, and the dealers' room was stripped as if by locusts within a few hours. On the last day, the organizers had to give up charging admission. Over four thousand people attended.

Paramount knew about the convention—they'd hired out thirteen episodes of the series to be shown in the screening room—but they were clearly caught out by the success of the event. Four thousand people was an impressive number to gather in one place, and clearly indicated that *Star Trek* had a following, but ultimately it told the studio nothing about whether there was a mass audience hungry for more. For them, the measures of success were the column inches in the newspapers, and that it justified a front page story in *Variety*. There was something there.

The next year, a second event was held in New York, at a far bigger venue, and James Doohan and George Takei were the official star guests. Seven thousand tickets were sold. Leonard Nimoy happened to be in town and popped by, to find himself mobbed. By this point, there had been conventions almost as large on the West Coast. The next few years saw similar events around the country. With the biggest conventions offering four-figure appearance fees, James Doohan bought a recreational vehicle and made more money touring the convention circuit than he ever had playing Scotty on television.

Attending the 1972 New York convention, where he addressed 1,500 fans in a room with a fire safety limit of 500, was no road-to-Damascus moment for Roddenberry. By now, he knew that *Star Trek* was thriving in syndication. He and Majel were aware there was a vibrant *Star Trek* fandom because they ran Lincoln Enterprises, and because he continued to receive a huge volume of fan mail. He was realistic—no show had ever been revived. Paramount had told him again and again that the show had lost money. On a purely practical note, they had disposed of most of the costumes, props and sets from the original run, and replacing them would be prohibitively expensive. Roddenberry was cautious in his message to fans, and hoped that the attention *Star Trek* was getting would persuade television executives that if Gene Roddenberry had created one hit show, he could create plenty more.

After a weekend basking in the adulation of *Star Trek* fans, Roddenberry called in on various television executives, then returned home to Beverly Hills. In 1972, with no work on the horizon, he was running low on money. He successfully appealed to have his alimony payments cut (and, once again, failed to persuade his ex-wife that his rights to *Star Trek* were worth $1,000). *Inside Star Trek* reports:

> He even needed to sell his sailboat. But he couldn't; there were no buyers. James Doohan, however, felt that Roddenberry wasn't going about the sales process correctly and volunteered to sell the boat, as his friend's agent, in return for a sales commission of ten percent. Roddenberry jumped at the offer. Doohan ran ads in several papers and soon found a buyer for $19,000. Roddenberry was elated, took the deal, and when reminded of the ten percent sales commission, wrote out a cheque to Doohan for $1,900. But Roddenberry cautioned "Listen, Jimmy. Hold onto the cheque for a while, Okay?"[1]

With every bridge to working in cinema burned, Roddenberry had rediscovered his love of working in television. Or, as he phrased it to journalist Richard Shull in a November 1972 interview:

> "When *Star Trek* went off, I was so irritated with television I stayed completely away from it for four years. My creative juices must have stored up during that time. When I decided to come back, I had four ideas at once . . . Obviously, I can't do four shows at once. Oh, I suppose I could try, but there'd be a tombstone with the inscription: 'He tried to do four TV series at the same time.' So I'm doing two and putting the other two aside for the time being."[2]

The two series he started work on were *Genesis II* and *The Questor Tapes*. Pilot episodes for both were filmed and both came tantalizingly close to being picked up for a full series. It's telling, though, that this November 1972 newspaper interview with Roddenberry, ostensibly about his new TV projects, bore the headline "Creator of *Star Trek* comes back to TV." Eleven months after the New York convention, *Star Trek* now had the reputation of "the show that wouldn't die." Asked whether it would be revived, Roddenberry told Shull: "My own feeling is not to go back into television. I'd like to have a series of *Star Trek* feature films in the theaters, like *Planet of the Apes* has done. The statistics show there's a ready made audience of at least three million who would go to a *Star Trek* feature."[3] His thinking seems clear enough: he wanted to make movies and Paramount wanted to bring back *Star Trek*—so they'd have to put him in charge of the movie version.

And it really could have been as easy as that. Just weeks later, early in 1973, Herb Solow took Roddenberry to meet Frank Yablans, president of Paramount, and they pitched an idea for a *Star Trek* movie. The story, "The Cattlemen," was an old idea—it had appeared as one of the suggested plots for *Star Trek* episodes in the original pitch document, back in 1964, as "A Question of Cannibalism": a colony planet that relied on selling meat discovered the alien cattle were intelligent, but they were reluctant to give up their lucrative trade—with Kirk and Spock going on to learn that it was part of the creatures' life cycle to be eaten, as it allowed them to lay their eggs in whatever ate them, converting their hosts into aliens.

Solow was skeptical, and worried that the proposed story was far too bleak. Yablans, though, "was enthusiastic and estimated that the film could gross a minimum of $30m."[4] Thirty million dollars at the box office would have made *Star Trek* one of the top ten highest grossing movies of 1973. Perhaps the bleak tone was what sold it—a number of dark science fiction movies had been released or were in production. Charlton Heston had rather cornered the market, appearing in *Planet of the Apes* (1968), *The Omega Man* (1971), where he was the last man left on Earth, and *Soylent Green* (1973), where the solution to overpopulation was problematic. *Westworld* (1973) saw androids run amok in a theme park (the movie had a small role for Majel Barrett), *Silent Running* (1972) was an eco-fable in which a lone astronaut tried to protect the Earth's last surviving plants. Almost unnoticed, George Lucas had released his first movie, *THX1138* (1971), set in a dystopian future police state. Whatever his thinking, Yablans gave the go-ahead on the spot. He wanted Roddenberry to write the script and Solow to produce.

Then Roddenberry blew it. He demanded to be the producer, and when Yablans refused, Roddenberry had Leonard Maizlish take over the negotiations. Maizlish demanded $100,000 for writing the script—as much as Roddenberry had received for writing *and* producing the Vadim movie. Yablans walked away. For his part, Herb Solow—who was more than happy with the terms being offered—was baffled by Roddenberry's behavior. He never worked with him again.

Very soon after that, in March 1973, it was announced that a new *Star Trek* television series would be made, with the first episode airing in September. It would feature almost all the original regular cast, and many of the original writers. The twist was that this was a cartoon series—and that Roddenberry wasn't involved.

The first Roddenberry heard about the animated series was when Lou Scheimer, the co-founder of Filmation, approached him. One biographer claims that Scheimer approached Paramount because he was a fan of the series.[5] Everyone agrees that rival animation studio Hanna-Barbera were also pitching to make a *Star Trek* show. Whether anyone at either studio was a Trekkie or not, adapting *Star Trek* fit their business model: around this time, many old shows from the Sixties that had done well in syndication were being resurrected as animated series. In 1973 alone, Filmation produced Saturday morning cartoons of *Lassie*, *Gilligan's Island*, and *My Favorite Martian*, and Hanna-Barbera made versions of *The Addams Family* and *I Dream of Jeannie*.

Roddenberry told Scheimer that he could not make *Star Trek* without Paramount's cooperation and Paramount could not make it without his. (Contractually, Paramount had every right to make *Star Trek* without him, but Roddenberry sincerely thought otherwise, and Paramount felt that he should be involved in any revival.) Roddenberry and Paramount quickly came to a deal, one where Roddenberry had, or at least believed himself to have, complete creative control of the show.

Roddenberry had no interest in running the series on a day-to-day basis but wanted to ensure the new show stuck closely to the original *Star Trek* format. He did not like one early idea, which was that Kirk, Spock, and the other officers would each be assigned a teenage cadet to mentor. William Shatner was approached to reprise his role as Kirk. He, too, made it clear he wasn't interested in making a "kiddified" version, and would only return if the ethos of the original show was retained. In similar circumstances, other animated shows had simply given the part to a different actor (none of the cast of the original *My Favorite Martian*, for example, returned for the cartoon), and perhaps it was here that the existence of a stubborn creator backed by a loyal and vociferous *Star Trek* fandom influenced Filmation's plans.

In the Seventies, most cartoons were intended for very young viewers. Two decades before the premiere of *The Simpsons*, the idea of an animated show broadcast late in the evening on weekdays was extremely unusual but not unprecedented: *The Flintstones*, for example, had run for six seasons and 166 episodes in the Sixties. In 1973, there was fresh proof that primetime animation was possible: *Wait Till Your Father Gets Home* had debuted the year before, and would run for three seasons. Its 10:30 P.M. slot was actually later than *Star Trek* had ever been shown. Notably, it was a sitcom about a fairly ordinary suburban family—there were no talking animals, or other fantasy elements. The show was quite spiky, and the fact it was animated perhaps allowed the writers to get away with a little more than they would have if it had been live action—the same thing Roddenberry claimed he could do with science fiction. So it was just about plausible that the *Star Trek* animated series would get a similar timeslot to the original show. In actuality, virtually every other cartoon on television was firmly for children, and that had always been the plan for this incarnation of *Star Trek*—the new audience for the show created by syndication was skewed towards pre-teens, and it was this audience that NBC wished to tap into.

At Roddenberry's suggestion, D.C. Fontana was hired as associate producer. She quickly corralled a group of writers from the live action show, including David Gerrold, Margaret Armen, and Marc Daniels, as well as writers who were also fans. One coup was commissioning a script from SF novelist Larry Niven, fresh from the publication of his masterpiece *Ringworld* (1971). She gave the writers copies of the original *Star Trek* series bible and her intention was that this was effectively to be the fourth year of the *Enterprise*'s five-year mission, as close to the original series as the format allowed. As she put it, "none of us ever said cartoon."[6]

While this was to be a Saturday morning cartoon, the writers knew that there was a loyal, organized group of *Star Trek* fans, and they did plenty to cater to fandom. The original series had striven to be self-consistent—the show knew better than to cheat its audience by changing the rules of how transporters, warp engines, and so on worked—but had only made a few nods towards what fans now call "continuity." On the whole, episodes were broadly self-contained and even the recurring threats didn't recur half as often as you might think: the Romulans, for example, made a total of three appearances. The animated series was clearly set in a more coherent, consistent "*Star Trek* universe," brought back characters from previous episodes, and—like the series of *Star Trek* novels written by science fiction author and critic James Blish—was happy to smooth gaps in the backstory. The opening script was by Sam Peeples, a deliberate act of self-mythologizing on Fontana's part, as he'd written "Where No Man Has Gone Before," the first episode to feature Captain Kirk. Many of the stories included references to familiar characters— they were often direct sequels, such as "Mudd's Passion" by Stephen Kandel, or David Gerrold's "More Tribbles,

More Troubles." The animated series featured appearances by the Klingons, Romulans, Andorians, Orion slave girls, Tellarites, and Sarek, and made reference to the Eugenics Wars and more.

Fontana was also keen to move the show forward and expand its horizons. It paid more than lip service to diversity, using the medium of animation to make the locations and aliens more elaborate and exotic. Two alien crew members, an exotic cat lady and a three-legged, three-armed navigator, were introduced, something that could never have been achieved in the live action show when Vulcan and Romulan extras had to wear helmets to disguise that the budget didn't run to giving everyone pointy ears.

It was an ambitious show, and at $75,000 an episode Filmation's most expensive to that point, but it was still a Saturday morning cartoon. It was made quickly, and relied on the reuse of stock sequences. Scenes set on the bridge of the *Enterprise* were noticeably repetitive, but the limitations of the form were most painfully obvious during action sequences, when every scene of characters running or fighting looked identical. Characters' faces had a handful of standard expressions—surprised, angry, sad, happy. William Shatner had little room to improvise or find his signature twists on line readings, and so for perhaps the only time in his long and varied career there are places where he can be accused of sounding subdued.

A key indication that the animated series was authentic *Star Trek* was the plethora of jostling egos and behind-the-scenes shenanigans. At the first session, Gene Roddenberry was present, and gave a speech. William Shatner says now that Kirk had "been locked away inside me for almost four years, but as soon as I opened my mouth to read his first line he was back. Slipping back into that character was like putting on a comfortable old sweatshirt."[7] This spirit of bonhomie was not universally shared. The day was an uncomfortable one for Leonard Nimoy, who had been reluctant to take part. The makers saw Spock's presence as vital to the show and bent over at least a little way backwards to accommodate him. It was agreed that rather than interrupt any filming schedule or theater run with a trip back to California, in future he would be allowed to record his lines at recording studios more convenient for him, and mail the tapes in. He was present for the first session, but was surprised that Nichelle Nichols, George Takei, and Walter Koenig weren't, and confused when he saw that James Doohan and Majel Barrett were to play the roles of Sulu and Uhura, as well as Scotty and Chapel (between them, the two were slated to play the vast majority of guest roles).

With episodes half the length of the live action ones, it was felt extravagant to pay voice actors to deliver the sort of "business" dialogue Sulu, Chekov, and Uhura typically had in the original show. Nimoy understood this, but felt it was offensive that Roddenberry was allowing the parts to be played by other actors. He also felt he'd been conned into coming back—he'd been told the rest of the cast had agreed to do it, and had felt a little churlish to be the only holdout. Technically he hadn't been lied to—he was the only member of the cast actually asked back who'd turned it down. Takei, Nichols, and Koenig had never been asked. Nimoy added this to what he saw as a growing pile of instances of Roddenberry's unethical behavior.

He also doubted whether Roddenberry's insistence that Majel Barrett, rather than Nichelle Nichols, be the one female voice in the cast had been purely based on merit. Nimoy told the producers he would only proceed if the missing cast members were involved. One happy consequence was that, once Nichols and Takei were hired, the writers gave Sulu and Uhura a little more to do than had been typical in the live action show. In "The Lorelei Signal," Uhura takes charge of the *Enterprise* following a disaster and Nichols clearly relishes the line "I'm taking command." Ironically, given that the character had been introduced to appeal to youngsters, the budget did not stretch to hiring Walter Koenig to play the youthful Chekov, but the actor was commissioned to write an episode, "The Infinite Vulcan."

The series was put together fast: the voice tracks for the first three episodes were recorded in a single day at the beginning of June 1973 and the series began broadcast on September 8. At no point during the making of the animated series were Shatner, Nimoy, Kelley, Doohan, Nichols, Takei, and Barrett ever all in the same room as a group.

Roddenberry had a prominent credit, pocketed a total of $55,000 for reading the scripts, and offered many dialogue suggestions and other pieces of advice. For "The Infinite Vulcan," Koenig reports, "Gene required a great many rewrites, the reason for which neither Dorothy or I could fathom, and I was quite weary of the whole thing by the time I was finally done with it. I was later invited to write a second episode but decided to pass on the opportunity."[8] The truth of the matter was that D.C. Fontana and the writers she hired understood what made for good *Star Trek*, possibly better than Roddenberry himself. Fontana and Gerrold in particular were in touch with the new *Star Trek* fan groups, and knew what made them tick. Gerrold's book *The World of Star Trek*, in which he explored the lasting appeal of the show, had just been published. Fontana and her writers were certainly more invested than Roddenberry in the process of making the animated show. They knew the format and reveled in creations that simply wouldn't have worked in live action—underwater cities, zero-gravity fights, plant people, an alien with detachable limbs, giant dragons—but they understood that the core of the show depended on the interaction of the familiar characters as they encountered seemingly all-powerful foes who personified ethical standpoints or seemingly intractable philosophical conundrums.

The show's tight deadlines limited Roddenberry's scope for involvement. Each episode took three months from a blank page to twenty-two minutes of completed animation. Scheimer recalls that some weeks, they would still be editing the film on Friday, the day before it was due to be shown. There came a point, early in the production process for each episode, where Roddenberry had to step back and let them get on with making it.

Roddenberry was not part of the production's conveyor belt, and clearly had no strong emotional attachment to the series. He was genuinely busy with *Genesis II* and *The Questor Tapes*, and the "other two" shows he'd mentioned in his interview with Richard Shull. By the 1980s, he'd made it known that he didn't consider the animated series "canon," and references to events in the series were excised from books, comics, and games. His attitude infected fandom, and while—as was typical for cartoons—the animated series was frequently repeated by various stations over the years, fans tended to downplay it.

There are several candidates for the "two" live action shows Roddenberry told Shull he'd put aside. Roddenberry wrote down a number of his ideas for series, and in most cases they were little more than single-page summaries. So, for example, he wrote a half-page summary of a show called "Battleground Earth," a series set after aliens have arrived on modern-day Earth. After his death, this note would be adapted and dramatically expanded upon until it became the series *Gene Roddenberry's Earth Final Conflict*.

Some sources mention "Magna One" as a possible series. Roddenberry's secretary Susan Sackett, though, says it was a rewrite of a movie 20th Century-Fox were working on: "set in the year 2111, the story concerned an underwater mining city. The eponymous 'Magna One' (were there to be others?) was a Stephen Kingesque sub-oceanic bulldozer gone amok."[9]

The other two shows were *Spectre* and *The Tribunes*. The

former was a horror series, pitched to CBS in January 1972. He wanted it to be a detective show where the ghosts were real, rather than "someone trying to drive the heiress mad so they can get her money."[10] It didn't become a series, but he went on to co-write a *Spectre* TV movie with Samuel A. Peeples, which was made and shown in 1977.[11]

The Tribunes was a science fiction police procedural, also developed with Peeples (a fellow ex-cop). In *The World of Star Trek* it was described as:

> a 90 minute pilot for NBC. It will be a police show unlike any on the air. It's about an experimental police division of 40–50 men and women, equipped with the latest scientific and technological developments to aid them . . . these special officers will no longer carry guns, but weapons that are non-lethal, such as high intensity light which temporarily blinds a suspect or sprays of non-lethal chemicals. The officers would also be magistrates; they can take testimony, settle cases on the spot, issue subpoenas, and so on.[12]

At the end of his life Roddenberry said,

> "I never had any doubt that one of the great problems of modern times was how to force people to obey the law. It seemed to me at one time in my life that the best way to do that was to have policemen that were justifiable—policemen that were very *good* . . . At one time I had decided that when I became Chief of Police . . . I would bring along with me new attitudes and new uniforms, and that the only weapon

you carried was one with which you could choose to injure or
kill someone . . . I believed that we should legalize drugs . . .
I would have done something like I have done in *Star Trek*
for law enforcement."[13]

There were 4,730 LAPD officers when Roddenberry served on the force in the Fifties. He never rose above sergeant. Despite his claim to be "in line" to be chief of police, there were thousands of officers ahead of him in that line. It is possible that he is talking here about *The Tribunes*, rather than real life. Back in 1973, he'd said of the proposed show, "our hope is that some of these ideas will filter into actual police work."[14]

It's worth noting that before *Star Trek*, Roddenberry had pitched cop shows, military shows, and Westerns, but that as far as we know, everything he came up with in the Seventies was some form of science fiction or fantasy. He complained about this in a 1979 interview: "They said 'you're a science fiction type,' I said, 'hey wait a minute, I used to write Westerns, I wrote police stories,' and they said, 'No, you're now science fiction.' I don't feel bitter about that. That's the way Hollywood is, and that's the way mediocre people think."[15]

But this may be a rare instance where Roddenberry failed to see a more positive spin: writers for detective shows were a dime a dozen but very few could come up with workable science fiction formats. Roddenberry may have been a victim of typecasting but at least he was thought of as successful in a particular genre.

One idea that Roddenberry was clearly convinced would be a winner first emerged under the title *Genesis II*. It's the show specifically mentioned in the Shull interview. Roddenberry worked on it for almost two years, from spring 1972, and it's fair to say the series came as close as it possibly could to being made.

By the Seventies, networks still made pilot episodes of drama series, but now tended to offset the expense by running them as movies-of-the-week. If the network liked the result, and the ratings were good, they would commit to a full season. *Genesis II* was commissioned on those terms, filmed from November 1972 to January 1973, and shown in March.

The story begins in the twentieth century, deep in a cave system, where NASA astronaut Dylan Hunt is taking part in a test of suspended animation technology. There is a rockfall, and the sleeping Hunt is buried alive. He is revived 150 years in the future to discover that industrial civilization has collapsed and mankind now lives in isolated communities which dot a verdant planet. People face hardships that include the need to eke out a living without modern technology and cope with groups of marauding bandits. There are mutated animals and people, and vestiges of ancient machines and knowledge.

Hunt has been woken by a team from PAX, an organization that champions diversity and preserves technology and art that has survived the disaster, hoping to be a beacon of peace and progress. PAX hate "lust" in all forms. They are committed to non-violence to the point that their guns only fire stun darts. A number of them are "unisex" (asexual) including Harper-Smyth, a young woman who is assigned to help Dylan settle in. Hunt is wary, and easily swayed by a more conventionally beautiful woman, Lyra'a (Mariette Hartley, who'd played Zarabeth in the *Star Trek* episode "All Our Yesterdays"), who says she's a spy from another city and PAX are actually intent on conquering the world. Hunt takes this at face value, even when she tells him her city is called Tyrania. He is only a little suspicious when Lyra'a shows no concern for a group of starving stragglers. When he learns that there's a ruling elite of superhuman mutants who consider themselves superior to ordinary men, he seems more disturbed by the fact that this means Lyra'a has two bellybuttons (a Roddenberry in-joke). He is even accepting when he sees that while the Tyranians live in luxury, they operate work camps.

Hunt does come to see the error of his ways. To the horror of a team from PAX who help him escape (one of whom, the noble savage Isiah, is played by the giant actor Ted Cassidy, who'd appeared in *Star Trek* but was best known as Lurch, the butler for *The Addams Family*), Hunt reactivates an ancient nuclear device close to Tyrania and sets it to explode, so destroying the Tyranians.

Roddenberry had not stumbled across a wholly original idea. As long as humans have told stories, there have been tales about worldwide disasters and the struggles of survivors emerging from their shelters to rebuild—the biblical account of Noah's Ark was building on an already ancient myth. After the first atomic bombs were dropped, there was a particular interest in new stories about the aftermath of a global holocaust. George R. Stewart's *Earth Abides* (1949) was a successful early example. Roddenberry read science fiction magazines, so he was probably familiar with Walter M. Miller's *A Canticle for Leibowitz* (1960), about a group of Catholic monks preserving artifacts and scientific knowledge that have survived an atomic holocaust millennia before.

The premise of *Genesis II* was a strong one: the idea would be that Hunt would lead a team from PAX who would explore the world, encountering different communities who'd learned to survive in unusual ways. It would transpire that Lyra'a had survived the nuclear explosion, and she would be a recurring adversary. *Genesis II* would be a vehicle for adventure stories that could include social commentary and satire, with each community embodying a particular issue.

As part of his pitch, Roddenberry came up with a number of story ideas, and even before the show was made, we can see him falling back on ideas from *Star Trek*. Hunt would meet super soldiers from the 1990s who've emerged from suspended animation, a "god" that turns out to be the priesthood using advanced technology to con their followers, and a space probe that has returned in search of its creator. The idea for one story, "Poodle Shop," in which men are treated like pets by the domineering leaders of a matriarchal society, recycles an idea in the original *Star Trek* pitch document, where it was called "The Pet Shop." The plan for *Genesis II*, though, was—like *Star Trek*—to open the series to many writers, who would bring their own ideas to the table.

Genesis II did well in its timeslot, and was given positive reviews. Afterwards, Roddenberry was prone to exaggeration on these points, claiming it was "the highest rated Thursday night Movie of the Week"[16] and that he'd lost a bet with Majel because it had received no negative reviews whatsoever. In fact, the pilot had done well enough that, in the normal course of events, a series would have followed. CBS weren't entirely convinced, and told Roddenberry they might commission it as a mid-season replacement. They paid for four scripts to be written. When they decided not to pick up the series that year, they took the unusual step—albeit one Roddenberry had encountered before—of ordering a second pilot. Changes were made, and from these we can infer where it was felt the problems with the original lay.

The biggest change was the recasting of Dylan Hunt. It's clear Roddenberry wasn't happy with Alex Cord's performance in *Genesis II*, telling *The Monster Times* in 1976 he was "a very capable actor . . . but not for this series, as it turned out." He'd wanted Lloyd Bridges (as he had for *Star Trek*) but this was vetoed by the network, as were, according to Roddenberry, "all twelve" of his choices. He didn't get his way second time around either, with the network assigning John Saxon, who gives a far more physical, exuberant performance (one that seems consciously Shatneresque). The whole look and feel is less gloomy and faster-paced than *Genesis II*.

The second pilot had a peculiarly generic title: *Planet Earth*. It was shown a little more than a year after *Genesis II*, in April 1974. The makeover gave Roddenberry the opportunity to revamp a few aspects of the format. The story is a sequel to *Genesis II*, with Dylan Hunt now part of PAX, but it plays rather loosely with what was established before. Ted Cassidy returns as a more articulate Isiah; Harper-Smyth returns, though now played by Janet Margolin, not Lynne Marta. Majel Barrett also gets a small role as a PAX officer, but apparently not the same one she played in *Genesis II*. PAX no longer live in caves and wear drab overalls—now they have a futuristic city and dress in colorful, floaty William Ware Theiss creations.

The story is a meld of two ideas from the original *Star Trek* pitch: "Kongo," where white men are taken into slavery, and "The Pet Shop," the "women rule over men" plot. *Planet Earth* skips the introductions and setup, launching straight into an adventure where Dylan Hunt is captured and sold as a slave in a society of domineering women who drug their men and set them to work in the fields, the kitchen, and—inevitably, given who wrote it—the bedroom. The community is being menaced by Kreegs, mutants who have the same head ridges and bumps the Klingons end up with in the later *Star Trek* movies and television shows. Hunt realizes the male slaves are being drugged to keep them meek. He removes the drug from their food supply, and the men help the women fight off the Kreegs.

Roddenberry occasionally said that the reason *Genesis II* didn't become a series was because CBS opted to make the *Planet of the Apes* TV series instead. It's clearly not that simple. CBS did make *Planet of the Apes* for TV, but crucially it ran in the autumn of 1974. *Genesis II* was shown in March 1973, *Planet Earth* in April 1974. So CBS made *Planet of the Apes* *after* giving *Genesis II* its second chance. Twenty stories from various writers were commissioned, at least six scripts were completed and ready to be filmed. CBS invested time and money in the project, and clearly wanted it to work. So why didn't it?

There's no doubt that *Planet of the Apes* was, as it were, the gorilla in the room. The 1968 movie had led to a series of sequels, and the movies had thrust the concept of a bizarre post-apocalyptic Earth of the distant future into the heart of popular culture. Over at DC Comics, editor Carmine Infantino had failed to secure the rights for *Planet of the Apes*, but set legendary artist Jack Kirby—who'd recently left Marvel, where his creations and co-creations included the majority of the superheroes who made up the Avengers, the X-Men and the Fantastic Four—the task of coming up with a similar series. Kirby hadn't seen *Planet of the Apes*, but he knew the premise, and created *Kamandi*, set in a lurid, densely packed world where all sorts of animals had been mutated following a "Great Disaster" long ago which had bathed the world in radiation. *Kamandi* started publication in autumn 1972, as Roddenberry was writing *Genesis II*. There's no evidence Roddenberry was aware of the comic, and it's virtually impossible Kirby knew anything about Roddenberry's plans. They are very similar not because one influenced the other, but because many people who published or broadcast science fiction were looking for ideas like *Planet of the Apes* at the time.

Genesis II got good ratings, but when CBS showed the original *Planet of the Apes* movie in the same slot, the ratings were far higher. *Genesis II* had the same kind of setup as *Planet of the Apes*—a NASA scientist returns to Earth in the future to find a world settled after an apocalypse. The network executives thought the *Genesis II* series would be better if it was more like *Planet of the Apes*. Many producers in such a situation would have talked that through, tried to understand what the network was after, and come to some form of accommodation. Roddenberry's belief that he shouldn't compromise left both sides a little exasperated by the process. Roddenberry would go on to tell an anecdote silly enough that it may well have been completely true:

> "At that time a junior executive came up with one of those great front office suggestions: he suggested that we consider the possibility that man's best friend had evolved into a hind-legged species of talking dog, and intending to be sarcastic, I said 'no, I have something much better. I have in mind a turtle-man creature and it may turn out to be even better than apes because it will give our show an underwater dimension.' I knew it was all over when they were taking that suggestion seriously."[17]

Having made two pilots and paid for twenty scripts, CBS were still not convinced. They pulled the plug on *Genesis*

II/Planet Earth, and simply commissioned *Planet of the Apes* instead. As well as having a title audiences recognized, the show was a cheaper option than Roddenberry's series, as many of the costumes and props from the movies could be reused. The series would star Mark Lenard, who'd played the first Romulan we saw in *Star Trek*, as well as Spock's father Sarek, as the main antagonist, the gorilla General Urko. CBS expected great things when it debuted in September 1974, but the reviews and ratings were poor, and the show was ignominiously canceled after fourteen episodes.

With *Planet of the Apes* out of the way, a third attempt at the same basic concept was aired. *Strange New World* was broadcast on March 23, 1975. Despite lifting its name from *Star Trek*'s opening title voiceover, Gene Roddenberry was not involved. This version kept John Saxon as the lead, but made him a new character, Anthony Vico, one of three astronauts in orbit when Earth is hit by an asteroid. It's easily the dullest of the three versions. Two months before the transmission, in January 1975, Roddenberry had already publicly declared that *Genesis II* was "dead."[18]

Gene Roddenberry had spent two years working on some form of *Genesis II*. It came at an odd time for him: he'd failed to move into movies, but saw the renewed interest in *Star Trek* as proof he was great at making serial television. He'd remarried and was trying to start a new family, but Majel Barrett suffered a series of miscarriages. He was getting paid to develop television shows, but nothing like the number he'd become accustomed to while producing shows that were on the air. He told plenty of people that *Star Trek* had been "ahead of its time." The corollary of that, surely, was that his hour had now come. Roddenberry saw the signs. The public were interested in science fiction, perhaps because of the moon landing, perhaps because they wanted escapism from the Vietnam War and the troubles of the Nixon era, or perhaps because it was a genre that could hold a satirical mirror up to confusing, uncertain times. Whatever the reason, Roddenberry looked to be on the right side of history. So what went wrong?

While *Genesis II* clearly meant a lot to Roddenberry on a number of professional and personal levels, it's just not very good. *Planet Earth* is far more entertaining, but it's endearingly terrible, rather than impressive. There's some baffling storytelling in both pilots—elaborate explanations of details that aren't important to the story while major characters and plotlines disappear for long stretches. Both are extraordinarily pompous. *Genesis II* is as airless as the tunnels of the subterranean travel tubes that allow our hero to propel himself around the world. *Planet Earth* has a very odd problem with tone—the serious stuff is brushed away, we dwell on trivia (it's explained to us that the travel tubes move at 1,135 miles an hour) and the pacing is slow. The story beats are so obvious that you can set your watch to them and it's almost impossible to make any emotional investment in Hunt, PAX or anything else that's going on. The direction, performances and dull design work play their part, but it can't be a coincidence that a lot of the faults are also evident in *The Lieutenant*, "The Cage," *Star Trek: The Motion*

Picture, or the first season of *Star Trek: The Next Generation*—all of which were started from scratch by Roddenberry and laden with some fairly humorless worldbuilding.

Then there are the "issues." There's some interesting subversion—nowhere in the various societies we see in any of the proposed storylines was there anything resembling democracy, let alone capitalism. But, given two chances to put his money where his mouth is, and make a television movie that's bold and political and has a clear message, Roddenberry blows it. *Planet Earth*'s depiction of a society run by women is clearly meant to be "about" feminism, but the treatment of gender politics—perhaps best summed up by John Saxon's growled line "Women's Lib . . . or Women's Lib *gone mad*?"—is so bizarre that most modern viewers would probably be too busy being bewildered to remember to be offended. There's some nuance: the women have various leadership styles from cruel dominatrix to more playful and forgiving. But Roddenberry wants to have his cake and eat it: to portray how humiliating it is for a man to be treated as a sex object, but also how hot it is when a man bends a babe to his will. *Planet Earth*'s killer flaw is that a description of TV listings length makes it sounds rather kinky and fun, but when he fleshes it out, Roddenberry manages to make it astonishingly dull.

Innovation Publishing, a company who produced a number of comic-book titles based on old TV shows and movies, such as *Lost in Space*, *Dark Shadows*, and *Forbidden Planet*, bought the rights to adapt *Genesis II* in the early Nineties, but the company folded before the series was developed.

Could it have worked? Yes. The idea's perfectly good. It's easy to see how a format about visiting different models for how to run a society could be a fascinating, smart show. Here, rather than in *Star Trek*, Roddenberry hit on the perfect template for a modern take on *Gulliver's Travels*. *Genesis II* and *Planet Earth* are frustrating to watch mainly because, although it's clearly a good idea for a television series, the episodes themselves somehow manage to be both heavy-handed and lightweight. It's very hard not to place a lot of the blame on Roddenberry himself.

Roddenberry had a second series in the works at exactly the same time. This was *Questor* (retitled *The Questor Tapes* by the time it was shown). He delivered the first draft on November 29, 1972, and a revised draft by December 12,[19] which fell during the filming of *Genesis II*. The pilot episode was broadcast in January 1974 (coming neatly between *Genesis II* and *Planet Earth*) with Robert Foxworth in the title role. Because Roddenberry was busy with *Genesis II*, much of the day-to-day work on *Questor* was done by Gene L. Coon, who'd been such an important force on *Star Trek*.

Questor was an android, one we see assembled by an international team of scientists at the beginning of the story. The scientists have not designed Questor, but are completing the work of the late Dr. Vaslovik, who was so far ahead of his field that the scientists don't fully understand what they are building. In an attempt to keep some control over the experiment, they decide not to upload all of the tapes Vaslovik planned to program Questor with into the android's brain. Questor activates anyway, and—after the scientists have gone home for the night—uses machines to adopt an appearance that's indistinguishable from a human, even on quite close inspection. Questor escapes from the lab, quickly learning to speak and act like a person, barring a few mannerisms. We're briefly led to think that the android might be hostile, but one of the scientists, Jerry Robinson (played by Mike Farrell, soon to end up as B.J. Hunnicutt in *M*A*S*H*), knows otherwise, and works with Questor as he travels the world trying to discover what was on the missing tapes—including a trip to a "London" that looks suspiciously Californian, complete with mountains in the background). In the last act of the pilot episode, Questor reaches a mysterious cave full of deactivated androids, and encounters Vaslovik, who reveals he is also an android. As he expires, Vaslovik explains that Questor is the last of a line of androids built by mysterious aliens to carefully guide and protect the progress of the human race. By the time Questor's life ends, humanity will have either destroyed itself, or its civilization will have attained the next level of development.

Star Trek fans will spot that Questor is, as Questor himself might put it, 99.9997 percent identical to Data from *The Next Generation*, particularly in the early seasons of the latter show, when the android was preoccupied with exploring "the human equation"—the mysterious factor that makes humans unique. Data looks a little more artificial than Questor, but shares the same superior physical and mental abilities. They both say "humor is a quality which seems to elude me," and assure a female acquaintance that they are "fully functional" lovers. As *The Next Generation* progressed, Data's backstory was developed and we learn he was built by a human being, Dr. Soong, but according to the writers' guide (and a couple of the early *Next Generation* books and comics) he was built by mysterious aliens. While the series took another direction, it's entirely possible Roddenberry's original plan was to reveal that Data was on an identical mission to Questor, shepherding the human race to its next stage of development. This was a recurring theme of the early episodes of *The Next Generation*, with the godlike Q being worried about the destiny of humanity in the pilot episode, and young Wesley Crusher singled out as important by the Traveler in "Where No One Has Gone Before." It was a theme that faded away as *The Next Generation* settled in. Brent Spiner became popular with fans for his portrayal of Data, in part because he found a way to bring a lighter touch and a slightly arch quality to the character.

At the time it was made, the obvious parallel to Questor in Roddenberry's other work was, of course, Mr. Spock, another logical being whose role was often to comment on the foibles of human beings. There was a good reason for this—it was intended as a vehicle for Leonard Nimoy. As Nimoy related it in *I Am Spock*,[20] he'd left *Mission: Impossible* at the end of its fifth season, and the head of production at Universal told him, "we've just hired Gene Roddenberry to write a project for you." Nimoy signed a one-year contract with Universal "with the understanding that I was to star in this new series." Later, Nimoy was in makeup for another project, and saw people at work on an old life cast of his. After he hadn't heard anything for a while, he spoke to Dick Colla, the director, who told him the part had gone to Robert Foxworth. Nimoy called Roddenberry, who insisted he'd had nothing to do with the decision, but Nimoy was secretly relieved, as he'd been getting a fair amount of work on stage, TV, and the movies, and preferred it to being a regular on a production-line TV show.

For Nimoy, the continuing success of Star Trek was a little irritating. While waiting to play Questor, he'd become aware just how closely identified with Spock he now was. He'd started to worry that playing another logical humanoid in a Gene Roddenberry science fiction show would hurt his career.[21]

At the beginning of 1972, Roddenberry had been able to write to Hal Clement that he knew Leonard Nimoy would return to Star Trek if it was revived, but that William Shatner may have moved on.[22] Being passed over for Questor marked the point where Nimoy decided to have as little as possible to do with Roddenberry, something that would remain true for the rest of their lives.

The network wanted more Questor, and Roddenberry was commissioned to write a series bible. D.C. Fontana was involved in the process (and would write the novelization of the pilot episode). Roddenberry wanted to avoid the sort of stories that involved "monsters trying to conquer man," and suggested one in which Questor calculated that a brilliant young scientist would go on to cure cancer as long as he wasn't distracted by marriage, and so would plot to split him up with his fiancée. Having succeeded, he would then realize he'd miscalculated, that the man's wife would have been very supportive, and would then try to get them back together. Questor and Robinson would run an international organization from a hi-tech base.

A number of scripts were written but Universal weren't happy.[23] They'd suggested a major change to the format: losing the Jerry Robinson human sidekick character and making the show more like *The Fugitive*, where the main character would be on the run from the authorities, arrive in a town or city, and struggle to solve a local difficulty before his pursuers caught up with him. It had become a tried and trusted format for a TV show. It's not a bad suggestion for adding urgency and movement to the format—but it wasn't the show Gene Roddenberry wanted to make. He saw the dynamic between Questor and Robinson as the whole point.

At conventions, it was part of Roddenberry's schtick that the network bosses were too dumb to get his shows. When he replied to a letter from a nun, Sister Margaret Clarke, who'd written to say she enjoyed the exploration of the human condition in *Star Trek*, he talked about his new show, and seemed irritated at some of the network changes:

They wanted it to become a robot, Superman show which would draw its entertainment from Questor's ability to leap tall buildings in a single bound, or something like that. They insisted on entirely deleting the back story of *The Questor*

Tapes, more particularly Questor's mission to help mankind and his computer-logic perspectives on mankind by which the weekly episodes would have aimed at seeing ourselves as others might see us.[24]

As with *Genesis II*, it's easy to believe that a different producer might have found a way to persuade his bosses that the Jerry Robinson character was a vital cog in the series, or to navigate a course that created plenty of room for "Superman" antics *and* philosophical scenes. Questor might even have had that man in Gene L. Coon, but Coon had died in July 1973, from throat and lung cancer. He was forty-nine (younger than Roddenberry) and had continued to chain smoke even after he'd started using an oxygen tank to breathe. His death clearly cast a shadow over the project. Even by the time the pilot for *The Questor Tapes* aired in January 1974—to good ratings and reviews— it was extremely unlikely the show would ever be made.

As 1973 started, things must have looked incredibly bright for Gene Roddenberry. *Star Trek* now had the reputation as "the show that didn't die," and Roddenberry was getting the credit. The animated series was in the works and providing a useful income for very little effort. There was discussion about a *Star Trek* movie. Roddenberry had two pilots in production, both promising to build on the potential of *Star Trek* to deliver smart science-fiction action stories. In modern marketing parlance, a Roddenberry brand was developing. Majel was pregnant—she would give birth to their son, Rod, in February 1974.

But by the start of 1974, his career was in tatters. Over and over again, Roddenberry had played "crazy Gene," insisting to the network executives that it was his way or the highway, and they'd consistently chosen the highway. *Genesis II* and *The Questor Tapes* weren't going forward. There wasn't going to be a *Star Trek* movie, and the animated series was canceled. No one was interested in any of Roddenberry's other ideas.

Meanwhile, *Star Trek* had only grown in popularity. When Roddenberry reconnected with *Star Trek* fandom, he would be amazed by what he found . . .

CHAPTER SIX

FAN-TOPIA

There are still people in the United States who've never seen an episode of *Star Trek*. Even they, though, know that *Star Trek* attracts a devoted following and that these fans gather in their thousands at huge conventions, where they dress up as characters from the television shows and movies, meet their heroes, and stock up with merchandise. For a very long time, now, *Star Trek* fans have been at least as visible a presence in the world as *Star Trek* itself.

The fans have been an important part of the equation for almost all of *Star Trek*'s history. Gene Roddenberry and the cast were worried how little fan mail was showing up at first—possibly the network wasn't forwarding it to the studio—but clubs, newsletters, and fanzines were beginning to spring up by the end of the first season. In August 1967, an NBC booklet stated that twenty-nine thousand items of fan mail had been received, second only to *The Monkees*.[1]

It wasn't unusual for some letter writers to be obsessed with a favorite cast member. William Shatner received his fair share of fan mail, but it was Mr. Spock who proved to be the show's real heartthrob. This was something that Roddenberry, Shatner, and Leonard Nimoy all failed to anticipate and found horrifying, albeit for radically different reasons. Even here, *Star Trek* wasn't entirely unusual. Ilya Kuryakin on *The Man from U.N.C.L.E.*, the cerebral, cool Russian played by David McCallum, ended up with more fan mail than his co-star Robert Vaughn's more conventional American hero, the one the women were "meant" to be going for.

The first effect the fans had on the show was that *Star Trek* clearly changed to accommodate the popularity of Spock. It's no coincidence that the second- and third-season premieres were both Spock stories. The second season saw a conscious effort to cater to the "Spockians," as the writers termed fans of the character. Two second-season stories in particular sought to explore the nature of Spock's alien heritage: "Amok Time" portrayed Vulcan society as sternly matriarchal, whereas "Journey to Babel" showed Spock's father acting in a domineering manner towards his wife. With two episodes that rather contradicted themselves as stars to steer by, *Star Trek* fans plotted a course that encompassed Spock as a being of ferocious sexual potential, but one who needed to be nursed; from a stoic race who could, if his father was anything to go by, be swayed by an exceptional woman; someone who'd die for Kirk, but occasionally got so horny he'd kill him if he got between Spock and his mate. The disparity between "Amok Time" and "Journey to Babel" was purely down to writers not comparing notes, but if the production team had been setting out to accommodate every possible sexual fantasy involving Spock they couldn't have done so more efficiently.

By the end of the second season, it was clear to everyone that the fan response was abnormally intense for a television show. As Lincoln Enterprises started replying to letters it became obvious that people were going beyond the standard requests for autographs of the cast or asking whether they could have a part on the show. Something about *Star Trek* resonated with the audience.

The primary evidence that *Star Trek* had a particularly devoted fanbase was, of course, the letter-writing campaign in December 1967 to February 1968 that—for the sake of argument—saved the show from cancelation at the end of the second season. As a result of that, Gene Roddenberry and Bjo Trimble ended up with a list of twelve thousand avid fans of the show.[2] That campaign had connected and, to use a *Star Trek* word, energized a group of likeminded people who were dispersed around the country. This network would live on, even after *Star Trek* was taken off the air.

The studio weren't expecting *Star Trek* to disappear overnight after its cancelation. There was still a little more to be squeezed out of the show. Comics and books were still being published, toys produced. This was entirely typical for a show of its type—*The Man from U.N.C.L.E.*, *Dark Shadows*, and (a few years down the line—it would only end its run in 1973) *Mission: Impossible* all lived on as novels, comics, and toys for several years after the television shows ended.

There were signs that it would be a while before the line was drawn under *Star Trek*. One of the first was that the model kit of the USS *Enterprise* was proving to be a perennial seller. As one aficionado, Jay Chladek, has put it:

> In all of science fiction modeling, the one kit that has been produced the longest and one which probably almost every modeler with at least a passing interest in science fiction has built at one time or another has been the classic 18" U.S.S. *Enterprise* kit from AMT. The model stayed in AMT's catalog for almost 30 years, which has to be something of a record.[3]

AMT sold well over a million models of the *Enterprise*, and their Klingon battlecruiser was also very popular. In the early Seventies, they expanded the range with models of Spock, a Romulan Bird of Prey starship, and the *Enterprise*'s shuttlecraft. Chladek has noted that AMT retooled the *Enterprise* kit in the early Seventies. Molds for model kits eventually wore out, and making a new one was an expensive process. AMT must have been confident that sales weren't trailing off to make such an investment.

The second indication of the scale of the phenomenon was the success of the *Star Trek* books. James Blish had written three volumes published by Bantam (imaginatively titled *Star Trek*, *Star Trek 2*, and *Star Trek 3*, published in January 1967, February 1968, and April 1969 respectively) that each adapted six or seven television episodes into short stories. These had sold "several million copies" according to one source,[4] "four million" according to another,[5] and certainly enough to have been reprinted numerous times by the early Seventies. For 1970, Bantam asked Blish to write a full-length original novel. *Spock Must Die!* was a sequel to the TV episode "Errand of Mercy," and featured the start of a massive war between the Federation and the Klingons, with Spock accused of treason. It was an epic story that would have been hard to make as a blockbuster movie, let alone for television.

This commercial activity was just the tip of the iceberg. Around the country—and now in a few other countries—*Star Trek* fan clubs thrived. Dozens of fanzines were being published, with titles like *Babel*, *Stardate*, *Quadrant*, and *LNSTFCCF* (it stood for *Leonard Nimoy* Star Trek *Fan Club of Concerned Fans*). The 1968 fanzine *Star Trek: An Analysis of a Phenomenon in Science Fiction* was a forty-eight-page, heavily illustrated survey of the show that drew up histories of the characters and the Federation, technical details of the phasers and communicators, behind-the-scenes information on the special effects, with a long essay trying to put the show in a social context. In 1969 Bjo Trimble published the first edition of her *Star Trek Concordance*, an essential A–Z of the show. Fanzines cataloged the episodes and the careers of its cast, and they reviewed stories. Some publications were lists of fan clubs and other fanzines. Fan clubs tended to have newsletters that kept people as up to date as possible. There was a massive amount of *Star Trek* fan fiction. The quality of all of this ranged from slapdash and amateur to (rather more rarely) glossy publications that looked as good as a professional magazine.

Since the 1940s, there had been a full calendar of general science fiction conventions, where fans gathered to discuss the work of Isaac Asimov, Robert Heinlein, Arthur C. Clarke, and many others. The very first public showing of *Star Trek* had been at Tricon, the 24th World Science-Fiction Convention in Cleveland on Labor Day weekend, September 2–5, 1966. When *Star Trek* had been on, science fiction fans had tended to champion it, certainly compared to the general standard of the genre on television and at the cinema. No doubt because a few "proper" SF authors, like Harlan Ellison and Theodore Sturgeon, wrote for the show, science fiction fans put it on the same approved list as *Destination Moon*, *Forbidden Planet*, and, more recently, *2001: A Space Odyssey*, rather than counting it as "dreck" like *The Time Tunnel* and *Lost in Space*. Gene Roddenberry had courted these science fiction fans, understanding how important it was to get them on side. Isaac Asimov and Arthur C. Clarke had given *Star Trek* their seal of approval, and both became regular correspondents with Roddenberry.

Star Trek brought science fiction to a mass audience, a younger audience, a female audience. Before long, conventions started seeing more and more *Star Trek* fans, and they tended to be interested only in *Star Trek*. The more traditional science fiction fans were a little put out by this, and a slight backlash started. With the show off the air, but with the number of *Star Trek* fans who showed up to conventions only increasing, *Star Trek* fandom was now viewed "with alarm."[6] While many young viewers were introduced to science fiction by *Star Trek*, going on to discover Heinlein, Asimov, and so on, many were interested in *Star Trek* alone. The "subset" of science fiction fandom soon contained more exclusively *Star Trek* fans than it did "mainstream" fans of the genre.

Bjo Trimble was a long-time attendee of science fiction conventions, as were many other *Star Trek* fans. They saw a very obvious solution: organize a science fiction convention exclusively dedicated to *Star Trek*. The New York event was so successful that soon the calendar filled up with dedicated *Star Trek* conventions.

The same pattern occurred with science fiction magazines. In his 1973 book *The World of Star Trek*, David Gerrold estimated that the number of hardcore fans actively organizing conventions or fan clubs, or producing fanzines, "touches about five thousand people in the United States."[7]

So what was the appeal? Early on, the character of Mr. Spock was a huge part of it. Looking back from our vantage point, from where there are four *Star Trek* television series which barely mention Spock, it's striking just how prominent he is in the early merchandise, and how much of the early fan culture was dedicated specifically to Spock, Leonard Nimoy, and Vulcan society. There were Mr. Spock model kits bearing the tagline "*Star Trek*'s Most Popular Character." The titles of three of the first five original novels were (complete with exclamation marks): *Spock Must Die!*, *Spock, Messiah!*, and *Vulcan!*.

Gene Roddenberry fought to keep "the guy with the ears" in the face of network objections. Not only was Mr. Spock the only character who made it from the pilots to the regular series, Nimoy's Spock would go on to be— as far as we know—the sole survivor of the original *Star Trek* universe when its timeline split off in the 2009 *Star Trek* revival movie. Nimoy played Spock for almost fifty years, from the pilot episode "The Cage" to a cameo appearance, two years before his death, in the 2013 movie *Star Trek Into Darkness*.

That's not to say, though, that Mr. Spock sprang fully formed into existence. In "The Cage," he has the pointy ears, but also a full range of emotions. For the series, Spock took on the bridge duties and personality of Number One, the austere female second-in-command dropped after the pilot. The script of the second pilot, "Where No Man Has Gone Before," called on Spock to be annoyed by Kirk's occasional irrationality—in their first scene, Kirk beats Spock at chess by making, in Spock's opinion, the "wrong" move. Over the course of the episode, Spock shouts, sulks, and is clearly not quite the character we're familiar with.

During the filming of the next episode to be made, "The Corbomite Maneuver," the director, Joseph Sargent, suggested that while the rest of the crew were alarmed by the arrival of a vast alien spaceship, Spock should react with scientific detachment. Leonard Nimoy was a Method actor. Before taking the *Star Trek* job, he'd taught Stanislavski and Strasberg's techniques to classes in Hollywood (and made more money teaching acting than from acting work). Nimoy took this suggestion for one line reading and made it the character note: from that point, Spock would approach *everything* with scientific detachment.

Over the course of the series, Mr. Spock's alien nature permitted the writers to give him all sorts of hitherto unsuspected abilities that allowed him to save the day: it turned out he could merge his mind with someone else's, he had a special inner eyelid that saved his sight when bombarded by intense light, and he could render people unconscious by pinching their neck. Gradually, more details of his family and home planet were revealed.

Spock was a sex symbol. A glance at pretty much any early *Star Trek* fanzine demonstrates that we shouldn't dismiss or underplay "kinkiness" as a big part of his appeal. Just try unpacking this paragraph from 1973's *The World of Star Trek*:

> [Spock] touched a particularly responsive chord in a lot of little girls—and a lot of big girls, too. The pointed ears and arched eyebrows suggested great strength and masculinity, with a healthy hint of controlled *evil*. But Spock's conscious suppression of emotion, as well as his unavailability as a sexual object, made him (in the words of one of these young ladies), "A safe rape. You could love him without risking your virginity."[8]

So pressing was the question of what made Spock so attractive that author James Blish had Kirk ask it in the first full-length *Star Trek* novel. Again, the answer is somewhat jaw-dropping and involves the word "safe":

What was the source of the oddly overt response that women of all ages and degrees of experience seemed to feel towards Spock? Kirk had no answer, but he had two theories, switching from one to the other according to his mood. One was that it was a simple challenge-and-response situation: he may be cold and unresponsive to other women. But if I had the chance, I could get through to him! The other, more complex theory seemed most plausible to Kirk only in his moments of depression: that most white crewwomen, still the inheritors after two centuries of vestiges of the shameful racial prejudices of their largely Anglo-American forebears, saw in the Vulcan half-breed—who after all had not sprung from any *Earthly* colored stock—a "safe" way of breaking with those vestigial prejudices—and at the same time, perhaps, satisfying the sexual curiosity which had probably been at the bottom of them from the beginning.

One in-joke or shibboleth that developed at conventions involved adding a slice of cucumber to any cocktail which had the word "Spock" in its name, a reference to him being a healthy, green-blooded male.

Spock's father was also a source of particular fascination—Sarek was, after all, the only known Vulcan to have shown interest in an Earthwoman. His stated reason for marrying Amanda left just enough to the imagination: "At the time, it seemed the logical thing to do." Mark Lenard, an actor with a CV encompassing an episode or two of virtually every American network show from the Sixties and Seventies, was rather surprised that of all the roles he'd played, Sarek most caught the imagination of fans, particularly female fans.

Sarek appeared in one episode of the original show, but in its afterlife he became a central part of the mythology, appearing in the animated show and three of the movies, and was the focus of the first major crossover with the original series in *The Next Generation* (a third-season episode called, naturally enough, "Sarek"). Sarek's death was such a momentous moment for the mythology of *Star Trek* that it was a turning point in the twenty-fifth anniversary episode, "Unification."

In 1976, Gene Roddenberry was approached to record a spoken-word album about *Star Trek*, a project which became *Inside Star Trek* (to be confused neither with *Inside Star Trek: The Real Story*, the 1996 book by Herbert F. Solow and Robert H. Justman, nor with *Inside Trek*, Susan Sackett's 2002 tell-all memoir). Roddenberry curated a rather odd collection made up of recordings of speeches he'd given at conventions, interspersed with dialogues between himself and characters and actors from the show. William Shatner met Kirk on the bridge of the *Enterprise*, Dr. McCoy spoke up in favor of holistic medicine. The album was made at the time when Leonard Nimoy was least keen to revive Spock, and most distrustful of Roddenberry's "cashing in" on the series. Mark Lenard stepped into the breach for the track "Sarek's Son Spock," in which Roddenberry interviewed the Vulcan ambassador. Here, Roddenberry was able to satisfy the curiosity of a section of *Star Trek* fandom, and was quite playful about it:

RODDENBERRY: I have many new questions, Ambassador. Much more intimate, and personal, than I have ever had to ask before.

SAREK: About my son Spock, I presume.

RODDENBERRY: Well, yes, if you include the beginnings of Spock. There are some things I must know, Ambassador, in order to continue with my *Star Trek* journey. Forgive me, but how were you able to overcome the Vulcan *pon farr* mating drive? I presume you did overcome it, Spock's mother Amanda was human, and somehow she was impregnated by you—

SAREK: Roddenberry, are you asking if we coupled?

RODDENBERRY: Er, yes, sir. We know that Vulcans normally mate only once every seven years—

SAREK: And since it is known that we pay for our sexual repression during these years by an almost animal madness, this has aroused a . . . a prurient curiosity among humans.

Sarek goes on to explain that Spock's gestation had required all sorts of medical experimentation in order for the fetus to remain viable as it developed. Both Roddenberry and Lenard were well aware that there was a subset of fans keen to tame a Vulcan male—they'd met women at conventions very keen to inform them of that. "Sarek" takes his opportunity to announce that much "depends upon the woman. Not just her strength, but also her wisdom. Her patience . . . Ordinarily an Earth woman could not endure that. If she survived, she might be severely injured, both physically and emotionally."

Perhaps the most surprising development was that Mr. Spock became a strong identification figure for sections of the *Star Trek* audience. Even before he was "logical," Spock's character was defined by his status as an outsider. In Spock's first scene in "Where No Man Has Gone Before," we learn that he's not purely alien, he has "human ancestors." It's halfway through the second season, in the episode "Journey to Babel," before we learn that Spock's mother is human. When his parents visit the *Enterprise*, we hear for the first time that he had a difficult childhood. Spock isn't just "alien" because he comes from another planet, he doesn't fit in among Vulcans, either. He is perpetually alienated.

The cliché that all *Star Trek* fans are basement-dwelling virgins was never quite true—evenings at Seventies *Star Trek* conventions were notoriously debauched. It's fair to say, though, and not a criticism, that *Star Trek* fans have tended to be bookish to the point of being nerdy, to be more scientifically than emotionally literate. They are often the sort of people who look at the world and the people around them with an air of detached mild despair. All the human characters in *Star Trek* were clever—the *Enterprise* had a crew of engineers, doctors, and scientific specialists, and it's made clear more than once that simply to be posted on the ship was evidence of the highest achievement in your chosen field—but in a show about smart people, Spock, the kid who sits in the corner and doesn't know how to have fun at parties, was a clear identification figure for many viewers.

Spock was certainly an identification figure for Leonard Nimoy. More surprising, perhaps, Gene Roddenberry saw Spock as an ideal version of himself.

Roddenberry and Nimoy both admitted that they talked to Spock. *Star Trek* fans who've read either of Nimoy's autobiographies, *I Am Not Spock* (1975) or *I Am Spock* (1995), know that the books wrestle with questions like: "I am not Spock. But I'm close to him. Closer than anyone. How much closer can two people be than to stand in the same body, occupy the same space?"[9]

Nimoy was always keen to portray himself as a serious artist. *I Am Not Spock* was his third published book, after *You and I* (1973) and *Will I Think of You?* (1974), which combined his poetry with his photographs and drawings. So it's fair to conclude that the two autobiographies are, at least in part, a form of performance art. Nimoy might have been using the Spock character to dramatize his inner conflict. However serious-minded Nimoy might get, there's room for us to imagine at least an element of play when he publishes these "dialogs." More than that, Nimoy's autobiographies frequently slip into lengthy dialog between the actor and the character where they question each other, score points off each other.

NIMOY: Spock . . . How does it feel to be popular?
SPOCK: I do not have feelings.
NIMOY: I'm sorry. I didn't mean to offend you.

SPOCK: I am not offended. I understand your tendency to judge me by your human standards. It would, however, facilitate matters if you would refrain from doing so.

NIMOY: I'll try.[10]

Gene Roddenberry told Yvonne Fern he did exactly the same thing, that he had a "relationship" with Spock, and he seems to have meant it entirely literally:

> "It's very profound. Very powerful. In some ways, Spock is my best friend. I have long conversations with him. We're both trying to figure out the same problems . . . the meaning of the universe. Who we are. Why we're here. The time and space of it all. Where we're going and how we can prepare ourselves for the journey."[11]

We all have an inner monologue, and use it to rehearse what we're going to say or do. We're familiar with the idea that our "heart" and our "head" don't always steer us in the same direction. The pop culture version of Spock is that he's a being of pure logic, and his narrative purpose in many *Star Trek* scenes is as the "reality check." So on the face of it, when Roddenberry and Nimoy say they "talk to Spock," we might imagine they just mean they have a strategy of occasionally sitting back and analyzing a situation dispassionately. Every so often, much like Captain Kirk, they pause and turn to Spock for a logical explanation, or to suggest the rational way forward, as a way of calming down. But this is not how either Nimoy's or Roddenberry's conversations with Spock went.

Gene Roddenberry might have once said, "I have had so much trouble with emotion in my life I thought it just would be fun to write someone who didn't have that problem."[12] But that's not actually quite the character he created. Roddenberry and Nimoy knew better than anyone else that the famed Vulcan calm is essentially a façade. As *Star Trek* progressed, we learned that Vulcan logic was not the result of Spock's people being born with computer-like brains—it was a state reached as a result of lifelong training and self-discipline. In a number of stories, we see Vulcans abandon austerity as their bestial nature comes to the surface. Famously, in "Amok Time," we learn that Vulcan males go into heat and have to return to their home planet to mate, or they will go mad and die. The ultra-rational race are, essentially, slaves to the same impulses as salmon.

The most telling scene in that episode, though, comes at the end. Driven by his mating instinct, and thanks to some rather odd Vulcan by-laws, the bestial Spock is forced into a fight with Kirk, and his rage only subsides when he kills his captain. We cut back to the *Enterprise*, where it turns out that McCoy has injected Kirk with a drug which feigns death. Kirk wakes up in sickbay. Spock is summoned, still believing Kirk is dead. The moment he sees Kirk is alive, Spock's eyes light up, he grins, blurts out "Jim!" He immediately collects himself, resumes his usual air of sangfroid, but we've seen through it.

So Spock's key character trait is not "logic" or "a computer-like nature." As Roddenberry put it: "Spock is, to me, the essence of evolution in a sense . . . he's not distracted, he doesn't excuse himself. He's very hard on himself, very disciplined . . . he solves problems by refusing to allow himself to do anything other than focus on the problem."[13]

Spock represents a striving for self-control, for discipline. Actors and writers need a great deal of both. Spock was the ideal.

Leonard Nimoy and Gene Roddenberry had a long falling out, one that can be characterized by Nimoy's increasing awareness of how often Roddenberry failed to live up to his promises: "Gene always had an agenda—his own. I didn't see him step up to bat and be the decent, honorable humanist that he portrayed himself to be."[14] There were business disputes too: when Roddenberry learned that Nimoy was going to command $2,000 for a personal appearance, he tried—and failed—to get a 20 percent cut, on the grounds that all bookings had to go through Lincoln Enterprises.[15]

At various low points in their relationship, Nimoy would go as far as using roundabout phrases to avoid saying the name "Gene Roddenberry" in the answer to a question. In turn, Roddenberry would talk about his "dreamworld" version of *Star Trek*, a thought experiment about what the future might look like, freed from the constraints of television budgets, or censorship, or the need to put his ideals in concrete form. "When I say '*Star Trek*,' I'm often not talking about the shows. I'm talking about my dreamworld, my philosophy, the one I wanted to put on television."[16]

Gene Roddenberry had a "dreamworld" version of Mr. Spock . . . and he didn't look like Leonard Nimoy. When he talked about the character, "Spock has for me so much significance, such personal and impersonal appeal. My Spock—not the one you see in *Star Trek*—although they are similar."[17] It wasn't Nimoy who said the following, it was Roddenberry: "I know Spock so well that I have actually turned out pages of dialogue with me and Spock. And I say, 'why do you think this way?' and he answers. With Spock it comes very close to telepathy. But that is because I am Spock."[18]

More than their business dealings, or broken promises about involvement in the third season of the original series, the treatment of others during the animated series, the casting of Questor, or any one of dozens of similar slights and perceived slights—the deep-seated reason for the animosity really seems to be that both men laid claim to saying "I am Spock."

We see now, though, that the appeal of *Star Trek* is far broader than one character or one performance. David Gerrold hit on something when he noted that *Star Trek* was building up its universe very slowly. You had to watch a few weeks to understand what was going on and "at the end of the first year only the broad outlines had been sketched, the details still had to be filled in."[19] There was a vast universe to explore. If the USS *Enterprise* had the registration number NCC-1701, did that mean there were at least another 1,700 Federation ships exploring the galaxy? Fans were keen to exploit gaps in *Star Trek*'s narrative.

Beyond a glimpse in the pilot episode, we never saw Earth in the original series; what was it like in Captain Kirk's time? The USS *Enterprise* was a large ship, a community, but across seventy-nine episodes, we saw a fraction of the crew. What was it like for "ordinary" crew members who served under Kirk and Spock? What happened between adventures? What would it be like working on a smaller ship, or on a remote starbase? Beyond that were the alien cultures—the logical Vulcans, the belligerent Klingons, the noble Romulans. What did the home planets of the alien races look like?

Fan fiction rushed to fill in the gaps. Some of this—a lot of it—involved stories that were "too hot for TV." Many of them involved Spock's mating frenzy, *pon farr*. That was by no means all of it, though. *Star Trek Lives!* notes that "one of the most immediately striking things about *Star Trek* fan fiction . . . is that most of it is written by women."[20] In the last-ever episode, "Turnabout Intruder," it had been said that women couldn't be starship captains, and that was inevitably a target for fan writers. Laura Basta's *Daneswoman* stories and Judith Brownlee's *Saratoga* series were about female captains rising to the challenge of starship command. Others were such startlingly simple high concepts that you can imagine the people who made the show kicking themselves they never thought of them—Claire Gabriel's "Ni Var" saw a transporter accident split Spock into two beings, one human, one Vulcan.

There were plenty of "what happened next?" stories that returned to planets where Kirk's intervention had overthrown a tyrant. Bantam, who held the *Star Trek* fiction licence, published two volumes of *Star Trek: The New Voyages* (1976 and 1977) in which fans Myrna Culbreath and Sondra Marshak curated selections of the best fan fiction. Each story came with a brief introduction by the actor who played the main character. The first volume of *New Voyages* had a foreword by Gene Roddenberry in which he celebrated the emergence of *Star Trek* fandom, saying, "Certainly the loveliest happening of all for us was the fact that so many others began to feel the same way. Television viewers by the millions began to take *Star Trek* to heart as their own personal optimistic view of the human condition and future."[21]

Every television series—every story—has narrative gaps. What was it about *Star Trek* in this respect that particularly appealed?

Nowadays the word Roddenberry uses, "optimism," is part of the standard answer. The February 9, 2016 press release announcing a new *Star Trek* television series (later given the title *Star Trek: Discovery*) spoke of "Gene Roddenberry's optimistic future, a vision that continues to guide us as we explore strange new worlds." When a movie is called *Star Trek Into Darkness*, it's meant to feel oxymoronic, unsettling. Optimism is meant to be the unique selling point of the franchise, the secret sauce that makes a project a *Star Trek* project.

This hasn't always been how *Star Trek* fans would have responded. *Star Trek Lives!* (1975), a wide-ranging survey of the state of early *Star Trek*, of fandom, of the whole phenomenon at the time, pretty much dismisses it on the way to suggest a different magic ingredient: "*Star Trek* shared with the old wave of science fiction the romanticism, the heroism, the concern with themes and ideas, the optimism. What it added to science fiction was an absolutely startling new element: it did *not* keep its distance from emotion."[22]

The word "optimism," though, was always part of the mix. In 1973, David Gerrold asserted: "The subvocal message of *Star Trek* was optimistic—there *will* be a future. And it will be a good one. We will all live in it together. We will all accept each other as equals."[23]

Star Trek, the original series, had a positive view of the future ... to the extent that viewers could infer the world had not been destroyed or devolved into a Planet of the Apes. Actually, pay close attention to the television episodes, and we're told the near future is going to be rather grim. Between now and the period in which *Star Trek* is set, there will have been a Third World War, and a Eugenics War, a future which had seen dictators like Khan and Colonel Green. That's before atomic war with the Romulans. James Blish's books managed to add a couple more disasters, like the mysterious "Cold Peace" referred to in his version of "Miri."

These were footnotes. In the *Star Trek* future, our present ideological struggles have been resolved. While it's an American show—they're flying around in the "USS *Enterprise*," after all—the bridge crew represent groups emblematic of divisions in twentieth-century US society—a woman of African descent, a man from the

Deep South—and/or America's geopolitical enemies—a man of Japanese descent, and (from the second season onwards) a Russian, all working together in harmony.

The Federation was presumably democratic—although this isn't actually said at any point. It was certainly broadly peaceful and prosperous. It resembled, in many ways, H.G. Wells's projection of the future at the end of *The Outline of History* (1919), and similar depictions of the future in his *The Shape of Things to Come* and its movie adaptation (with a screenplay by Wells himself), *Things to Come*. A peaceful, clean world, a "united Earth," ruled over not by the old superstitions and elites, but by technology and reason.

Tolerance was always part of the mix. In "Plato's Stepchildren," Kirk could tell a little person bullied by the other inhabitants of his world, "Alexander, where I come from size, shape or color makes no difference." Many stories were resolved by having Kirk actively seek his antagonist's side of the story, and treating his opponent with respect and dignity. Giant lizard men, lava creatures, Romulans—Kirk never hated them. While Gene Roddenberry disapproved of some of the attitudes on display in *Star Trek VI*, Kirk's private log confession in that movie—"I've never trusted Klingons, and I never will. I can never forgive them for the death of my boy"—and his blurted "They're animals!" are treated, by Kirk as well as his comrades, as a startling lapse of judgement. The movie is about breaking down prejudice. If you can trust a Klingon, who can't you trust?

Roddenberry consistently preached some variation on the following sentiment: "If man is to survive, he will have learned to take a delight in the essential differences between men and between cultures. He will learn that differences in ideas and attitudes are a delight, part of life's exciting variety, not something to fear."

In "Is There In Truth No Beauty?" Spock held up an IDIC—a brooch symbolizing the Vulcan concept of Infinite Diversity in Infinite Combinations. As it happened, he did this because Gene Roddenberry wanted to sell replicas of the brooch through Lincoln Enterprises. Nimoy argued furiously with him about having to film the scene, and the lines were cut down. The sentiment, though, stuck with *Star Trek* fans.

Star Trek conventions were not utopian paradises, but they were inclusive. Everyone there had something in common, a shared love. *Star Trek* fans tended to be socially progressive and open-minded. People considered to be "minorities" in the outside world found themselves part of one big community. The more introverted or weird kids found themselves in big rooms full of people like them. The extroverted ones loved the attention they would get in an outrageous costume. There were always ways to strike up conversations, there were many experiences to enjoy, friends to meet, ways to impress. And so it came to pass that the main hall of a *Star Trek* convention came to resemble, in the real world, the diverse, optimistic society that the Sixties TV show could only hint at.

Roddenberry was aware he was a product of his times and his upbringing, that he had prejudices. Kirk's toast in the same scene is also telling: "I think most of us are attracted by beauty and repelled by ugliness. One of the last of our prejudices. At the risk of sounding prejudiced, gentlemen, here's to beauty. To Miranda Jones, the loveliest human ever to grace a starship."

Roddenberry grew up prejudiced against gay men. He served as a police officer at a time when two men who had consensual sex in their own homes could be arrested, tried, and given lengthy prison sentences, often hard labor. Roddenberry admitted that his attitude to homosexuality changed, mainly when he became friends with the openly gay William Ware Theiss, *Star Trek*'s costume designer. David Gerrold reports that Roddenberry's friend and lawyer Leonard Maizlish remained virulently homophobic: "To my face, he called me 'an AIDS-infected cocksucker. A fucking faggot.'"[24] By the end of his life, Roddenberry claimed he regretted never having had a homosexual relationship.[25]

Needless to say, there's no depiction or allusion to homosexuality in the original 1960s television show. Here, again, fan fiction took up the challenge of saying what couldn't be said on the networks. As with their fictional antecedents Holmes and Watson, some of the audience inferred a homosexual relationship between Kirk and Spock. Today, "slash fiction" depicting gay encounters between characters is common to the fandoms of every show with a fandom. It started with *Star Trek* fan fiction, where it was known as K/S—"Kirk slash Spock." In his novelization of *The Motion Picture*, Roddenberry had Kirk himself rule out the possibility that he and Spock were lovers, by commenting on his enjoyment of women, although with open-mindedness and humor.

Later, writers on *Star Trek: The Next Generation* would grapple with the same problem when they tried coming up with stories involving gay characters, or stories that were allegories of issues like coming out and AIDS. In the 1980s, it was still genuinely difficult to depict homosexuality on network television in the USA. The fifth season of *The Next Generation* eventually "tackled the issue" of same-sex attraction with the story "The Outcast," in which William Riker fell in love with . . . a beautiful woman, from a race who were androgynous.

In practice, the original *Star Trek* is not especially diverse, even for the 1960s. Most shows on American network television of the time cast people of color in supporting roles and managed to incorporate female characters in "traditionally male" roles. *Star Trek* was not radically ahead of the game. Even if we accept for the sake of argument how remarkable it is that *Star Trek* could "get away" with having Uhura and Sulu on the bridge, the paradox was that the stories could never talk about it, because the future society depicted in *Star Trek* wouldn't think it remarkable at all. Uhura was visible on the bridge, and that may have been a powerful statement, but it was the only statement the format of the show allowed her to make. There are a few references to her race, such as when Trelane, an immortal being posing as a foppish aristocrat, says in "The Squire of Gothos" she's "a Nubian prize . . . She has the melting eyes of the queen of Sheba. The same lovely coloring." There's only one place where we can say her race is addressed in a meaningful way, and even that's fleeting: in "The Savage Curtain" Uhura meets Abraham Lincoln, and Nichelle Nichols gets to echo her lines from *The Lieutenant*:

LINCOLN: What a charming Negress. Oh, forgive me, my dear. I know in my time some used that term as a description of property.

UHURA: But why should I object to that term, sir? You see, in our century we've learned not to fear words.

Star Trek portrays a better future, one that's better because humanity has learned to celebrate diversity, to work together for the great good. The original series depicts neither the Federation nor the future Earth as a utopian civilization. It doesn't depict Earth at all, except by showing us people who have come from there. Kirk's is plainly not the perfect society. More than that, it makes no real effort to depict the broader culture. *Star Trek* is a primetime action adventure serial, not a lecture series on alternative politico-economic systems.

While Roddenberry and others involved with the show talk about episodes that are allegorical, or satirical, there's surprisingly little social commentary. We see a number of alien societies and they're usually modeled along the lines of some extreme rule or code—a good example would be "A Taste of Armageddon," where warfare is ritualized and people trudge dutifully into disintegration booths if the computer simulations demand it. Kirk finds this repugnant, as do we, although it's hard to explain exactly why it feels even more inhumane than using real bombs and hearing the casualty figures on the evening news. In "This Side of Paradise," crew members, including Spock, are infected by spores that make them forget their duty and surrender to blissful hedonism. It's a (rather heavy-handed) allegory for drug dependency and, again, almost all of us will side with Kirk as he seeks to free his crew; the story certainly does nothing to challenge the idea that he has chosen the right course of action. In other words the show's social values are broadly our own.

In places the overt message may be a little more controversial to some sections of the audience. There are religious groups in modern America who might object to Kirk's offer to supply contraceptive devices to an overpopulated planet in "The Mark of Gideon." The portrayal of a pacifist in "The Savage Curtain" makes him appear naïve to the point of suicidal stupidity because he seeks a diplomatic solution to a problem. But the most devout Catholics and dedicated pacifists in the audience would probably agree Kirk is espousing normative liberal American values of the 1960s. There's very little to suggest his future Earth has adopted radically different social models. The economic implications of living in a society where machines supply every material need would be immense, but they're barely touched upon in the original series.

It's ironic that perhaps the most sophisticated examination of utopianism in the original series is in the much-reviled "The Way to Eden," which *Star Trek* fans invariably describe as "the one with the space hippies." It's interesting because it features a group who have renounced the lifestyle of the United Federation of Planets, an otherwise unchallenged society where self-determination and freedom seem absolute. Spock asks why, and their leader answers: "Because this is poison to me. This stuff you breathe, this stuff you live in, the shields of artificial atmosphere that we have layered about every planet. The programs in those computers that run your ship and your lives for you . . ."

They seek "Eden," a primitive paradise. Spock sympathizes. In real life Spock was popular with hippies, he was so square he was cool. In the episode, while Kirk and Scotty get flustered, Spock chills out with the interlopers, plays music for them. In the end, when their plans have, as we might predict, been dashed, Spock sends them on their way with this farewell: "It is my sincere wish that you do not give up your search for Eden. I have no doubt but that you will find it, or make it yourselves."

Spock was a countercultural figure, a weird guy, someone who didn't fit in. It was natural enough that this should find its fullest expression only once *Star Trek* was canceled, once it was out of the hands of the money men and had been passed on to those who approached *Star Trek* with no agenda beyond love and enthusiasm. By definition, you can't be part of the counterculture if you're on a primetime show on network television.

After *Star Trek*'s cancelation, Gene Roddenberry began to adopt a lot of utopian ideas, started to find imagining the practicalities of a better future increasingly interesting. By 1976 he was calling *Star Trek* "something very personal to me—my own statement of who and what this species of ours really is, where we are now and something of where we may be going."[26] The notion of *Star Trek* as model for a better society is not tackled in any depth in the original series, but when the fans take control of the agenda, it becomes absolutely central.

The young female fans who saw *Star Trek* and a very few years later began living through the early years of the Women's Liberation movement could have taken *Star Trek* as Exhibit A in the crass way women were depicted on network television in the dark ages. It's a show with a parade of beautiful "girls of the week" who wore tiny outfits and—despite being high fliers in their field, rulers of worlds, or possessing great powers—always fell for Kirk's charms. Instead, the message that educated women took from *Star Trek* was that they were looking at an entire universe full of amazing, empowered women, whose stories we had barely scratched. They saw *Star Trek* as forward-looking because it engaged with emotions. As William Shatner's biography put it:

> Women's lib groups damn Kirk as a male chauvinist pig. Women's lib groups hail Kirk as a liberator. Then you notice that the "damners" are damning Kirk by standards he and *Star Trek* helped to set. The "hailers" are recognizing an almost explosive interaction between Shatner's Kirk and women. Singly or in groups, in or out of the women's movements,

many women have recognized that what they want most from men—or for their sons—is emotional openness.[27]

The primary appeal of *Star Trek* may be as simple as this: it looked like a great place to live. This was central to science fiction author David Brin's argument as to why he preferred *Star Trek* to *Star Wars*:

Star Trek generally depicts heroes who are only about ten times as brilliant, noble and heroic as a normal person, prevailing through cooperation and wit, rather than because of some inherited godlike transcendent greatness. Characters who do achieve godlike powers are subjected to ruthless scrutiny. In other words, *Trek* is a prototypically American dream, entranced by notions of human improvement and a progress that lifts all. Gene Roddenberry's vision loves heroes, but it breaks away from the elitist tradition of princes and wizards who rule by divine or mystical right. By contrast, these are the *only* heroes in the *Star Wars* universe . . . when it comes to portraying human destiny, where would you rather live, assuming you'll be a normal citizen and no demigod? In Roddenberry's Federation? Or Lucas' Empire?[28]

Star Trek always had little touches that made the *Enterprise* seem like a real place—signage, recreational areas, crew quarters with personalized decoration. It was easy to picture yourself on the *Enterprise*. And because it was a tolerant future, it didn't matter who you were,

what you looked like—there would be a place for you.
A better you.

At times, *Star Trek* fans could get carried away at warp
speed:

> The depth of William Shatner's Kirk leaves us speechless.
> But only figuratively, for throughout this book we have
> tried *heroically* to restrain the outpourings of boundless
> admiration that Mr. Shatner's achievement has aroused in us.
> Captain Kirk is, as we have indicated, an almost ideal man
> to millions of viewers. How much of Kirk is William Shatner?
> We judge: a prodigious amount.[29]

In 1968 William Shatner released an album called *The
Transformed Man*, the title track of which is a spoken-word
piece where the narrator "quietly walked out of the life
they had planned for me," traveled up into the mountains
and, "Cutting myself adrift from the past and the future,
I became immersed in the living moment. The eternal
now." This was something, the early *Star Trek* fans believed
anyway, that the show promised. Transcendence. Beaming
up. If that was the case, it made Captain Kirk and Mr. Spock,
and their present-day avatars William Shatner, Leonard
Nimoy, and Gene Roddenberry into visitors from the
future. It made conventions a place to meet these future
people. They seemed to be intelligent, forward-looking,
glamorous. It explains why fans were quick to defend
Roddenberry against any and every complaint. David
Gerrold's descriptions of behind-the-scenes discord at *The

Next Generation were said to be sour grapes from someone who'd lost his job. When Joel Engel's biography appeared in 1994, *Entertainment Weekly* declared,

> Joel Engel is the Salman Rushdie of Trekkies. An entertainment writer for *The New York Times*, this infidel has dared to defile the memory of worshiped *Trek* creator Gene Roddenberry—who died of a stroke more than two years ago—with a tell-all biography, *Gene Roddenberry: The Myth and the Man Behind Star Trek*, that is supposed to rip the lid off the legendary producer's untold private life. Already, hard-core fans are on red alert: One outraged Trekker has even been faxing protest letters to the press, presumably trying to drum up an Engel boycott.[30]

By the late Seventies, Gene Roddenberry was finding that convention audiences were asking fewer questions about *Star Trek* anecdotes, and more and more about where he saw the future heading. In discussions with a number of people, notably Isaac Asimov and Carl Sagan, he began to think of himself more firmly as a "humanist," or at least came to understand that many of his positions and opinions could be so classified. He began honing his answers to questions about the future, and soon made the subject part of the speech he would make when invited to university campuses or other speaking engagements. This was proving to be a lucrative sideline for him (he charged around $1,500 per appearance). The "hook," of course, the reason he'd been invited, was that Roddenberry had created *Star Trek*, so when he described a "better future," he would often elide this with the show, call it "the *Star Trek* future," whether his predictions had ever been seen on the television show or not. In his lectures, he used a phrase: "The human adventure is just beginning." This would become the tagline for *Star Trek: The Motion Picture*.

So while there's very little evidence of utopianism in the original series, the idea of perfecting society has always been key to *Star Trek* fandom. Fans wrote articles and stories about the fictional worlds of *Star Trek*, but they went one further than that. As David Gerrold put it in 1973, "With rare exceptions, the *Star Trek* fans are trying to bring that kind of future about by living in it now."[31]

It was no coincidence that NASA sent a huge display to that first major *Star Trek* convention in 1972. Gene Roddenberry and Bjo Trimble and the vast majority of *Star Trek* fans were utterly committed to the human exploration of space. It was through exploring and coming to understand the universe that we would come to understand ourselves. Roddenberry saw this as imperative, the purpose of our existence. "Why our space program? Why, indeed, did we trouble to look past the next mountain? Our prime obligation to ourselves is to make the unknown known. We are on a journey to keep an appointment with whatever we are." [32]

The culmination of this was in 1976, and *Star Trek*'s second triumphant letter-writing campaign, again organized by Bjo Trimble. This time, 200,000 fans wrote to President Ford asking him to name the first space shuttle *Enterprise*.

OV-101 never flew in space, it was an elaborate test vehicle, but it's counted by NASA as the first space shuttle. Roddenberry and the *Star Trek* cast were present at the unveiling on September 17. Three years later, *Star Trek: The Motion Picture* would feature a display of previous vessels named *Enterprise*—one of them was the space shuttle. In 1985, the council of Riverside, Iowa (with Roddenberry's permission) erected a monument claiming their town as the "Future Birthplace of James T. Kirk." Every June, the town holds an annual Trekfest and parade to honor their most famous future son. *Star Trek* fans were connecting the present day with the better future *Star Trek* promised them. In 2002, William Shatner would co-write a book, *I'm Working on That*, which charted progress towards the technology seen in *Star Trek*. With everyone now owning a computer and a cellphone, with a space station and the Hubble telescope in orbit, and with many scientists, engineers, and astronauts more than willing to credit *Star Trek* with inspiring them to take up a science and engineering career, Shatner was able to report good progress.

Roddenberry was himself transformed by *Star Trek*. Materially, this is obvious: it would make the son of a New York cop rich and give him a star on the Hollywood Walk of Fame. There's more, though: Roddenberry was enthusiastic and invested when he made the original *Star Trek*, but it was "just a TV show." Later he saw for himself that it had empowered its fans, made them better people. Many of the teenagers he met at the early conventions became highly accomplished people—artists, scientists, doctors, inventors, politicians, activists. All of them credited *Star Trek*. For other *Star Trek* fans, the results were less spectacular, but they were immeasurably valuable—for the first time, they were accepted for what they were, found friends, were able to look forward to something.

By 1979, when he was writing the novelization of *Star Trek: The Motion Picture*, Roddenberry, putting words into Admiral Kirk's mouth, asserted this had been the plan all along:

> "I have always looked upon the *Enterprise* and its crew as my own private view of Earth and humanity in microcosm. If this is not the way we really are, it seems to me most certainly a way we ought to be. During its voyages, the starship *Enterprise* always carried much more than mere respect and tolerance for other life forms and ideas—it carried the more positive force of love for the almost limitless variety within our universe. It is this capacity for love for all things which has always seemed to me the first indication that an individual or a race is approaching adulthood."

Roddenberry himself, asked whether he liked the idea of a *Star Trek* that wasn't his own creation, said, "I would hope that there are bright young people growing up over time who will bring to it levels and areas that were beyond me. And I won't feel jealous of that at all . . . It'll go on without any of us, and get better and better and better. That really is the human condition—to improve."

CHAPTER SEVEN

BIGGER THAN *STAR WARS*

Star Trek: The Motion Picture was perhaps the purest expression of what Gene Roddenberry wanted *Star Trek* to be, and also of the strengths and weaknesses of the man himself.

Despite almost certainly being the most expensive single film ever made to that point, and despite the fact that it cost the studio around three times the initial estimates, *Star Trek: The Motion Picture* did not go over budget. This was for one simple reason: it was impossible to plan the cost of bringing its script to life, because the film went into production before the script had been completed. The film never went over budget because a budget had never been set.

A number of reports of the press conference at which it was announced, held on March 28, 1978, stated that the first *Star Trek* movie would cost $15m. This seems to be based on an over-literal interpretation of a light remark from the president of Paramount Pictures, Michael Eisner, when he said the film would be made "at a cost at least equal to all the original seventy-nine episodes put together." That would add up (not allowing for inflation) to around $14.5m. Early in the process, the studio would tell the director, Robert Wise, they had allocated "between fifteen and eighteen million dollars," but "they didn't exactly expect we'd be able to actually spend that much."[1] No one, including the studio's accountants, ever knew exactly what the first *Star Trek* movie ended up costing, and estimates range from $25m to nearly twice that.

The film was an extravagant production. The studio was complicit in this. Following the success of *Star Wars* (1977), Paramount promised investors and distributors early in 1978 that a *Star Trek* movie would be in cinemas the following year. This was an extremely tight deadline, and it quickly became clear that original plans to release the movie in April or June 1979 weren't viable. Soon, the premiere was set for December 7, and the studio struck deals with distributors that meant, if the date was missed, they would have to repay at least $30m (some reports suggest that there were also penalty clauses which would have raised the payout to $75m). December 7 became the absolute, non-negotiable release date.

Star Trek had predated *Star Wars*, of course. Even the idea of bringing back *Star Trek* had predated *Star Wars*. While it clearly felt to fans like *Star Trek* endured a long time in the wilderness, in fact the show had quickly become a major cultural force, a valuable studio asset. Paramount had started talking about making a movie or TV series within a couple of years of the show going off the air. The only delay was because they weren't able to find the best way to bring it back. A number of different ideas for major movies were pitched, without involvement from Gene Roddenberry. The rumor that Paramount would recast Kirk and Spock (the names of Robert Redford and Dustin Hoffman came up) seems to have originated from Roddenberry. He understood that William Shatner and Leonard Nimoy were hero figures to *Star Trek* fandom, that both actors had fervently devoted fans. Roddenberry wanted to be involved in the remake, and felt that riling up the fans into writing letters would scare the studio back into line—and make it clear to them that only Gene Roddenberry truly understood what made *Star Trek* tick.

In early 1977, the first serious attempt to make a *Star Trek* movie was underway. This was *Planet of the Titans*, directed by Philip Kaufman (*The Right Stuff*). The sets were to be designed by Ken Adam, designer of the most memorable James Bond supervillain lairs. Ralph McQuarrie, an artist who'd done so much to establish the "look" of *Star Wars*, redesigned the *Enterprise*. A fair amount more design work was done, but the studio didn't like the first draft of the script.

The plug was finally pulled in the early summer. Paramount had a new plan: they were going to set up a fourth American TV network, and *Star Trek* was to be the centerpiece. Roddenberry returned to his old job as executive producer, and a two-hour pilot and thirteen episodes were commissioned. He brought back as much of the team from the original series as he could, including D.C. Fontana, William Ware Theiss, and Matt Jeffries. The studio called it *Star Trek*, the fans would come to call it *Star Trek: Phase II*. To Roddenberry, it was *Star Trek II*.[2]

Leonard Nimoy would not be returning as Spock. Although Spock was the character featured most heavily on the covers of comics, books, and magazines, Nimoy received no money for this use of his image, nor for the constant syndicated repeats. He was particularly affronted to find a British billboard ad which featured Spock's limp ears perking up when he drank a pint of a particular brand of lager. Bernie Francis, his business manager, investigated, and learned that Paramount had lost the rights to use his client's likeness when they'd canceled the show. When Gene Roddenberry's promise he would be playing Questor failed to materialize, it confirmed Nimoy's growing sense that Roddenberry was not to be trusted. Ever since Roddenberry had tried to take a cut of his proceeds from the *Mr. Spock's Music From Outer Space* album, Nimoy had been wary. He felt a little swindled by his involvement with *Star Trek* as he noted how others—the studio, Roddenberry— were exploiting Spock.

Nimoy was aware that Gene and Majel were selling *Star Trek* merchandise through Lincoln Enterprises (and he almost certainly overestimated by some way how much the couple were making). Bernie Francis and Paramount were unable to agree a figure to compensate Nimoy for their unauthorized use of his likeness. As Nimoy said,

"I wound up having to file a lawsuit ... perhaps you can understand why I wasn't champing at the bit to get involved with Paramount and *Star Trek* again."[3] That said, it seemed Nimoy might possibly be a series regular. He did sit down to discuss terms. Nimoy was more offended by the proposed compromise whereby he would appear in only a couple of episodes as a "guest star," than by the prospect that he would not appear at all.

There was little secret that Roddenberry was lukewarm about Nimoy's involvement. William Shatner sums it up best:

Whatever the sometimes difficult dynamics of their relationship, without question, Roddenberry and Leonard both lived long and prospered because of it. They needed each other—we all needed each other—and looking back, it is far more important to focus on Gene's creative genius than the family fights we endured.[4]

Neither Roddenberry nor Nimoy held that opinion in the late Seventies. This was the perfect opportunity for Roddenberry to prove that there was more to *Star Trek* than Mr. Spock.

The studio were a little concerned that William Shatner would prove too old to be a dashing action hero, and they also wanted a new female character to add to the show's sex appeal. Roddenberry created three younger characters: Xon would take Spock's place as science officer, Decker would be a young first officer who could handle some of the running and fighting, and there would be an exotic new navigator, Ilia. The rest of the regular cast—McCoy, Scotty, Uhura, Sulu, Chekov, and Chapel—would return, all with more experience and added duties.

The pilot episode was to be "In Thy Image," by Harold Livingston, based on a story by Alan Dean Foster, in which the newly refitted *Enterprise* was sent to intercept an immensely powerful spacecraft that was on a direct course to Earth. Scripts were written, sets built. A start date for filming the series was set for November 28, 1977. And then, in late July, Paramount's plans to set up a fourth television network collapsed.

Star Trek bounced back almost immediately. Production was never halted, but the plan for a few months was simply to produce a one-off TV movie—mainly as a way for Paramount to recoup some of their investment. In September, the former Miss India, Persis Khambatta, was cast as Ilia, David Gautreaux as Xon. (Decker proved harder to cast.) The test footage that was shot looked like a mild Seventies update of the original show.

The success of *Star Wars* made something obvious to Paramount's executives: the return of *Star Trek* should be "like *Star Wars*." On October 21, 1977, they decided that the project would be upgraded to a full, big-budget cinematic release.

Close Encounters of the Third Kind (1978) proved *Star Wars* was no fluke—there was a huge audience hungry for science fiction movies. Even James Bond got in on the act, taking a space shuttle to the villain's orbiting lair in *Moonraker* (1979).

The studio wanted, if anything, a movie bigger than *Star Wars*, and were happy to spend a lot of money to make a lot of money. They were not the only studio trying to do this. Disney was pouring vast amounts into *The Black Hole*, a movie that would eventually come out two weeks after *Star Trek: The Motion Picture*. *Star Trek* was an existing science fiction franchise, and was immensely popular with a broad audience, in America and abroad. This was exactly the right time to make a *Star Trek* movie.

This was part of a pattern. The industry was changing, and a new approach to making movies was developing. Instead of producing a lot of medium-budget ($5m–$10m) movies that nearly all made modest profits or modest losses, with the occasional smash hit, studios now planned to spend $25m to make $200m. Such movies would be spectacular, crowd-pleasing, and designed to be blockbusters. *Moonraker*, in production at the same time as the *Star Trek: The Motion Picture*, cost $34m, well over twice as much as the previous entry in the James Bond series, *The Spy Who Loved Me*, but it made $210m worldwide. Every other movie budget was dwarfed by the period's most expensive film, *Superman: The Movie* (1978), which was made back-to-back with *Superman II* (1980), the two together costing about $95m.

Spending so much on a single project was a risky strategy for a movie studio—a flop could bankrupt them. In 1980 this happened to United Artists, who bankrolled *Heaven's Gate*, a Western made at the same time as *Star Trek: The Motion Picture*, and possibly costing as much. When it was released in November 1980, it made a mere $3.5m at the box office, bankrupting the studio.

In the late Seventies and early Eighties, Paramount was on a winning streak, with a team of rising star executives like Barry Diller, Michael Eisner, Jeffrey Katzenberg, Dawn Steel, and Don Simpson, all of whom had a hand in bringing *Star Trek* to cinema screens, and all known for a swaggering, confident approach to the business. The studio had recently put out hits such as *The Godfather*, *Saturday Night Fever*, and *Grease*, and would soon go on to make *American Gigolo*, *Airplane!*, and the Friday the 13th and Indiana Jones series.

As Paramount knew, *Star Wars*, *Close Encounters*, and *Superman* showed that audiences wanted spectacle, movement, striking visual effects. The *Star Trek* movie couldn't just look like a TV episode . . . and the original sin of *Star Trek: The Motion Picture*, the root cause of almost every single one of its subsequent problems, was that it started out as a TV episode.

To meet the release date, it was felt there was no time to start a new script from scratch. The pilot episode of *Star Trek II* already had many of the features any new script would need. "In Thy Image" was two hours long and gave an in-story reason for getting the gang back together. It included the launch of a refitted, modernized USS *Enterprise*, explaining why it didn't look exactly like the ship from the TV show. The story reintroduced the characters (and a couple of fresh faces) and conformed to the basic format of a brave crew of space explorers heading out to face the unknown. The threat was greater than Captain Kirk and his crew had faced on television, with Earth itself in direct and immediate jeopardy, a plotline never used by the original series. The "high concept" of the antagonist—an augmented NASA probe, returning to judge its creator—was timely, as the *Voyager* missions were underway. *Voyager 1* sent back images of Jupiter from January to April 1979, *Voyager 2* arrived in late April and beamed back images until August. The movie would go on to include a sequence where the *Enterprise* flew past Jupiter, created with the cooperation of NASA using data from the real *Voyager* probes. All in all, the potential was there for an epic adventure, and plenty of visual spectacle.

At a practical level, the script was a known quantity, one that had been discussed, worked on, and reworked. Gene Roddenberry redrafted Harold Livingston's script himself—to the point that copies of it circulating when *The Motion Picture* was announced bore only his name.

The script had problems. No one had ever thought any of the drafts had a satisfying ending. The story started by establishing that the vast alien ship (at this point, it was a giant spaceship, not the vast energy cloud it would be in the finished film) could easily annihilate Klingon battlecruisers, that it was an unstoppable force . . . and this painted the story into a corner, as the only way it could possibly be defeated would be by contriving some form of *deus ex machina*. Roddenberry further limited the story's options by insisting that the solution could not rely on violence. This would become a pattern with the *Star Trek* movies: Roddenberry was dead set against "space battles," often in the face of demands from the studio, director, actors, and other writers. Roddenberry liked *Star Wars*, saw it four times at the cinema, and saw its box office success as proof he'd been right all along that there was a market for science fiction movies. The *Star Wars* movies, of course, were—as the name suggests—packed with thrilling sequences of dogfights in space, large ships bearing down on small ones, and chases through asteroid fields. That was *Star Wars*, it wasn't *Star Trek*. Roddenberry wanted Kirk and his crew to prevail using brains instead of brawn, he wanted the characters to have rich inner lives, not to be action heroes.

While the movie began production without a usable third act, everyone was optimistic that a solution would be found. The lack of an effective ending was seen as an opportunity—they could start with a blank page and go wild, with none of the limitations of the small screen. These limits were, as Roddenberry saw it, not simply those of special effects technology. Unbeknown to the studio, the version of *Star Trek* that Gene Roddenberry had started to talk about at conventions and in lectures was an exercise in philosophy, in ethics, in depicting a human race that had developed from the awkward adolescence of the twentieth century. Finally, he thought, he'd get to make *that Star Trek* without having to listen to TV executives and their silly demand that Kirk's life should consist of a procession of love interests and fist fights.

The switch from a TV pilot to a Hollywood movie

necessitated a huge culture shift. A fairly large number of British TV shows had been remade as movies in the Sixties and Seventies—everything from *Doctor Who* and *Thunderbirds* to a host of sitcoms like *Porridge* and *Dad's Army*. There were very few precedents for American TV shows that became movies, though. In the US, there had been *Dragnet*, *Batman*, and *Dark Shadows*, all films made while the TV shows were in production, using the existing casts and sets. There had been a handful of TV reunion movies, including *Gilligan's Island* and *Peyton Place*. There had been television spinoffs of movies, such as *Planet of the Apes* and *Logan's Run*. There had never been a movie intended for cinemas which was a revival of a canceled TV show.

Since the dawn of the television age, studios had maintained an iron curtain between television and movie production. Movies were seen as the superior form. This operated on every level. Actors and directors might start off in television: Clint Eastwood, say, appeared in eight seasons of *Rawhide* (1959–65). But once he had moved up to movies like *A Fistful of Dollars*, that was it: if he returned to television, it would be an admission that his career was over (regardless of the fact that he earned ten times more per episode of *Rawhide* than he did for starring in *A Fistful of Dollars*). The same was true in reverse, as when Rock Hudson found himself "demoted" to television when his box office appeal diminished (as we've seen, Roddenberry played his part in this). Many of the new breed of Paramount executives had started out in television and success there had seen them "promoted" to movie production.

By definition, *Star Trek: The Motion Picture* was going to bridge the divide. The movie would use the original cast of television actors but the studio was pragmatic—they would be cheap, they were (with the exception of Leonard Nimoy) already under contract, they were the familiar faces of *Star Trek*. In any case, it was to be a spectacular special effects adventure, not something driven by movie stars or the need for particularly nuanced performances. The fans would object if Kirk, Spock, and so on were recast . . . and which movie stars would be both available immediately and interested in playing characters from a TV show? The success of *Star Wars* reassured Paramount that they didn't need "big name" actors in their science fiction movie.

Having tried and spectacularly failed to make the leap into cinema with *Pretty Maids All in a Row*, Roddenberry understood that his poor track record would normally mean he had no clout at all with the movie studios. But this seemed to be different. The way he saw it, hiring him was an admission that Paramount needed the existing *Star Trek* fanbase on side. For years, Trekkies had been writing letters and running campaigns in which they pledged to see a *Star Trek* movie many times over, and promising to drag their friends and families along. If the television show's creator was unwilling to give the movie his imprimatur, the *Star Trek* fans would boycott the movie, ruining its chances. Gene Roddenberry gleefully told his friends the studio were paying him half a million dollars, and that he'd finally been vindicated.

Roddenberry was to be the producer of the movie. He clearly went into *The Motion Picture* thinking that his role hadn't changed since the television series, that he would be in charge of making a version of "In Thy Image," but on a budget of $15m instead of $8m. He already had a script, he had his cast and production team, he even had sets and props built.

In the film, Admiral Kirk convinces his boss that he should return to active duty because he is the one man with the experience and leadership qualities needed to deal with the massive challenge they face. The most powerful entity in the universe believes the most important being in existence is "the Creator." It's not too much of a stretch to imagine Roddenberry seeing this as semi-autobiographical. But his rude awakening would come quickly.

One of the young Turks at Paramount, Jeffrey Katzenberg, was appointed Vice President in Charge of Production for the *Star Trek* movie, the studio executive whose role was to oversee the project. Katzenberg would go on to a ten-year stint (1984–94) as chairman of Walt Disney Studios. During his tenure what had been a moribund company would achieve a massive revival of fortune, before he left to become CEO of DreamWorks Animation. He was twenty-seven when he joined the movie, less than half Roddenberry's age at the time.

The moment *Star Trek* became a motion picture, Katzenberg wanted experienced movie makers behind the camera. The original director, Robert Collins, who had only ever worked in television, was replaced by Robert

Wise. Editor on Charles Laughton's *Hunchback of Notre Dame* (1939) and on *Citizen Kane* (1941), Wise had subsequently enjoyed a long career as director of movies like *West Side Story* (1961) and *The Sound of Music* (1965), as well as science fiction movies such as *The Day the Earth Stood Still* (1951) and *The Andromeda Strain* (1971). He was not a *Star Trek* fan, although his wife and daughter were. What appealed to Wise was that new movies like *Star Wars*, *Close Encounters of the Third Kind*, *Superman*, and *The Black Hole* were using innovative ways of combining optical and model effects with live action. Wise was intrigued by the challenge of telling a story using new special effects technology like computer-controlled cameras.

Gene Roddenberry was not consulted about the hiring of Wise—Katzenberg drew up a shortlist of people he felt could handle the project and whose schedule was free. Roddenberry had met Wise at a science fiction seminar at Arizona State College. "So when I saw Bob's name on the list, there was no doubt in my mind that he was the one." Wise, for his part, recognized that the show's creator knew the heart of the show and its characters. Roddenberry was "elated" that someone of Wise's stature was on board,[5] and there was none of his customary jostling to establish himself as the alpha male. It would take Roddenberry a while to understand that this wasn't TV, where directors are "brought in" to film a script, and to add a few distinctive touches. The studio trusted Wise and considered him to be the person in charge of the day-to-day running of the project.

Wise's friends and family told him, "You can't possibly think about about doing *Star Trek* without Spock. I mean, that would be as bad as trying to tell it without Kirk. It's impossible, it's crazy to make the film without him."[6] Roddenberry told Wise he had spent three or four years failing to overcome Nimoy's reticence to return to the role. The actor had fears of typecasting; he had internalized the character of Spock; he wrestled with his relationship with the character; he took himself very seriously as an artist; he was a man of integrity; he felt the studio had exploited his image, limiting his opportunities as an actor while not giving him a fair share of the proceeds. And he distrusted Roddenberry.

Robert Wise cut the Gordian knot, and he did it in a few hours. Nimoy had not wanted to be a regular on a TV show, but being co-star of a big budget movie was an entirely different proposition. Although he was diplomatic about it, Nimoy had far more respect for Robert Wise than he did for Gene Roddenberry. This was evident when Roddenberry, Wise, and Katzenberg visited Nimoy at his home on a Saturday afternoon. Nimoy recalled: "Gene and I greeted each other cordially, and the tone of our conversation remained pleasant, but in all honesty, he appeared agitated, haggard, and preoccupied. I got the impression that he had only come reluctantly, at Katzenberg's insistence."[7]

Nimoy had been sent a copy of the script, and was asked what he thought. His response was a masterpiece of passive-aggression: "Well, is this the screenplay you plan on shooting?"[8] Spock, of course, wasn't featured in the script as he hadn't been due to appear in the *Star Trek II* TV show. Roddenberry's idea was that Spock had returned to Vulcan and had a nervous breakdown, which didn't appeal to Nimoy in the slightest. Katzenberg ushered Roddenberry out of the room. An hour later, Wise had persuaded Nimoy to come onboard.

Leonard Nimoy did not engage in lengthy negotiations, he simply asked for the same contract as William Shatner, knowing it had a "favored nations" clause that meant no actor could be paid more for appearing in the movie. "This meant that they were co-leads, each receiving equal treatment, equal dressing rooms, and equal salaries."[9]

With so much money on the line now, Paramount were able, literally overnight, to conjure up a check that matched the figure Nimoy's agent had put on a fair cut of past merchandising revenue. Nimoy reportedly received $2.5m in total, including his fee for the movie. Shatner, safely under contract, might have been upset to have gone from lead to co-lead, except that the "favored nations" clause instantly triggered the same payout for him. Now the studio had finally admitted they were making money from *Star Trek* merchandise, there was also a windfall for Roddenberry.

Nimoy signed his contract as soon as the legal department sent it over, on March 27, 1978. A press conference was held the very next day. Wise, Roddenberry, Michael Eisner, and the full cast were assembled at Paramount studios. Adverts were taken out in the trade press. Roddenberry wrote to all the major fan groups and fanzines. Both the banner at the press conference and the ads used concept art of the *Enterprise* as redesigned for *Star Trek II*.

The production team now had twenty-one months to make a movie. Robert Wise set to work. He watched old *Star Trek* episodes in a screening room. He toured the sets and reviewed the costumes and props, to see what had already been built for the *Star Trek II* television series/TV movie and what he could use. He instantly decided he had to start again from scratch. One of his first decisions was to dismiss Roddenberry's long-term associate, costume designer William Ware Theiss. He quickly replaced the television production team with his own people, including the production illustrator Maurice "Zuby" Zuberano, whom he'd worked with for nearly thirty years, and the production designer Hal Michelson. Most people brought in had worked with Wise before at some point.

The director would later complain that the "$45m" figure touted as the final cost of the movie included the money which had already been spent on the *Star Trek II* series. But it was his decision to ditch what had already been built. That said, it was almost certainly the right thing to do, technically and artistically. The photos we have from *Star Trek II* make the sets look a little creaky, even for television, and their limitations would have been immediately obvious on the big screen. The movie was coming out weeks before the 1980s began, and anticipating the new decade, fashion had shifted away from the flowing fabrics and bright colors of the early Seventies to far more austere palettes and clean lines. *Star Trek II*'s future already looked a lot like the past.

Wise had identified the same problems with the script as everyone else. Rewrites were needed anyway to accommodate Spock, and Gene Roddenberry would not be doing those rewrites. When Harold Livingston learned that the studio were making a *Star Trek* movie, he managed to acquire a copy of the script. He believed that what he read was his work, with a series of alterations by Roddenberry which consistently weakened the story. Livingston complained to the studio; the studio took his side, and rehired him to strip the script back and rework it as a feature. Livingston had assurances from Katzenberg and Wise that Roddenberry would not be allowed to interfere with his work. Tellingly, Leonard Nimoy started spending evenings at Livingston's house. There would be a new draft of the script by July 19, 1978.

The fixed release date meant it wasn't possible to wait for the script to be completed before designing and building replacement sets, props, models, and costumes. Although not everything had been locked down, the basic storyline of the film was set and it was clear that, once the *Enterprise* launched, almost every scene of the movie would take place on the ship. The studio wanted a spectacular movie, so the *Enterprise* needed spectacular interiors. The *Star Trek II* sets were almost identical in size to those of the old TV show. Wise set his new team to work on designs that were generally faithful to the basic layouts established in the original series, but on a far grander scale.

The best example of the scale of the upgrade was the recreation area, the place crew members of the USS *Enterprise* relaxed when off duty. Mike Minor had painted concept art of a "recreation room" for *Star Trek II*: a square set with about half a dozen comfy chairs, a few exotic potted plants and a couple of electronic games. For *The Motion Picture*, this was transformed into the "recreation deck," or rec deck, a vast communal space on various levels with a panoramic view of space. The set that was built had walls twenty-four feet tall, and was large enough to accommodate 300 extras for a scene where Kirk gave the entire crew a pre-launch briefing. It took up the whole of Paramount Stage 8, a hangar-like soundstage that would later hold standing sets for *The Next Generation*.

At this early stage, Roddenberry and Wise were on the same page. Wise was acclimatizing himself to the project, the cast and crew, the script, and *Star Trek* more generally. There's the distinct sense that Roddenberry reveled in getting the *Enterprise* looking just the way he wanted. The subdued color scheme of both the new *Enterprise* and the uniforms is noticeable similar to the *Enterprise* of the first pilot, "The Cage," rather than the primary colors of the broadcast series and *Star Trek II*.

But, unconsciously or not, Gene Roddenberry was still making a television pilot. The script had been structured in a very canny way, in those terms. It ensured that characters visited various rooms in the ship we would have seen week after week in a television series: the bridge, the transporter room, sickbay, Captain Kirk's living quarters (which could be re-dressed to serve as anyone else's room), main engineering, a set of corridors, the recreation area. This tour of the *Enterprise* wasn't done purely for story reasons, it was financial: if this had been TV, the first episode would be very expensive, but every one which followed would be able to make use of sets that had already been built and paid for. It's exactly what Roddenberry would later do with *Star Trek: The Next Generation*, the first episode of which featured new crew members exploring the *Enterprise-D* and spending time in such out-of-the-way places as the holodeck and battle bridge.

Over the course of a TV series, the recreation deck, the transporter room, Kirk's quarters, and sickbay would have ended up appearing hundreds of times, shot from every angle. This approach made very little sense for a one-off movie. Huge and elaborate sets were built. They're solidly made, interesting spaces, packed with little details. In *Star Trek: The Motion Picture*, most areas of the ship are only in a couple of scenes each. The huge rec deck appears in the scene early on where the whole crew is assembled (and the mass of people obscure the set), and in a single later scene, when Decker shows the robot Ilia around and explains the concept of "recreation." If a television writer had put that in a script for the original show, Roddenberry would have scolded him and told him to relocate it to Decker's quarters or even a corridor.

Across the whole project, a great deal of time, money, and effort was spent on things that either don't appear on screen, or which barely appear. The table in Kirk's quarters has four chairs stowed in it, each on a rail that allowed it to glide out and lock into place. At some point in a running

TV show we'd see someone use it. They don't in *The Motion Picture*. (Roddenberry perhaps expresses his own frustration in his novelization of the movie, when he has Kirk decide to have the thing removed at the earliest opportunity.)

As the props people began their work, it was a similar story. It was assumed that the crew would need phasers. Dozens of prop phasers were built using state-of-the-art electronics (few props at the time contained printed circuits). They lit up, the exact color and configuration of the lights depending on whether the phaser was set to stun or kill. As with the TV phasers, a smaller unit about the size of a bar of soap could be detached from the "gun" part of the device, to act as a more discreet weapon. In the movie, the guns hang from the belts of the security guards. No one ever draws their weapon—the two scenes where that happened were both edited out.

An ingenious seam was designed for the tricorders, so that no hinge was visible when the prop was opened. We never see anyone open a tricorder in the movie. A beautiful "computer clipboard" was designed and an etching technique was used that meant when lights were played over its plastic surface, it appeared to be a sophisticated animated computer display. This is never seen on screen. In all, 1,200 phasers, tricorders, clipboards, and similar tools and gadgets were created. The designers were told not to skimp by using dummy wood or rubber props, even if they were to be held by background characters, but to cast them all in fiberglass or plastic. Almost every prop had some sort of lighting feature or clever trick.

Again, this would make perfect sense if a TV pilot were being made. The phasers would have been used at some point. Replacement props would have been needed for those lost or damaged over the course of filming a whole season. Many of the props built for *The Motion Picture* would end up being reused in the sequel movies, and in the four TV shows that followed (the most prominent example was that the corridors were repainted to become those of the *Enterprise-D* in *The Next Generation*). At this point, though, it represented a vast amount of expenditure of precious time and effort, and therefore money, for very little screen time.

The irony was that *Star Wars* had been made on the cheap. The special effects were state-of-the-art in places, George Lucas's movie pioneering computer-controlled cameras which allowed very complicated composite model shots to be accomplished, but the models used in those shots were "kitbashed"—made by putting together pieces from existing model kits. Virtually all the iconic *Star Wars* props are existing items with a few pieces of junk glued on to them. Luke Skywalker's lightsaber was made from the handle of an old flash gun, bits of a broken calculator and four strips of rubber (the bits kept falling off, so are different from scene to scene). The sets were rarely much bigger than what was seen in shot. Lucas's technique was very simple: move things along so fast you don't have time to spot that C3PO's leg is falling apart as he walks, or that they were forced to use a take where one of the Stormtroopers banged his head against a door frame, or that there are at least two places where members of the production team have wandered into shot. Lucas was acutely aware just how ramshackle his final movie was. Audiences, though, didn't care—indeed perhaps what's guaranteed to make *Star Wars* fans angriest is that every time the movie is re-released, Lucas has fixed things and improved the special effects.

One place where *The Motion Picture*'s extravagant approach was justified was the bridge set. About half the scenes of the movie were set on the bridge, and the story called for extensive use of controls, computer displays, and so on. A great deal of planning went into building a set that allowed Wise flexibility in framing his shots. A flaw with the design of the television series bridge set was that the stations were positioned so all the characters had their backs to Captain Kirk. For the new bridge, consoles were moved around, placed at subtly different angles. The floor was given different levels, a vaulted ceiling was constructed.

A lot of thought was put into background displays and into making the controls and screens and other instruments visually interesting. Instead of the old random arrangements of flashing lightbulbs and rocker switches, each station on the bridge of the movie *Enterprise* was given a set of ergonomic controls, all carefully labeled. It had been designed by a team with experience in laying out control panels for submarines and aircraft. This was actually a pared-down version of the original plans. Gene Roddenberry was keen that the controls should be elegant and minimalist. Even on the bridge, though, the design went far beyond what could be seen on screen. When the ship went to red alert, headrests would emerge from the back of the chairs, a system that required a dozen pieces of sophisticated hydraulics and a computer-controlled system to synchronize them. How many viewers even noticed?

By the end of July, all the key personnel had been hired and there was a shooting script of a sort, albeit without a workable third act. Stephen Collins was cast in the role of Commander Decker, the young commander displaced from the captain's chair by the return of Kirk. Persis Khambatta's initiation as Ilia came on July 26, 1978, when her head was finally shaved for the role. The occasion was filmed and photographed, and was reported in the press at the time.

Most of the actors were a little bemused to be handed manuals explaining what each button on their control panels did. Most conceded, though, that the elaborate sets immersed them in their role. Walter Koenig was delighted to discover that pressing a button would often activate a row of lights, a display of some kind, or even cause a new device to emerge from a side panel.

Following the fanfare of the press conference, and having been told how tight the deadline to deliver the film was, the cast had been essentially sat on their hands for ten weeks, waiting for the new sets and costumes to be made. There had been a reading of an extremely unfinished script, costume fittings and makeup tests, and very little communication. Morale was high, though, with each of the regulars thinking the gaps in the script would be filled by the expansion of their own role (they all had suggestions).

It didn't hurt that checks from Paramount started showing up. The cast had all been bought out of their *Star Trek II* television contracts—James Doohan claimed that this was his biggest *Star Trek* payday. The studio had originally wanted to fold that payment into the fee for appearing in the movie, but the cast had successfully revolted over the issue: they would be paid for the television series *and* get a fair rate for appearing in a big Hollywood movie. For all the talk of "the show that wouldn't die," this was the first money any of them had received from the studio in almost ten years.

Gene Roddenberry was present when filming began on August 7, 1978, with scenes involving Sulu and Chekov, then later Kirk and Uhura, on the bridge. As scripted, the crew of the *Enterprise* were rushing to prepare the starship for launch, and these scenes showed technicians frantically fitting components to the bridge. Art mirrored nature, as the set wasn't quite completed when the first scenes were filmed.

The cast's initial enthusiasm quickly began to dissipate. The new shooting script still lacked a workable ending but the main objection was that, in the completed pages, most of the returning cast had very little to do. Once again, promises that Nichelle Nichols would get a meatier part were broken. A subplot explaining that Uhura was now Head of Starfleet Communications, a very senior officer, and on Kirk's mission as a favor to him, were dropped.

Walter Koenig felt Chekov's first appearance on screen was important enough that it deserved a closeup. Robert Wise quietly disabused him of that. James Doohan was given more scenes, but one of his favorites was cut out.

It escaped no one's notice that Stephen Collins and Persis Khambatta, playing new characters, had plenty of lines, a little backstory and character progression. Both were involved in the climax of the film, and Ilia appeared on the posters with Kirk and Spock. A lot of the publicity concentrated on the striking image of a bald alien woman—a former Miss India—in a very short kimono. Shatner was later dismissive: "Khambatta, a stunningly beautiful model, was also a stunningly bad actress, once proving that assertion by requiring a whopping nineteen takes of a single line, 'No.'"[10]

But Khambatta was able to assert at the time that "everybody was so nice and helpful to me."[11] Whatever her merits as an actress—and a role in which she was transformed from a navigator reporting what her instruments were saying into a stiff, monosyllabic robot possibly wasn't the best way to assess those—Khambatta suffered for her art. Having already had her head shaved, she burned her throat on the dry ice used in a shower scene, and almost fell fifteen feet through a gap in the set. Most horrifically of all, the xenon lights used in her final "ascension" sequence were so bright they seared off a layer of her eyes, blinding her for a few days.[12]

It was less harrowing for most of the cast—indeed their main issue probably was staving off boredom. Every scene, except for a couple of shots where geysers in Yellowstone National Park were used to stand in for Vulcan, was filmed on the Paramount soundstages. Most of the actors spent the vast majority of their time on the bridge set. Every shot required elaborate rigging of lighting and electronic gear. Apart from Ilia, the crew were dressed in virtually identical uniforms that were, by general consent, uncomfortable and unflattering. There were many technical glitches—the actors could give a great take, but if a lightbulb blew, the footage couldn't be used. Some of the mechanisms proved so noisy that the voice track had to be redubbed.

The bridge scenes were shot for the most part in script order, but it was slow going. All the cast had worked on movies before, but not on such a long shoot. They were used to filming television:

> The pace of making films is startlingly, amazingly slow in comparison to television. It all has to do with the lighting. On television, the shots are designed for a small screen, and you can get away with a great deal of cheating in lighting a scene. Block the scene, string up some lights, bring the actors in and shoot that sucker. Get an hour show out every week.[13]

They were completing about two scenes a day, on average. Making what was essentially a TV script at the pace of a movie was the worst of both worlds, and William Shatner complained that "our production schedule became a work of fiction, and our already turtle-esque pace became downright snailian."[14] At least Kirk was the center of attention. For people like George Takei, Walter Koenig, and Nichelle Nichols, who were in every bridge scene but with barely anything to say or do, the days dragged on and on. Koenig started keeping a journal and struck deals with *Starlog* magazine and Pocket Books to publish it.

The scenes were repetitive—slight variations on staring at a viewscreen and reporting what they were looking at. Early on, there wasn't even any concept art to guide the actors, so they literally didn't know what they were meant to be looking at. The last act of the script was still being written. The cast assumed the pace and spectacle would emerge in the finished film, that the live footage would be snappily edited and intercut with amazing visual effects, but they had all noticed that every revision seemed to edit out a joke or trim a few lines of banter.

The actors' ire focused on one scene in particular: the wormhole sequence. Ironically, this is one of the few scenes in the finished film where there's a sense of urgency or imminent jeopardy. The first time the *Enterprise* goes to warp speed—almost an hour into the movie—a problem with the engines traps the ship in a wormhole, subjecting the crew to time distortions. It's a sequence that lasts exactly three minutes on screen, with less than twenty lines of dialogue. To achieve their vision of the scene, the special effects people needed a great deal of footage, from a variety of angles, filmed with different lighting and on different film stock. Stephen Collins remembers it being composed of "48 set ups, but each set up was shot four different ways: at regular speed, and then again in slow motion, and then with a 65mm camera, and then again in 65mm slow motion."[15] Which meant two hundred shots, before taking into account retakes necessitated either by an actor forgetting a line or by a technical problem. According to various reports, it took between two and three weeks to shoot. The performances had to be identical every time, and the scene required the cast to be thrown around, so all of the actors were soon covered in bruises. The scene was to be overlaid with swirling lights (painstakingly animated by hand, a process that would take many weeks), the soundtrack was to be loud and electronically distorted. Without any of that, the raw footage was of actors jiggling themselves about and shouting. Nichelle Nichols has said, "everyday we would look at the dailies and cringe; it was awful."[16]

Even after breaking free of the wormhole, filming dragged on. There still wasn't a completed script. Harold Livingston had stormed off the project after finding that on multiple occasions Roddenberry had edited his work before passing it on to Wise and Katzenberg. The dispute between Roddenberry and Livingston meant that multiple, conflicting script pages would appear, bearing the initials GR or HL, often specifying to the minute when they'd been written. At one point Livingston rewrote a scene not knowing it had been filmed three weeks before. Each rewrite had the potential to change the production schedule or add a special effects shot and this all cost money. By November, Roddenberry was the sole writer, and the budget stood at \$24m.[17] One extra, Billy Van Zandt (nowadays an established playwright), was hired for a single day to play an alien crew member (he wore contact lenses and a wig). By the end of filming, he'd been there twelve weeks and been paid \$16,000.[18]

Everything about the movie was becoming stiff, slow, and joyless. Even the title had caught the disease—it shifted from *Star Trek*, to *Star Trek: The Movie*, then changed again, because of *Superman: The Movie*, to the rather pompous *Star Trek: The Motion Picture*. The model for a "serious" science fiction movie was *2001: A Space Odyssey* and *Star Trek* was following its template: a first act defining the problem, the spaceship launched at the start of the second act and then settling into a routine, an encounter with an alien leading to transcendence at the end. The novelization made the link explicit, with Kirk talking about a mysterious monolith being discovered centuries before on the moon.

Roddenberry had a tendency to lapse into long, philosophizing speeches in his work and the various pressures and deadlines were bringing out the worst in him. He was determined to make something more morally worthwhile than *Star Wars*. Meanwhile, Wise was keen to avoid the colorful camp of the original television series.

Other hands would have given a lighter touch to the twist that the great threat turns out to be a returned *Voyager* probe. It's a concept that's easy to understand: quirky, a little reminiscent of the reveal of the Statue of Liberty at the end of *Planet of the Apes*; and it links the world of the future with the NASA missions of our own. V'Ger turns out to be simultaneously mundane and utterly weird. The fact that it sends its own probe to scout out the interior of the *Enterprise*, "disguising" it as a remarkably beautiful woman, is an idea, in however deadpan a manner the characters have to treat it, that is *funny*. Roddenberry was determined to treat the reveal with utter solemnity, as a way to ponder the nature of god and creation, and the limits of knowledge.

When they saw the movie, fans were quick to note that the twist was the same as the episode "The Changeling" from the second series of the original run, in which an ancient space probe from Earth, *Nomad*, was driven mad after being repaired by aliens. One reviewer felt the movie should have been called "Where Nomad Had Gone Before." That story was light on philosophy, featuring a robotic probe stalking the corridors of the *Enterprise* and casually killing anyone who interfered with it (including Scotty at one point, although Nomad resurrects him). The twist is not integral to the story but, because Nomad mistakes Kirk for its creator, it puts the resolution in Kirk's hands in a way that's concrete and direct.

Roddenberry's heart may have been in the right place. He wanted the movie to be a good example of science fiction tackling big ideas, to create something epic, thoughtful, deep. It's far more constructive to view *Star Trek: The Motion Picture* as a conceptual sequel to *2001*, and not a remake of "The Changeling." Ultimately, though, the big difference was that Stanley Kubrick worked with Arthur C. Clarke and masterfully used some jarring cinematic techniques.

Star Trek's DNA was in seafaring romps, in the character-driven narratives of network TV—the fans had declared "optimism" and "emotion" to be key to the appeal. In *2001* the dialogue was kept sparse and the audience were allowed to try to piece it together. Roddenberry's script often feels more like Gene Roddenberry's own monologues about the nature of the universe, broken up and divided between the characters.

Roddenberry was feeling the pressure. George Takei noticed that his boss was gaining weight. Susan Sackett reports that Roddenberry was smoking more pot, and—for the first time—was seeing a therapist in Beverly Hills because of "his obvious stress and mounting depression."[19] Roddenberry was also, for the first time in his life, using cocaine.

More to the point, he hadn't produced an ending, and filming—even as far beyond schedule as it had fallen—was about to run out of pages to shoot. The studio had finally lost patience. Robert Wise was tactful, but consistently came down on the other side whenever Roddenberry argued a point. Roddenberry found himself outvoted on something as basic as how to pronounce the name of the antagonist. It was spelled "Veejur" in the script (most of the time), and Roddenberry said it with emphasis on the second syllable: "Vay-JAW." Nimoy and Shatner decided "VEE-juh" was better. The official spelling changed to "V'Ger." Roddenberry's novelization retained "Vejur."

Roddenberry was hardly Robert Wise's only headache. It gradually dawned on members of the cast and crew that

William Shatner and Leonard Nimoy were both taking their "favored nations" clause so literally that they were counting lines and insisting on having the same number in any given scene. Ironically, this tension was eased in early October, when another clause was activated that allowed them a say in the script once filming had reached a certain number of days. This led to an uneasy truce between the two leads, and they began suggesting lines and whole scenes. Nimoy effectively imposed a character arc on Spock, one in which the Vulcan gradually came to understand the emptiness of V'Ger's reliance on pure logic. Shatner, for his part, toned down Kirk's bickering with Decker.

Together, Shatner and Nimoy came up with a scene where Kirk treats V'Ger like a child, ordering his officers off the bridge. Wise liked it. Roddenberry hated it, and was angry that he was being overruled. Wise took the dispute to Jeffrey Katzenberg, and Katzenberg rehired Harold Livingston—who demanded $10,000 a week and the promise of future work from the studio. The official reason given for Roddenberry's disappearance from the set was that he needed time to write the novelization.

Virtually the last part of the shoot Roddenberry attended was the filming on October 16 and 17 of the "briefing session" scene, where Kirk gathers the entire *Enterprise* crew on the rec deck to explain the nature of the threat to the Earth. The scene involved 300 extras in Starfleet uniforms, around 125 of them long-term *Star Trek* fans and friends and family of the crew, such as Susan Sackett and Robert

Wise's wife Millicent. After that, Roddenberry was rarely, if ever, seen on set. By the end he "was in terrible physical shape, and was drinking more than ever."[20]

Filming caught up with the finished script pages in early November and production was put on hold for a couple of days. The final script was only ready on November 29—to put this in perspective, about a week after Walter Koenig, Nichelle Nichols, and George Takei had completed filming. The scenes from the climax of the film, featuring just Shatner, Nimoy, Kelley, Collins, and Khambatta, were filmed after a short Christmas break with principal photography ending on January 26, 1979. The original plan had been for filming to be complete three months earlier, by the end of October. A number of sequences that didn't feature the main cast had yet to be filmed—scenes on the Klingon ship, the Federation space station destroyed by V'Ger, and some background crowd scenes for the San Francisco sequence. Freed from the pressure of movie production, a New Year's resolution led Roddenberry to quit smoking and take up jogging.

The worst was yet to come. The live action filming had dragged but everyone had been assuming that, once the special effects were added, the movie would come alive. The studio had paid Robert Abel's effects house $6m, about twice *Star Wars*' special effects budget, and the script required twice as many effects shots as any previous film. By February, Robert Wise had become extremely concerned that he'd not seen any effects footage. Around February 20, he insisted Abel show him everything his team had produced. A screening was arranged. Wise had dealt with every problem so far with a calmness and professionalism that had impressed the cast and crew and steadied a lot of nerves. All reports have him emerging from the screening of the special effects footage incandescent with rage.

There was nothing usable. Millions of dollars had been spent but so little had been produced by Abel's team that there's some debate whether a single frame of theirs appears in the final movie (it's thought that, if there is anything, it's the shot of the asteroid exploding at the end of the wormhole sequence, a test explosion that no one had intended to make it to the finished movie).

Because the movie was locked into the December 7 premiere date, and had been promoted to the studio, distributors, licensees, fans, and the general audience as a special effects spectacular, this represented a major crisis for the movie. There were some in the studio who sought to write it off at this point. Instead, Douglas Trumbull, who'd worked on *2001: A Space Odyssey* and *Close Encounters of the Third Kind*, arrived in early March to take control of the film's visual effects. He was given $10m, and soon brought onboard his protégé John Dykstra, who had worked on *Star Wars* and *Battlestar Galactica*. Trumbull would shoot the *Enterprise* and the interiors of V'Ger, Dykstra would create sequences from early in the movie, including the V'Ger cloud, the Klingon battleships (the same model, filmed three times), and the Federation space station destroyed by V'Ger.

It was all hands on deck. Anecdotes abound. Surely it's apocryphal that footage shot of one large model was carefully framed to crop out the two model-makers, who were frantically painting the other end? Other props were held out of car windows as they were driven to the studio, in the hope that the paint would dry in time. The studio paid for hotels by the model-makers' workshops so the technicians didn't waste precious minutes commuting. By the end, hammocks were set up in the studio itself.

All of this cost money. When custom decals were needed overnight for one set of props, the supplier demanded and received $50,000 for work that would normally cost a few hundred.

There had been an ambitious plan for the interior of V'Ger. In Concept art from Abel's group, the scene looks like a prog rock album cover: a trippy, claustrophobic space, the *Enterprise* surrounded by a rippling field of screens that show it from every angle; giant eyes, cutaways of the ship, closeups of individuals. The crew would be in a nightmare environment where they were being scrutinized by an alien intelligence. It was nearly impossible to bring to life before the age of computer generated imagery. In the event, the final film shows the *Enterprise* in a vast, almost featureless space—a vast black cavern with a few distant lights . . . something that didn't feel claustrophobic at all, and wasn't that visually distinct from shots of the *Enterprise* traveling through space. The Marvel comic and novel versions portray the interior of V'Ger much more vividly and dramatically.

As Trumbull handed over footage, Wise edited each new sequence into the working print of the movie. The model work was technically some of the best ever seen in the movies. But there was no time to integrate the material with any subtlety, and obviously there was no time to reshoot or add sequences. Wise had to use what he was given and, perhaps because he knew the time and effort that had gone into the work, he seemed loath to cut a frame of it. The result is that the movie often rather crudely switches between long scenes of live action, to model work, and back to live action. The special effects shots take up over twenty-five minutes of the running time. There are almost five minutes' worth of footage of the *Enterprise* in spacedock, a series of long panning shots that seem designed to show off every angle of the model. But once the ship is underway, what we see isn't very varied or imaginative—the *Enterprise* flies though space, from the right of the screen to the left, almost always filling the screen, with little or nothing else to interact with.

Perhaps the ultimate indictment of the new work was that, when these new special effects shots were edited with the live action, Wise decided he needed to bring some of the main cast back for reshoots because their original horrified, awestruck performances now seemed like ludicrous over-reactions.

The last effects shot was delivered on November 29, 1979, a week before the premiere. Douglas Trumbull spent early December in hospital with nervous exhaustion. Things came down so close to the wire that Paramount had to charter planes to get the prints to some cinemas.

Roddenberry bears some blame, because a special effects team has to work from a script and the script had been subject to countless rewrites. But he'd warned Wise as early as July the previous year that he was skeptical that the effects could be achieved with the time and money allowed. And by the time things hit crisis point, Roddenberry had vanished from the set.

He was writing the novelization of the film and found some measure of revenge doing so. Harold Livingston did not receive an extra penny for the book rights, Roddenberry was paid $400,000. Roddenberry's name was prominent on the cover; Livingston's and Alan Dean Foster's names appear in a typeface less than half the size. Roddenberry starts the book with an introduction by Captain Kirk saying how wonderful Roddenberry is, and then another under his own name saying much the same thing. Knowing the production history of the movie gives an interesting slant to this line from the foreword, ostensibly written by Kirk himself: "While I cannot control other depictions of these events that you may see, hear and feel, I can promise that every description, idea, and word on these pages is the exact and true story of Vejur and Earth as it was seen, heard and felt by James T. Kirk."[21]

The book was written quickly and completed at 3:00 A.M. on the day before it had to go to the typesetters.[22] Even with a tight deadline, writing the book allowed Roddenberry a degree of freedom he'd never had before; he could allow his imagination free rein without worrying about the effects budget. The book starts very strongly, with Kirk on holiday in Alexandria (at a museum run jointly by Egypt and Israel, who had spent much of the Seventies either at war on or the verge of it). There's some world-building—the Mediterranean of Kirk's time has been dammed at the Straits of Gibraltar, the water used to irrigate the Sahara. Kirk receives a top priority alert and heads back to Starfleet HQ. The novel is peppered with details either cut from the script or dreamed up by Roddenberry to address shortfalls in the movie's story. A significant detail restored from an earlier draft is that Lori Ciani, the woman killed in the transporter accident alongside Mr. Sonak, was Kirk's ex-wife. Roddenberry clarifies that by Kirk's time, marriages are conducted on a fixed-term basis. Unlike the movie, the novel allows for inner monologues that flesh out the characters' thought processes and add new spins on the material. It makes for a much more dynamic, engaging story.

It is perhaps surprising that Gene Roddenberry would never complete another *Star Trek* novel. He started adapting an earlier story idea, "The God Thing," at one point roping in Walter Koenig to help. This was slow going and went on the backburner once *The Next Generation* started.

Roddenberry's absence was noted, but few in the cast and crew were clamoring for his return. The cast had received word that the special effects weren't going to save the movie. The film was edited together so hurriedly that Robert Wise had to carry the only existing print to the opening. It received a gala premiere in the MacArthur Theater in Georgetown, just outside Washington DC, and was attended by NASA officials and politicians as well as the cast and crew—including, of course, Roddenberry. The studio had prepared for three thousand *Star Trek* fans to be outside the private screening but only a couple of hundred showed up.

It was the first time even Wise had seen the completed film. Roddenberry had not been involved in the editing process—he'd accepted that there wasn't time for them to implement any changes he might have suggested. The reaction was not good. William Shatner fell asleep. Other cast members emerged baffled. The consensus afterwards was that the movie was a major misfire.

One studio executive described it as a "$35m turkey"— although, as we've seen, that probably underestimates what was spent by at least $10m. How much the movie cost depends on what you count. When asked, Robert Wise only counted what *he'd* spent, which didn't include the money spent on the *Star Trek II* sets, costumes, and salaries. Nor did he include the five million dollars or so paid to Shatner, Nimoy, and Roddenberry for merchandising royalties, a condition of Nimoy signing up for the movie. These were choices he and the studio made as part of the price for making *Star Trek: The Motion Picture*.

A more persuasive argument for reducing the price tag is to note that the *Star Trek* sequels (the movies and TV shows) saved a lot of money by using sets, props, costumes, and models built for *The Motion Picture*. While the studio say that the sequel, *The Wrath of Khan*, was far cheaper to make, they don't, as far as we can tell, take into account that the second *Star Trek* movie saved millions by reusing the massively expensive bridge set, the giant model of the USS *Enterprise,* and various props and other items. It's standard accountancy practice to amortize the cost of the sets and props when they're reused in other projects, but Paramount appear to have chosen not to do that, exaggerating the difference in cost between the first and second movies.

Any discussion of the huge budget should take into account the enormous guaranteed earnings: before the movie was completed, the distributors had paid Paramount $30m, ABC had paid at least $10m for the television rights, and a similar amount had been raised selling licenses for tie-in merchandise.

Fueled by the reaction of the cast, by Roddenberry himself, by the fact that the sequel saw a big change in direction for the series, and—yes—because it's a film where very little happens very slowly, *Star Trek: The Motion Picture* has gone down in fan lore as a flop. However, this is not the case.

Many more people saw it at the cinema than any other *Star Trek* movie until 2009's relaunch of the franchise. *The Motion Picture* was the fourth highest-grossing movie of the year and earned more than the smash hits *Alien*, *Apocalypse Now*, *10*, and *The Muppet Movie*. It did better in the US than *Moonraker*—the highest grossing entry in the James Bond franchise to that point. *The Motion Picture* opened at number one at the US box office. It earned $12m in its first weekend, a record at the time (although the movie industry placed nothing like same the emphasis on the opening weekend that they do now, with hit movies staying in circulation for many months). It went on to rake in $50m by the New Year, $82m in America and almost $100m more worldwide. *Star Trek: The Motion Picture* finished its first run in cinemas by scraping into the top thirty highest-grossing movies of all time.[23]

The movie appeared at the dawn of the home video cassette era and did exceptionally well in that market too. It was released in October 1980 on VHS and Betamax, and is one of very few films to be continuously available on home video for over thirty-five years. It did spectacularly well abroad. It received three Oscar nominations (Art Direction, Special Effects, and Original Score, losing to *All That Jazz*, *Alien*, and *A Little Romance* respectively). It made a lot of money. But the studio wasn't happy.

The main issue, of course, was that the movie had been ferociously expensive. Only three movies released in 1979 earned more than *Star Trek*, but they cost a fraction to make: *Kramer vs. Kramer* (which cost $8m), *The Amityville Horror* (with a budget of less than $5m), and *Rocky II* (around $7m). *Star Trek* couldn't even use the excuse that science fiction movies were always very expensive: *Alien* had cost $11m, and the sequel to *Star Wars*, in production at the time, was budgeted at $18m (although it too would go massively over budget).

Paramount had survived and *Star Trek: The Motion Picture* had pulled a profit... but the production had wasted vast amounts of money to produce a movie that no one involved liked very much.

The sheer scale of the box office success of *The Motion Picture* demonstrated a demand for *Star Trek*, but it also demonstrated just how insignificant the TV series' fan base was. It's impossible to define a "*Star Trek* fan" but, adding up every fan club member, everyone who attended a convention, or even owned a *Star Trek* book or toy, and assuming they saw it in the cinema more than once, and dragged a different set of friends and family members along each time, it's impossible to get anywhere near the thirty to thirty-five million tickets that were sold in the US. *Star Trek* could reach a far greater audience than the people obsessed with the old TV show.

The hardcore fans would be more likely to buy the novelization, the comics and toys, and this wasn't lost on Paramount or the comics or toy industries. The novelization stayed on *The New York Times*' bestseller list for six months. Its legacy was a series of *Star Trek* novels published by Pocket Books that continues to this day and now runs to several hundred volumes.

Star Wars had demonstrated that, for some movies, the box office was only one source of revenue. *Star Trek* merchandise was already a proven seller, but massive sales for *Star Wars* toys, books, and comics showed that the market for such things was orders of magnitude greater than the wildest dreams of Lincoln Enterprises. A December release tied *The Motion Picture* into the lucrative holiday season and the studio had flooded stores with *Star Trek* toys, games, models, comics, and books. After an energetic presentation from Dawn Steel, Vice-President of Marketing and Licensing, licensors queued up. Pocket Books planned to publish fifteen books tying directly into the movie. Marvel Comics would publish an adaptation. A range of action figures carefully modeled on the scale of toymaker Kenner's immensely popular *Star Wars* line would be released. *Star Trek: The Motion Picture* has the distinction of being the very first movie to tie in with a McDonald's Happy Meal. One of the commercials McDonald's aired has the distinction of being the first place the Klingon language was ever heard. Steel later estimated that $250m of *Star Trek* merchandise was sold.[24] Her achievement was all the more impressive because she didn't have a single clip of the movie to show potential licensors.

The novelization sold "close to a million copies." Marvel Comics' adaptation did well. The first movie generated more merchandise than the next five combined—but stores had dramatically underestimated the demand for *Star Wars* merchandise and, not wanting to be caught out again, they overcompensated with *Star Trek*. Many items didn't sell as well as expected, the action figures proving a particular disappointment. Pocket Books dropped a couple of the titles they'd announced and the planned second and third waves of toy lines were also scaled back.

The Motion Picture, then, produced a series of paradoxical results: it was a huge commercial success that the studio considered a financial disaster; it catapulted *Star Trek* from being a creaky old TV show with a vocal fan following into a fully-fledged state-of-the-art movie, even if one that few people liked. It proved the *Star Trek* name could sell toys, books and fast food . . . but the market had been flooded with stock that would take years to clear.

It also demonstrated Gene Roddenberry's limitations as a storyteller and manager. The studio were looking for a scapegoat, and Roddenberry had made very sure that his name was plastered all over the credits and the novelization. The studio concluded that they needed a radical change of direction if there was going to be a sequel. And that meant one thing: Gene Roddenberry could have no meaningful involvement.

CHAPTER EIGHT

THE BEST OF TIMES, THE WORST OF TIMES

As they contemplated a sequel to *Star Trek: The Motion Picture*, Paramount were faced with the same problem they'd encountered when making the first movie: finding a story that revolved around a big idea, but one that would allow for action and spectacle. They also wanted to keep costs firmly under control. There was talk of making the sequel a TV movie, but it quickly became clear that Shatner and Nimoy were only interested in coming back if it was shown in cinemas.

Gene Roddenberry pitched a story in which the Klingons went back in time to prevent the assassination of President Kennedy, forcing Kirk to ensure history stayed on track. It was swiftly rejected. While Roddenberry hadn't been responsible for every disaster that had befallen *Star Trek: The Motion Picture*, he certainly wasn't blameless, and the studio executives were happy to make him a scapegoat. He had redeemed himself a little by being a passionate and effective publicist for the movie in *Star Trek* fan circles. As before, it was felt that his "blessing" (Paramount actually used the word in memos) was vital to any *Star Trek* project. He was made executive consultant, a title that meant his name was featured prominently on the poster and credits, and that he was paid "a fee comparable to his producer's salary on the first film—and a percentage of the net profits."[1] He would receive the script, and his notes would be passed to the director. The making of the movie would be left to others. It was in both Roddenberry and Paramount's interest to portray *Star Trek*'s creator as deeply involved in the creative process. Publicly, Roddenberry was overseeing each movie, ensuring they conformed to his vision. In reality, he had next to no involvement. This is the deal that applied to the five *Star Trek* sequels made in Roddenberry's lifetime.

Barry Diller, chief executive at Paramount, turned to Harve Bennett to take Roddenberry's place. Bennett had worked in television, overseeing series that included *The Six Million Dollar Man* and *Bionic Woman*. At a meeting with Diller and Charles Bluhdorn, head of Paramount's parent company Gulf+Western, Bennett said he thought the first movie had been boring, and when he was told how much it had cost, said he could make five movies for the same money. A handshake later, and Bennett found himself in charge of making the sequel. When he was told of Roddenberry's role as executive consultant, Bennett "asked if that meant I had to report to him. The answer: 'absolutely not. Just consult with him; give him that to do.' That is all I was told."[2]

In November 1980, Bennett wrote a one-page synopsis of a story that involved Kirk discovering he had a son while fighting a revolution instigated by his old enemy, Khan. Within a month, Jack B. Sowards had developed this into a treatment where Khan plotted to steal the Omega System, a bomb the Federation was testing that could destroy a whole planet. Sowards was commissioned to write a script, and this first draft (delivered in February 1981) included Spock. Leonard Nimoy hadn't wanted to return to the role, but was lured back with the promise that the character would be dramatically killed off early in the movie. Spock was to have a protégé, a young Vulcan called Mr. Wicks, who would take Spock's place. Art director Mike Minor suggested that instead of a giant bomb, the Federation would create a device that transformed a world into an unspoiled, green paradise . . . even if it was used on an inhabited planet. Sowards's second draft, completed in April, renamed Spock's protégé "Savik," and showed the new recruit losing a no-win scenario in a flight simulator. In this version Spock died at the end of the first act, and it ended with an epic space battle and the formation of a new planet. Bennett still wasn't happy, and he brought in both Theodore Sturgeon and Samuel A. Peeples. In July Sturgeon wrote an outline featuring a female version of Savik (slightly renamed as "Saavik"), pairing up with Kirk's son. Peeples delivered a full script in August that didn't feature Khan, but introduced a subplot with Sulu and Chekov serving on a different Starfleet vessel. After a year's labor, there were five versions of the script, and none of them was working.

Nicholas Meyer was hired to direct in late August 1981. Meyer had written the smart, revisionist Sherlock Holmes novel *The Seven Percent Solution* (1974) and the screenplay for the 1976 movie version, and he'd adapted and directed the time-traveling Jack the Ripper movie *Time After Time* (1979). He admitted from the start that he knew nothing about *Star Trek* except that it was set in the future, what the USS *Enterprise* looked like, and that there was a character with pointy ears. (The movie would begin with an in-joke to that effect: it started with a caption announcing it's the twenty-third century, a display of the *Enterprise* on a screen, and a closeup of Mr. Spock's ears.) After that, Meyer was in uncharted territory. He had found *The Motion Picture* colorless and solemn, and although the sequel had a tight budget, he insisted on redesigning the Starfleet uniforms, and making the technology a little clunkier and more cluttered.

The studio's postmortem on *Star Trek: The Motion Picture* had concluded that essentially all the problems could have been avoided if there had been a completed script, and if the special effects team had been given a clear list of effects sequences early on, in order to have the time to carefully plan, test, and then integrate their work with the rest of the movie. When Meyer was hired, there was no approved script, and the movie had been booked into cinemas for a June 1982 release. The studio wanted the special effects team to start in two weeks. They suggested Meyer pick a favorite from the scripts, polish it, and make it, but Meyer had a proposal: "Why don't we make a list of everything we like in these five drafts? Could be a plot, a subplot, a sequence, a scene, a character, a line even . . . and then I will write a new script and cobble together all the things we choose."[3]

Meyer did this in twelve days, weaving together sequences from the various different drafts—the "no win" simulator sequence, Chekov's service on another vessel, Khan's search for the Genesis Device, Kirk learning he had a son, an epic space battle and Spock's death saving the *Enterprise*. Some things fell out of the mix entirely—in Sowards's script, Khan was to have developed psychic powers and drawn Kirk into a dreamscape where they fought hand-to-hand. Khan and Kirk never meet each other in final movie—Meyer brushed this objection aside, noting that Elizabeth I and Mary Queen of Scots never met, either. A romantic plot involving Dr. McCoy was dropped entirely. There are places in the final movie where the seams show a little—the story starts with the *Enterprise* being used as a training ship, and is manned with cadets, but there's very little to remind us of this once the *Enterprise* is underway. Khan steals the Genesis Device, but doesn't have a use for it beyond it being bait to lure Kirk to him. Kirk finds out he has a son and reunites with his lost love, but that storyline barely moves beyond the reunion.

Meyer brought out themes Bennett had been keen on from the start, such as an acknowledgement that the characters were aging. The movie had a clear villain, out for revenge. It had fun literary references—the heroic sacrifice of Spock echoes Dickens's *A Tale of Two Cities*, the book Spock gives Kirk as a birthday present at the start of the story; and Khan's famous "Klingon proverb," "revenge is a dish best served cold," is taken from *Les Liaisons Dangereuses*. The whole movie is a rough remake of *Moby-Dick*, at least the Gregory Peck movie version, with Khan's obsession matching Ahab's. Khan dies stealing Ahab's last words: "*From Hell's heart,* I stab at thee; For hate's sake, I spit my last breath at thee."

William Shatner wasn't happy with the script, a fact that horrified Meyer. Bennett had more experience dealing with lead actors, and after they met, he was able to assure Meyer that Shatner was merely protective of the character, that he wanted Kirk to be initiating the action, to be, in Meyer's words, "the first through the door" at the start of every scene. Meyer made some very minor rewrites, and Shatner was delighted with the results.[4] Nimoy enjoyed the script, recognizing that in this remake of *Moby-Dick* he was the exotic Queequeg, somehow prescient of his own death. George Takei and DeForest Kelley were unhappy that Sulu and McCoy had so little to do, and both hesitated to sign up.[5]

Meyer delivered his first draft on September 10, 1981, a second draft on September 16, and the third on September 29. Principal photography began at the start of November.

Rewrites continued, and the studio, happy with what they were seeing, authorized an increase in the special effects budget. The *Enterprise* bridge set had never been dismantled after the filming of *Star Trek: The Motion Picture*. It served as the ship's bridge, a starship training simulator and—slightly re-dressed and with some elements moved around—as the bridge of the starship Khan steals, the USS *Reliant*. The scenes on the *Reliant* were filmed first, meaning Ricardo Montalban, reprising his role in "Space Seed," completed his work on the film before most of the regulars had even started. While the regular cast once again spent almost all their time on the bridge set, and the action concentrated on Kirk and Spock to the near exclusion of everyone else, the actors were far happier with the pace of filming. Walter Koenig and James Doohan had interesting subplots (Doohan's, involving Scotty's nephew being assigned to the ship and dying in Khan's first attack, was cut from the cinematic release, but restored for most of the home video versions).

Although he claims it was entirely by accident, Meyer had written a script that had no scenes requiring crowds of extras or complicated and time-consuming matching up of live action and special effects. The bulk of the filming was completed on January 29. Two quick reshoots were made after a test screening. A scene was inserted clarifying that Kirk had known about his son, but had honored his mother's request to stay out of his life (the movie remains a little confused as to whether David always knew he was Kirk's son), and the final scenes were rejigged so the movie ended on a hopeful note, rather than a funeral one. The studio also rejigged Khan's last scenes without Meyer's consent.

The only big tussle with the studio was over the title. Meyer's first draft was titled "The New Frontier," but he wanted to call the movie *The Undiscovered Country*, a quote from *Hamlet* about death and a title he would use a decade later, when he returned to make the sixth film in the series. The studio ruled that the title would be *The Vengeance of Khan*. Very late in the day, rival studio Fox announced that the next *Star Wars* movie, released in 1983, would be called *Revenge of the Jedi*, and Paramount amended the name of their movie to *The Wrath of Khan*. The packaging for a few toys carrying the "Vengeance of Khan" title had already been printed. In the event, six months after *The Wrath of Khan* was released, the title of the *Star Wars* film was amended to *Return of the Jedi*.

Fans now hold *The Wrath of Khan* in very high regard, either citing it as the best of the movies, or knowing they have to carefully enunciate why they hold a dissenting opinion. The makers of subsequent *Star Trek* movies have been somewhat too enamored of it, with the tenth and twelfth, *Nemesis* and *Into Darkness*, being acknowledged near-remakes that manage to clutter up the simple story of the original. While *Star Trek* fans criticize the first movie for retreading the old episode "The Changeling," they don't seem to worry that *The Wrath of Khan* is pretty close in places to "Balance of Terror." And while most fans cite Gene Roddenberry's "optimistic vision" as the unique selling point of *Star Trek*, there is absolutely nothing utopian about Bennett and Meyer's version of the twenty-third century. There's no political message, philosophical or satirical allegory in *The Wrath of Khan* at all. It's a straight-up adventure story about a battle of wits between a seasoned naval officer and a mad pirate.

Meyer met Gene Roddenberry once during production, saying "our contact was limited to a brief meeting at which we shook hands."[6] Harve Bennett knew *Star Trek*'s creator from their TV days and met him a few times. Those face-to-face meetings were very cordial.

Roddenberry hated *The Wrath of Khan* at every stage of development, and hated the final film. Copied in on every outline and draft of the script, he issued long, often derisive memos. Bennett understood why Roddenberry put up what he characterized as "stiff-necked resistance"[7] to the interlopers who were making *Star Trek* without him; he considered every point made by *Star Trek*'s creator, and even altered a few details, usually those that touched on Roddenberry's understanding of the characters or established lore of the show. Roddenberry was quickly disabused of the notion that he had any power to insist that all the changes he put forward would be made. Some of the objections were old bugbears. Roddenberry didn't want space battles, and the last third of the movie was an extended battle between two Federation ships. He objected to a scene where Kirk used his phaser to vaporize an alien mind control worm that had crawled from Chekov's ear— Roddenberry felt that Kirk ought to be fascinated by the creature and would want to capture it and have it studied in a lab. He baffled Bennett and Meyer by objecting that Kirk and his crew were behaving like they were in the military. Meyer recalls that Roddenberry

> was emphatic that Starfleet was not a military organization but something akin to the Coast Guard. This struck me as manifestly absurd. For what were Kirk's adventures but a species of gunboat diplomacy wherein the Federation (read America, read the Anglo-Saxons) was always right and the aliens were—in Kipling's queasy phrase—"lesser breeds"? Yes, there was lip service to minority participation, but it was clear who was driving the boat.[8]

Bennett was not a *Star Trek* fan. Having been given the job of making a *Star Trek* movie, he'd sat down in a studio screening room, watched all seventy-nine episodes in order, and made extensive notes. *Of course* Starfleet was a military organization. The people in *Star Trek* wore uniforms and had ranks like captain and lieutenant, they were flying around in a ship that was armed to the teeth, and every week Kirk got into a fistfight with some bad guy. What Bennett wasn't aware of was how *Star Trek* had evolved after its cancelation. Roddenberry had embraced and built on those changes, and now saw the series as a projection of humanist views into a utopian future. His memos asserted that by the twenty-third century, every member of the human race would have resolved all personal and interpersonal conflicts. Bennett watched an old TV show where Starfleet crewmen bickered, defied orders, fought over women, behaved arrogantly and selfishly—some rogue officers even became tyrants or warmongers. Meyer and Bennett have independently said they shrugged, then made what was essentially a Hornblower seafaring tale set in outer space.

Roddenberry particularly hated the death of Spock, feeling that killing such a central character was a mistake that would undermine the series. Leonard Nimoy was keen to leave, but Roddenberry was more familiar with the actor than Bennett, and understood Nimoy had blown hot and cold over playing the character in the past. Roddenberry was, of course, right—after all the fanfare and tears shed, Spock was resurrected in the very next movie. But the death of Spock was part of the plan from the earliest days of the sequel. It had appeared in the very first outline Bennett wrote, as a shock twist at the end of the first act. Roddenberry made his position clear. The studio stood by Bennett's decision.

News spread like wildfire through the convention circuit that Spock was to die in the forthcoming *Star Trek* film, and fans were encouraged to write to producers to protest. Harve Bennett strongly suspected Roddenberry's involvement, and would later discover Lincoln Enterprises selling copies of the movie outline.[9]

Meyer felt that the story would work better if Spock's death came at the climax, but was faced with the prospect that his grand finale would be no surprise to a large chunk of the audience. While they were filming the flight simulator sequence that started the film, a way out of the no-win scenario presented itself: Spock—and almost every other regular—would simulate being "killed off" as part of the exercise. Fans would think they'd been hoodwinked, and breathe a sigh of relief . . . until the very end of the movie, when Spock heroically sacrificed himself.

Roddenberry was never confronted about his role in the leak and the subsequent fan campaign, but Bennett and the studio never had any doubt he was the culprit. Nowadays, studios go to great lengths to control movie scripts, routinely watermarking them so that the source of any leak can be traced, printing them using paper and ink that make the pages hard to scan or photocopy. Because the *Star Trek II* script had fallen into the hands of fans, two years later *Star Trek III* would have the distinction of being the very first movie where something like this was done. Everyone's script was secretly given a unique mark, so that the studio could see whose copy had been duplicated. The twist of the third film was going to be the destruction of the *Enterprise*. Roddenberry was as angry about that as he had been about Spock's death. Bennett was not particularly surprised to learn that, within days of the script being circulated, fans started writing letters complaining about this development—and that they'd somehow acquired copies of Roddenberry's version of the script.

The second *Star Trek* movie beat the record for the highest grossing opening weekend at the US box office, and ended up taking just under $79m during the course of its run. This was a little less than the first film's $82m, but it was impressive for two reasons. Sequels very rarely did as well as the first movie—a sequel was expected to make half the box office of the original, and was deemed a notable success if it made two-thirds of the previous film's total, as *The Empire Strikes Back* and *Superman II* had. Secondly, of course, the movie had cost far less, $11.2m compared with, for the sake of argument, $35m. The studio had spent far less promoting the movie (although they'd also received far less from merchandise licenses). The production process had been smooth. The studio, crew, cast, fans, and reviewers were almost all far happier with the end result.

The magic formula had been discovered. There would be a third (1984), fourth (1986), fifth (1989), and sixth (1991) movie, and following those, there would be four films continuing the story of *Star Trek: The Next Generation*. Budgets rose over time, but were subject to strict spending caps. *Star Trek IV* ended costing a million dollars less than the $22m the studio had allocated for it, but on *Star Trek VI*, there wasn't enough money to give the Starfleet uniforms trouser pockets.[10]

An unexpected windfall came from the emergence of home video rentals and sales in the 1980s. *The Motion Picture* had been released in October 1980. At the time, video cassettes were almost all sold to video stores to be rented out, and copies of *Star Trek: The Motion Picture* retailed for $80. They were quickly joined by five tapes each featuring two episodes of the original series. The studio probably anticipated that avid *Star Trek* fans would be renting these titles over and over again. What surprised them was how many fans were prepared to buy the tapes at that price. For *The Wrath of Khan*, they experimented with much lower pricing—$40, hoping to sell 60,000 copies in the first year. They sold more than twice that.[11] The price of *Star Trek III* was dropped further, to $30, and the studio began releasing all seventy-nine episodes of the original series on tape. Steady sellers since the dawn of home video, *Star Trek* titles have always been among the first "back catalog" releases on new formats from Betamax and VHS, through DVD to Blu-Ray. The shows are now stalwarts of streaming services like Netflix and Amazon Prime. The original series movies have all generated more money for the studio on home video than they did in the cinema.

The studio stuck with the team that made *The Wrath of Khan*. Harve Bennett produced the first four sequels, and made a cameo appearance as the admiral who gives Kirk his mission at the start of *Star Trek V: The Final Frontier*. After that, he left Paramount. Nicholas Meyer co-wrote the screenplay for the fourth movie, and wrote and directed the sixth. Leonard Nimoy became an important behind-the-scenes figure. He agreed to return to *Star Trek III* if he could direct it, and the studio were so impressed by his work that he took the helm of the fourth movie, too. After that, Nimoy went on to direct the hit comedy *Three Men and a Baby* (1987).

Because William Shatner and Nimoy's contracts specified they were to receive exactly the same billing and benefits, Shatner was now entitled to direct two *Star Trek* movies. He approached the task of making *Star Trek V* with great gusto, and he made the most Roddenberryesque of any of the *Star Trek* sequels: the story, in which the *Enterprise* travels to the heart of the galaxy to encounter God, was reminiscent of a specific idea of Roddenberry's, "The God Thing." This fact was not lost on Roddenberry, who vetoed the original idea that the crew would really meet God. Shatner and Nimoy had become good friends by this point, but this didn't stop Nimoy fighting to preserve his interpretation of Spock and demanding rewrites.

The result was disastrous. *The Final Frontier* was not a good movie. Shatner's analysis over a quarter of a century on is that "Between the demands of the studio, the authority of Roddenberry as protector of the canon, Leonard's Spockiness, and the limited budget I was given, the script never reached its potential."[12]

It's an action-packed movie, there is a big idea at the heart of it, and it's easily DeForest Kelley's biggest and most nuanced role in the *Star Trek* movies. The money, though, clearly ran out at some point before the special effects were completed—Industrial Light and Magic, who'd worked on the previous films, were busy on other movies, and it's missing their expertise. *Star Trek IV*'s fish-out-of-water comedy had found its way to a more general audience. *Star Trek V* sank in a summer crowded with blockbusters— *Indiana Jones and the Last Crusade*, *Ghostbusters II*, *Dead Poets Society*, and towering over them all, Tim Burton's *Batman*. There was, by that point, a new *Star Trek* television series with a fresh crew, and the original series—and its cast—were looking increasingly creaky.

Roddenberry's role diminished with each movie. His official biographer says,

> Gene's files tell the story. There are several storage boxes holding material from the first film. The amount of material generated by his consulting diminishes with each successive film. By *Star Trek VI: The Undiscovered Country*, there was less than half a small storage box of material, mostly scripts and script revisions.[13]

By now he'd told a number of friends and family he was reconciled to stepping away from *Star Trek*.

One important factor may have been that his starship had finally returned to port laden with treasure. By Paramount's calculations, the original series was now in profit: "between June 1984 and July 1987, [Roddenberry] received five profit participation payments for the original series totaling approximately $5,300,000,"[14] and money continued to come in regularly after that. Half went to his ex-wife, as had been agreed in his divorce settlement, but a substantial sum remained. While his role on the movies came with little to no influence over the product, it gave him an additional seven-figure sum every couple of years, both his consultation fee as executive producer and his share of the profits.

Roddenberry turned his thoughts to writing a science fiction novel, *Report from Earth*. This was the third novel he'd started in five years, following the unfinished *Star Trek* novel *The God Thing* and the novelization of *The Motion Picture*. It was a form of writing that allowed him control over the story, and he'd not sold the book to a publisher, so he had no pressing deadline. His authorized biography states he worked on it "sporadically" from early 1981.[15] *Report from Earth* was about Gaan, an alien who'd placed its consciousness in an artificial human body in order to explore our world. The idea was that the book would be told as a first-person narrative, Gaan struggling a little with fluent English and figures of speech. In November 1985's issue of *Starlog*, Roddenberry went into some detail, and considered it a current project, although over four years later, it was clear progress had been slow and he was still in the preliminary stages. "I'm in a period of growth and expansion. I'm taking long, hard looks at the world and what's happening in it and analyzing and thinking. I'm trying to become acquainted with the universe—with the part of it I occupy—and trying to settle, for myself, what my relationship with it is."[16]

It wasn't the first time he'd tried to articulate an idea like this. Creating an artificial body to investigate humans is exactly what V'Ger does in *The Motion Picture* when it duplicates Ilia. If we couldn't guess already, Gaan was another variation on the Spock/Questor character—the latest, and not quite the last, of Roddenberry's logical philosophers who are always polite, but have poor social skills and an outsider's perspective on the human race, and who wonder if such a prejudiced, immature species is likely to survive. Gaan's quest resembled Roddenberry's own. At the start of the *Starlog* interview he says, "Gaan finds us to be remarkable creatures, although he believes us to still be in childhood—or just barely getting into adolescence. But considering all we've achieved, we're remarkable!"[17]

At the end of the same interview, he gives his own view, and it's difficult to see much distance between him and the protagonist of his novel: "What we face is the excitement of evolving as a lifeform. We're still a very young form, and it seems to use that we make terrible mistakes and do so much wrong. But really, we're just growing out of childhood."[18]

Star Trek fandom had a word for it. In 1973, Paula Smith had written a story for the fanzine *Menagerie* that was a parody of a sub-genre of *Star Trek* fan fiction in which a plucky female character arrives on the *Enterprise*, everyone loves her, Kirk (or Spock) seduces her and then she saves the day with her amazing skills. The character in the parody was called Lt. Mary Sue, and the term "Mary Sue" caught on as a way of describing characters who were conveniently super-competent. As many early *Star Trek* fan fiction writers were young women—as were so many Mary Sues—the term soon evolved to mean a character who was a blatant, always idealized, version of the story's author. The term was perhaps a little sexist, and more than a little ironic, given that Roddenberry freely admitted that Lieutenant Rice, Captain Kirk, and Mr. Spock were all examples of him putting an idealized version of himself into his fiction (and he wasn't done yet:

Star Trek: The Next Generation would manage to incorporate three Gene Roddenberry surrogates).

In lectures and interviews, when he talked about a problem—personal, professional, or political—Roddenberry was fond of using some variation of the phrase "if a Martian had just arrived on Earth, he would see what we do and be unable to explain why we do things this way." Roddenberry felt a little like a wry, philosophical alien himself. In the *Starlog* interview, he admitted that not all the notes he was making would end up in *Report from Earth*. Asked when he would finish it, he said, "I'm a couple of years away, I think about these things, and I make notes. Being a computer nut, I put them in my computer and file them away and database them, so I'm accumulating a great deal of information."[19] Susan Sackett says that "he only completed about seventy pages,"[20] almost exactly as much as he wrote of *The God Thing*.

Roddenberry was ill. He continued to make many appearances at *Star Trek* conventions and for television interviews, and was reasonably good at hiding his poor health, but as he hit sixty, his lifestyle was catching up with him. He had always drunk heavily, chainsmoked tobacco, and since the mid-Seventies, he'd frequently smoked cannabis. He'd started using cocaine during the production of *The Motion Picture*, and this had become a habit. For twenty years, he'd popped all sorts of pills: amphetamines to increase his workrate, and various legal, illegal, prescription, and non-prescription antidepressants, painkillers, stimulants, and sleeping pills. He rarely exercised, barring a few short bursts of attempting to get in shape, and was overweight. Susan Sackett reports he was impotent. He had high blood pressure, and took medication for it that didn't sit well with alcohol or the other pills he was taking.

Roddenberry turned sixty-five in August 1986, *Star Trek*'s twentieth anniversary year. The fourth movie in the series, *The Voyage Home*, was in production, and would be the most successful to date at the box office. The original series was selling strongly on VHS, there was a vibrant series of original novels and a monthly DC comics series. There were *Star Trek* conventions all around the world, and the biggest were huge affairs, run professionally. *Star Trek* had never been more popular or high profile. *Star Trek* was firmly part of the pop culture world, with Roddenberry's role prominently acknowledged. The only slight cloud on the horizon, in fact, was that *Star Trek* was occasionally portrayed by the studio as coming solely from the mind of Gene Roddenberry, and other people who had worked on the series bristled a little at that.

Roddenberry played golf, a sport Majel had introduced him to. His wife was a great deal better at it than he was, one friend saying, "Majel was a great golfer. She won a lot of the putting events over the years." She was less than serene on the course. At Barrett's memorial service in 2009, "Regular golf companion Sue Anderson got a laugh from the crowd when she noted the first time she met Roddenberry at the Bel Air Club and how she 'had never heard a lady speak that way on a golf course before.'"

Roddenberry wasn't pushing for TV or movie projects anymore. He confided to friends that he didn't think he had the energy for the twelve or fourteen hour working days that making a television show required. He understood and accepted that his executive consultant role on the *Star Trek* movies was limited. Roddenberry was, in other words, easing into retirement.

Then, almost without warning, he was invited to create and produce a sequel *Star Trek* television show.

CHAPTER NINE

SECOND CHANCES

How and why Paramount decided to make a new *Star Trek* series says much about the changing landscape of television and its corollary, the growing symbiosis between a studio's movie and television divisions to "maximize assets." Television no longer means just the three networks. Paramount is making television programs this year for seven different entities—ABC, CBS, NBC, Fox Broadcasting, Showtime, USA Cable and first-run syndication.

The New York Times, November 2, 1986[1]

It was obvious why Paramount might want to revive *Star Trek* on television. *Star Trek* had accidentally pioneered the concept of a "franchise," showing how a series could be more profitable than a traditional network show, and for far longer. It remained the most popular syndicated series. It was a popular movie series, and generated revenue from books, comics, toys, and other merchandise. It was now making money on home video. In a new broadcasting environment where a show's "brand value" was important, *Star Trek* was one of the most valuable brands Paramount had. The old TV series had lasted a long time in syndication, but some stations had started to drop it. Fans with VCRs could tape the episodes now.

It's far less obvious why the studio would want to hire Gene Roddenberry, whom they considered "a pain in the neck . . . a has-been." But it was already clear that William Shatner and Leonard Nimoy wouldn't be reprising Kirk and Spock on television. Shatner was already playing Kirk in movies, and he had the starring role in a popular new police series, *T.J. Hooker*. He demanded a large pay rise for *Star Trek IV*, and this briefly held up production. The studio sketched out contingency plans, as *The New York Times* reported:

> The trigger for the new television series came when agents for Mr. Shatner and Mr. Nimoy asked sky-high salaries for the fourth *Star Trek* movie, *Star Trek IV: The Voyage Home*. "We thought of establishing new characters in a movie we called *Star Trek: The Academy Years*," says a Paramount executive who asked not to be identified. That idea was abandoned when the two stars signed for approximately $2.5 million each. But the seeds of "a new generation" had been planted.[2]

In fact, Nimoy didn't even need to ask. The "favored nations" clause in his contract meant he had pay equality with Shatner, so the studio had to pay out two dollars for every dollar Shatner managed to negotiate for himself. The movies were successful; above all else they were the nearest thing the movie business got to a safe bet. Shatner and Nimoy knew they had a great bargaining position—when the studio suggested halting production on *Star Trek IV* until Shatner had signed, Nimoy (who was directing the movie) laughed it off and carried on working.[3]

Nimoy, though, was Paramount's first choice to oversee the new television series. He quickly passed—he was happy directing movies. The new *Star Trek* show would need a new cast. The idea of passing the baton to the "second generation" took hold. The "Academy" idea mentioned in *The New York Times* report had been around since 1972, when the animated series was being developed. A vestigial form of it had surfaced in *The Wrath of Khan*, in which Kirk and his crew train cadets. After Nimoy had turned them down, Paramount asked producers Sam and Greg Strangis to develop a "Starfleet Academy" series.

The new *Star Trek* was to be an expensive, high-profile series. For the show to be as popular as the original, it needed to have the same magic ingredients, but it was starting out without any of the familiar characters or actors. Paramount knew the networks would bite their hands off for a show featuring Kirk and Spock. Instead they would be offering a series that was, in some senses, competing against the movies in which the pair featured.

They showed Roddenberry the Strangis' proposal. He said, "when I read what they'd written, I almost threw up."[4] Roddenberry had an effective veto over new *Star Trek* projects, although it's always been a little unclear if the studio were legally bound by that, or whether they just didn't want to generate bad publicity by making a form of *Star Trek* that its creator was publicly denouncing. At the meeting, Roddenberry told them that if anyone was going to make a new *Star Trek* television series, it would have to be him. By the end of the meeting, somewhat to everyone's surprise, that's what had been agreed.

Gene Roddenberry had created *Star Trek*, and his name was all over it. While his memos to Harve Bennett as executive consultant on the movies were mostly ignored, they demonstrated that he had thought long and hard about the spirit of *Star Trek*, and that he remained passionate and articulate in expressing his thoughts on the matter. As with the movies, the studio understood that they needed Roddenberry on the team, and knew he would be able to win over doubters among *Star Trek*'s avid fans. More importantly, in the short term, his name on the project would give it credibility as Paramount pitched it to the networks. The initial meeting had been in September 1986, and from there agreement came so quickly that the new *Star Trek* series could be announced at a studio press conference on Friday October 10, 1986. At that event, Mel Harris, president of Paramount Television, doubled down on Roddenberry's centrality to *Star Trek*: "Twenty years ago, the genius of one man brought to television a program that has transcended the medium. We are enormously pleased that that man, Gene Roddenberry, is going to do it again. Just as public demand kept the original series on the air, this new series is also a result of grass roots support for Gene and his vision."

Paramount offered Roddenberry a good deal. The studio were willing to give him a lot of money—a $1m signing bonus, plus about $2m a season; a large stake in the show (a reported 35 percent of the gross); and an extremely high level of creative control, with no one like Robert Wise or Harve Bennett calling the shots. Paramount would even renegotiate some of his old *Star Trek* deals. The contract set three levels of involvement, with proportionately increasing levels of payment, from advisor through to actively running the show on a day-to-day basis, and let Roddenberry choose which one to take, allowing him to change his mind further down the line.

The studio may have expected Roddenberry to be humble and grateful, or to meekly offer to be a part-time, semi-retired advisor on the new show. Instead, he was determined to have full control, that he would not be usurped or cheated out of anything. He set his attorney, Leonard Maizlish, to work. Paramount executive John Pike—fittingly, it's a name that sounds like he's the lead character in a Roddenberry pilot—described Maizlish as "a bullheaded guy who he himself could be a movie of the week."[5] Susan Sackett has the lengthiest description:

I had never been particularly fond of Leonard Maizlish. I'd met him when I first began working for Gene, and wasn't impressed. He was then in his late 50s, had slicked down, thinning dark hair, dressed in wrinkled shirts that were not always tucked in, and wore a perpetual look of melancholy. He reminded me of Mr. Magoo, scrunchy-faced and pudgy. He'd known Gene for years and they had become best buddies. Maizlish had handled all of Gene's contracts with

Paramount, and as far as I could tell, Gene was his only client. To me, he was a leech; to Gene, a lifeline. He depended on Maizlish to guide him through the mire of Paramount executives who wanted to take advantage of him.[6]

When Roddenberry set up his office at the studio, he moved Maizlish in, too.

Understanding that he was extremely lucky to have been given another chance, and that running a TV show had been an exhausting, stressful experience when he'd been twenty years younger, Roddenberry went into rehab at the weekends, starting in September. Various sources say this took place at La Costa, but Susan Sackett, who made the arrangements and visited him there, names the venue as Schick-Shadel Hospital in Santa Barbara. She reports that, for several months at least, he stayed "clean and sober."[7] He marked his turnaround in fortune by buying a new cream and tan Rolls Royce Silver Spur that cost $100,000.

Roddenberry wanted to surround himself with people he could trust. As he had with the *Star Trek II* television series, he hired as many people as he could from the Sixties show. In October 1986, he had a "core": two producers, Robert Justman and Eddie Milkis, and two senior writers, D.C. Fontana and David Gerrold. Costumes would be designed by William Ware Theiss, the music composed by Fred Steiner.

With Maizlish fighting the legal and financial battles, Roddenberry was free to concentrate on the creative side of his work, and clearly relished the prospect of reinventing *Star Trek* from the ground up. This is not to say he transcended office politics and petty disputes to dedicate himself to his art. This was a chance, after all, to demonstrate that the secret ingredient of the series was Roddenberry himself, not a particular character or actor.

Plenty remained the same—episodes would start with a "captain's log" voiceover, complete with stardate. The *Enterprise* was there, with a bridge, sickbay, and full complements of shuttlecraft and photon torpedoes. The crew would beam down from the transporter room, carrying phasers and tricorders. The key difference was in the personnel who would be beaming down. Roddenberry was keen to distance himself from the original crew, and none of the characters were literally the "next generation." The movies had seemed to be edging towards a direct continuation: they'd introduced—then discarded—a number of younger characters like Xon, Decker, Ilia, Kirk's son David, and Spock's protégé Saavik, who could easily have become a new cohort taking over after Kirk and his crew moved on. *Star Trek III* destroyed the *Enterprise* and introduced the USS *Excelsior*, a bigger, more advanced starship. Most fans assumed Kirk would take command of the *Excelsior* in *Star Trek IV*—and the DC Comics series showed this happening, in stories published between the third and fourth movies—but again, it would be the perfect vessel for the next crew.

Roddenberry moved things far further into the future. Precisely how far changed a little during production (it was reported at various times that the show would be set either 100 or 200 years after the original series), but the Writers' Guidelines of March 23, 1987 specified that "78 years have passed since the time of Kirk and Spock."[8] This was an exact number but not a precise enough answer for fans, as Kirk and Spock had been around for decades. Eventually, it was established that this meant seventy-eight years since *Star Trek IV*, the most recent movie. The show wouldn't feature a single familiar name from the old series—no descendant of Kirk or Spock, or any of the others. There would be no "whatever happened to?" stories. The Writers' Guidelines specified that "we are not buying stories about the original *Star Trek* characters," and there weren't even a handful of mentions in the first couple of seasons.

Up until now, a great deal of *Star Trek* had centered around Spock. Every effort had been made, millions of dollars spent, to persuade Leonard Nimoy to reprise his role in the movie series. The times Nimoy had been reticent, it had been taken for granted that *Star Trek* had to have another Vulcan character. For the *Star Trek II* series it had been planned to substitute a younger Vulcan science officer for Mr. Spock; at the start of *The Motion Picture* Kirk recruits another, Sonak, to take Spock's place. Many spinoff stories, official and fan fiction, had revolved around Vulcan society. Now, the Writers' Guidelines specified "No stories with Vulcans. We are determined not to copy ourselves and believe there must be other interesting aliens in a galaxy filled with billions of stars and planets."[9]

Roddenberry was making a conscious effort to decouple *Star Trek* from Mr. Spock and Leonard Nimoy.

Many elements *Star Trek* fans took for granted had changed: the Klingons, for example, were now allies of the Federation, and there was even a Klingon officer on the bridge—although early in the series, Worf is not a major character, and has only a few "business" lines in the pilot. Roddenberry's plans for the show were a mélange of ideas, some very old indeed. A couple of the "new" characters were familiar from *Star Trek II* and other earlier projects. The android Data was a barely disguised Questor from *The Questor Tapes*. Riker and Troi, an ambitious first officer on the verge of becoming a Starfleet captain, and his exotic, mildly psychic ex-lover, who unexpectedly found themselves reunited on the *Enterprise*, were Decker and Ilia from *Star Trek II* (and, of course, *The Motion Picture*). Roddenberry did attempt a more gender-balanced regular cast—there would be three female bridge officers, and they were all meant to be central to the action each week. Roddenberry wanted to give *Star Trek* fans with disabilities a role model, and he decided to make one of the officers blind—he was named after George La Forge, an early fan of the show with muscular dystrophy. New villains would be needed, and these would be the fearsome Ferengi, vicious traders who plotted to acquire wealth. They were set in direct contrast to the *Enterprise* crew, whose civilization was described piously by Picard in the episode "The Neutral Zone": "A lot has changed in the past three hundred years. People are no longer obsessed with the accumulation of things. We've eliminated hunger, want, the need for possessions. We have grown out of our infancy."

D.C. Fontana and David Gerrold threw important ideas into the mix. Gerrold had dedicated a whole chapter of *The World of Star Trek* to ways of improving the storytelling of *Star Trek*, if it returned. Some of those ideas, big and small, are clearly integrated into *Star Trek: The Next Generation*. It's Gerrold who first suggests that it might be good for the crew to bring a psychologist along, and that it was silly for the captain and first officer to both beam down on the same mission.[10] Gerrold is thought to have written the first draft of the series bible, the document that lays out the format of the show. He stated categorically, "I wrote the bible for that show, not Gene. He took credit for it, of course. And the idea of the older, more mature Captain—that was mine. That way we could keep the Captain on the bridge and make the first officer the Mission Specialist."[11]

But the early documentation clearly has Roddenberry's fingerprints all over it, too. While the new *Enterprise* crew would be politically correct, their creator was still a man capable of writing character notes like "Beverly Crusher's walk resembles that of a striptease queen." D.C. Fontana talked Roddenberry out of another idea: "I objected to Troi having three breasts. I felt women have enough trouble with two. And how are you going to line them up? Vertically, horizontally, or what?"[12]

At the core of the show Roddenberry placed . . . three versions of Gene Roddenberry. The captain was to be nearing the end of his career and (after he was originally called "Julien") Gene made him his phonetic namesake: Jean-Luc. The new captain would be an old sage offering advice to the up-and-coming William Riker, a clean-cut leading man—an idealized Gene Roddenberry firmly from the same mold as Lieutenant Rice, Captain Pike, and Dylan Hunt. Finally there was Wesley Crusher, a bright teenager about the same age that Roddenberry's son was at the time—and who was given Eugene Wesley Roddenberry's middle name. The three men represented "the three ages of Roddenberry."

The main change was one of attitude. The USS *Enterprise* was reimagined as a community, one where Starfleet personnel brought their families along as they traveled deep into the galaxy (although the show rather squandered this by only having one of the bridge crew actually do so). The new *Enterprise* retained echoes of the original designs, but everything had evolved along with the civilization that had built it. Large areas of the ship would be given aside to recreation and its crew would live in luxury. The uniforms were gender neutral. Men and women all wore one-piece uniforms . . . with the option for both men *and* women to wear "skants"—one-piece uniforms with skirts instead of trousers. The wellbeing of the crew was catered for, indeed one of the bridge officers was the ship's counselor, skilled in psychology and concerned with the feelings of the crew and the people they encountered. The fact that the new USS *Enterprise*, despite its legacy name, wasn't a military vessel was most obvious on the bridge, a huge carpeted space with ramps instead of steps and three chairs in the center (one of them for the counselor) instead of just the captain's, dominated by a curvy, wooden sculptural element that just happened to be the weapons and communications console. The computer panels were elegant ebony touchscreens. From the outside, the original *Enterprise* had been a modular design—a flying saucer, a stubby cylinder, and two missile-like rocket pods, connected together with struts. The *Enterprise-D* retained the basic shape, but made the ship into one seamless, curvy form. This was an elegant, beautiful, balanced future. The Federation was now explicitly utopian, post-scarcity, its people were unselfish, calm, concerned with self-improvement and serving the greater good (and, in the first season at least, keen to declaim this to anyone who'd listen).

The *Enterprise-D*'s relaxed vibe was in marked contrast to the tide in literary and screen science fiction in the late Eighties, much of which adopted the "cyberpunk" aesthetic of the novels of William Gibson and Bruce Sterling, or were grimy, violent stories like *Aliens* (1986). Most SF at the time depicted the near future as being in marked decay compared to the present day. The authorities were unaccountable (or non-existent), the environment was degraded, technology turned against its creators. Android contemporaries of Data were designed to imitate humans in order to infiltrate and murder, like the Replicants in *Blade Runner* (1982) or Arnold Schwarzenegger's character in *The Terminator* (1984). Roddenberry was well aware of the trend. Susan Sackett reports that they "saw virtually every contemporary (and some not-so-recent) SF film" as research for *TNG*.[13] His original idea for the character who would become security chief Tasha Yar was a specific lift from the movie *Aliens*—she was to be based on Vasquez, the macho Latina who was the only female space marine sent into battle. The original casting call for the character in December 1986 named the *TNG* character as "Macha Hernandez." By March the following year, the character was Tasha Yar: "born at a failed Earth colony of renegades and other violent undesirables, she escaped to Earth in her teens and discovered Starfleet, which she still worships today as the complete opposite of all the ugliness she once knew." In other words, Yar was consciously put in the show as a response to the "darker" forms of science fiction around at the time. Roddenberry would ram the point home in the pilot episode, where we see a recreation of a kangaroo court and drug-fueled soldiers from the "Mid twenty first century. The post-atomic horror." Tasha Yar makes it clear: "I grew up on a world that allowed things like this court. And it was people like these that saved me from it. This so-called court should get down on its knees to what Starfleet is, what it represents."

The *Star Trek* universe could encompass such places, but the utopian Federation offered a path to a brighter future—for the audience as well as the characters.

This was an aspect of the show that Roddenberry felt was central, but was often the subject of scorn from sections of the *Star Trek* world, including some of the people who would go on to make the show. Ronald D.

Moore would rise quickly from writer on the third season, to co-producer, to producer of the final season. Moore was particularly scathing of the humanist aspects of *The Next Generation*. He saw them as an indication that Gene Roddenberry was "starting to believe his own publicity," that the show's creator was determined to use it as "a vehicle to demonstrate this vision."[14] Each new iteration of *Star Trek* would end up drifting further from utopia: the next TV series, *Deep Space Nine*, was set on a space station far from the comforts of the heart of the Federation. The show after that, *Voyager*, was set on a starship smaller than the *Enterprise*, and compromised by being marooned on the far side of the galaxy. *Enterprise* was a prequel series, consciously bridging a gap between present-day NASA design work and the starships of Kirk's era. When the *Enterprise-E* was introduced in the second *Next Generation* movie, even Picard and his crew suddenly found themselves on a dark vessel with a clear military aesthetic, but no sign of the crew's families or airy recreational spaces. Moore later dreamt up a revamped version of *Battlestar Galactica* that took this process even further, making his vast starship clunky and prone to mechanical failure.

Star Trek: The Next Generation was a major investment for Paramount, whose executives would talk of it being "a $100m project."[15] The budget would average out at around $1.3m an episode, but this would include a lot of upfront costs, because the standing sets, models, costumes, props, and so on would all have to be ready for the opening episodes. In fact, Roddenberry insisted that the pilot should show the audience all the sets he had in mind, and he wrote in a tour of the ship. He knew from the first *Star Trek* series that if he waited to include a sequence in the engine room, battle bridge, or sickbay until the later episodes, the bean counters might stop him from building new sets.

Roddenberry's plan to do this with the pilot episode of the Seventies *Star Trek II* series had been one of the reasons *The Motion Picture*, based on the new series's intended script, had burned through so much money. This time, it was a perfectly sensible thing to do. As with the original series, virtually all the costumes, props, and sets had to be built from scratch, although imaginative use was made of a few older sets. The Klingon bridge from the first movie had been re-dressed as the photon torpedo bay for *The Wrath of Khan*, and would be called into service as all sorts of rooms, offices, alien ships' bridges, and so on. The most obvious bit of recycling was that the corridors of the *Enterprise* from the first movie were repainted, widened, and became the corridors of the *Enterprise-D*.

Roddenberry thought the show would only need a limited number of model shots of the USS *Enterprise*— flying through space, orbiting a planet, turning, going to warp speed, firing phasers, firing photon torpedoes, separating the two "sections" of the ship—and was sure to include all of these in the first episode. It was a sensible plan, but again it meant money was spent at the start of the season. As it happened, once the show was underway, it became clear both that modern audiences wanted fresh model sequences every week and that twenty years on from the original series, visual effects were far cheaper and more flexible than they used to be.

Paramount shopped the new *Star Trek* series to the three existing networks—NBC, ABC, and CBS—and the newcomer, Fox, which was launching in spring 1987. As it turned out, all four were keen, but there were issues. As would have been true for any new show, NBC and ABC wanted to see a pilot episode. Fox were interested in thirteen episodes, but wanted them by March 1987, and it was already late fall 1986. The huge upfront costs would see Paramount losing a minimum of $10m if a network dropped the show after thirteen episodes—much more, obviously, if all they made was the pilot episode. CBS came closest to meeting Paramount's needs, by offering to buy a six- or seven-part *Star Trek: The Next Generation* miniseries. Ordering fewer episodes than Fox might seem like an odd way to solve the problem, but at the time one-off TV movies and miniseries could be huge events for a network. Nicholas Meyer had gone from making *The Wrath of Khan* to a TV movie about a nuclear war, *The Day After* (1983), and over a hundred million Americans had watched it. The ratings of miniseries like *The Thorn Birds* (1983) and *North and South* (1985) justified their huge budgets. The *Winds of War* (1983) cost $35m to make, but averaged eighty million viewers. Miniseries could be sold to foreign television stations, and re-edited as TV movies and for home video. If the *Star Trek* series was popular, obviously there was potential for a follow-up.

All four networks wanted a great deal of say in the running of the show—and a share of the profits. Paramount were very wary of signing away any control or ownership of *Star Trek*. Lucy Salhany, president of Domestic Television at Paramount, came up with a more radical solution: "first run syndication." *The Next Generation* would debut on the hundreds of smaller stations already showing the original *Star Trek* . . . and those stations wouldn't pay Paramount for the show. Twelve minutes of commercials would run during each episode. Paramount would get the revenue from seven of those minutes, while the station would get the revenue from the other five. They had to commit in advance to broadcasting a full season, and only stations that agreed to the deal would be allowed to keep showing the lucrative original series.

It was not a tough decision. Many of these stations had been asking for new *Star Trek* material for years, and Paramount quickly signed deals with so many of them that 90 percent of the US population would be able to watch *Star Trek: The Next Generation*.

It would give Paramount full control over the show, and allow them to make a whole season. The worst-case scenario wasn't too bad: if a second season wasn't commissioned, then the *Next Generation* episodes would be added to the *Star Trek* syndication bundle, eking out at least a few more years for the original show. It was a brilliant solution, although not without its issues. For one thing, the shows that had been first-run syndicated before tended to be light entertainment—panel shows, variety hours very safe comedy. A television mini-series event, or a regular show that was the centrepiece of a network's schedule would have been far more prestigious and easier to attract talented cast and crew.

Bob Justman, though, relates that after some initial skepticism, the production team realized:

> This, this is heaven. This is heaven for a film producer. *There was no network*. There was no network, folks, no network. There was no Broadcast Standards Department. There were no censors. We censored ourselves, so to speak . . . Paramount tried to step in and get involved with the cutting of an episode, and Gene Roddenberry blew them away and told them "Don't come back again," you know, we'll take care of the creative end of everything.[16]

Roddenberry didn't get everything his own way. Once again, his casting choices were overridden by studio executives. He had a very clear favorite for the role of the *Enterprise*'s new captain: Stephen Macht. Known from roles on *Knots Landing* (1982–3) and as Christine Cagney's boyfriend in *Cagney and Lacey* (1985–8), Macht looked like a film star version of Gene Roddenberry, and had come to Roddenberry's attention when he'd auditioned for the role of Decker in *The Motion Picture*. The studio weren't happy with the choice, although this was clearly no reflection on his abilities, as Macht was later considered as a potential Riker. Other contenders for Picard, Mitchell Ryan and Barrie Ingham, could also have passed as

Roddenberry in a movie version of his life. Roy Thinnes, star of the Sixties show *The Invaders*—another old-school conventional lead—was considered. The studio spread the net a little wider, apparently offering the role to Edward James Olmos, who'd appeared in *Blade Runner* and would go on to play Adama in the twenty-first-century revamp of *Battlestar Galactica*. Olmos turned down the role because he was signed as a regular in *Miami Vice*. Yaphet Kotto was very seriously considered.

A memo dated April 13, 1987 lists Ryan, Thinnes, Kotto, and two actors called Patrick. Patrick Bauchau was a Belgian actor who'd started in New Wave cinema in the Sixties, but after appearing in the James Bond film *A View to a Kill* (1985) had begun to work steadily in Hollywood movies and American television. The other candidate was Patrick Stewart, a British actor who had been spotted by Bob Justman while reading to an acting class at UCLA. Stewart had an extensive background in British theater, twenty years in the Royal Shakespeare Company and the Royal National Theatre, but was somewhat overshadowed by others in his cohort, like Ben Kingsley, Ian Richardson, Paul Schofield, David Warner, and Ian McKellen. He had a memorable role as Sejanus in the television series *I, Claudius*, but his television and movie work had been limited to small, if often important, roles—he played Karla, the arch enemy of Alec Guinness's Smiley in *Tinker, Tailor, Soldier Spy* and *Smiley's People*, but had no lines and only appeared in a handful of scenes. He played Guinevere's father in *Excalibur* (1981),

Gurney in *Dune* (1984), and a doctor possessed by a space vampire in *Lifeforce* (1985).

Roddenberry hated the idea of Patrick Stewart as Picard. The English actor looked and acted nothing like the mental image he'd had of a gruff, French veteran explorer. John Pike liked him and, perhaps overestimating Stewart's place in the firmament, was amazed that a Shakespearean actor who'd worked with directors like David Lynch and John Boorman would consider a leading role in *Star Trek*. He was, though, very concerned that he looked too old. Stewart was forty-seven—hardly ancient, and actually a little younger than the character was meant to be—but he was bald.

The April 13 memo states that Bauchau read for the part "today" and the others would come in "next week," and listed Bauchau and Stewart as "favorites for the role." It came down to the two of them, and they both did a number of auditions and screen tests.

Stewart auditioned affecting a French accent he himself has said made him sound like Inspector Clouseau, and wearing a wig FedExed from London that he'd recently used in a play. Having finished the audition, and feeling he'd done very badly, he removed his wig and was leaving the building when he was called back in for another run through. This time, Roddenberry was convinced Stewart had the authority to be his captain, and he brushed aside the fact Stewart was bald by saying such things didn't matter in the future.

The same memo also states that "Denise Crosby seems

to be the only possibility for the role of Troi at this point; the same for J.D. Roth for the role of Wesley." Neither had signed a contract, and none of the other roles had been cast. The actors who would go on to play "Ryker" (the spelling changed late in the day), Geordi and Beverly— Jonathan Frakes, LeVar Burton, and Cheryl Gates McFadden—were on the shortlist. McFadden was up against Anne Twomey and British actress Jenny Agutter, well known from *Logan's Run* (1976) and *An American Werewolf in London* (1981). Wesley Snipes was one of those shortlisted for the role of Geordi. Rosalind Chao, who would go on to play Miles O'Brien's wife Keiko in *The Next Generation* and *Deep Space Nine*, was one of the contenders for Tasha, as was Bunty Bailey, a British actress whose most prominent role probably remains that of the girl in the pop video for a-Ha's "Take On Me."

Tasha and Data proved difficult roles to cast. A new casting call went out, and from that emerged Wil Wheaton (Wesley), Brent Spiner (Data), and Marina Sirtis (Yar). Sirtis was small, dark, and of Mediterranean ancestry, and so resembled the original model for the character, Vasquez from *Aliens*, more than anyone named in the April memo. It's clear from the actresses shortlisted that by this point Roddenberry wanted Yar to look either Chinese/Japanese, or somewhat Nordic. Denise Crosby now looked more like Yar to him than Sirtis, and the two actresses swapped roles. At this point, the Klingon character Worf was considered a minor recurring role, not a series regular— something akin to Billy Van Zandt's alien ensign in *The*

Motion Picture—and Michael Dorn was initially signed up to play him for only seven episodes.

Casting was completed in May, and announced on May 15. Filming began May 29, 1987. The first scenes shot saw Data and Wesley meeting for the first time on the holodeck.[17]

While bringing a new television series to air is always a fraught process, with lots of money and prestige very publicly at stake, and while almost every artistic production somehow manages to attract a battle of egos, the start of *Star Trek: The Next Generation* was almost legendarily messy. In 2014, a documentary about the making of the first season was released. It is called *Chaos on the Bridge*. And at the center of the chaos was Gene Roddenberry.

Virtually every television show takes a little time to find its feet, as the people making it build on what's working and drop things that don't. Watch the pilot episodes of most shows and compare them with one from two or three years later—you'll often see that major characters have disappeared, minor ones have been promoted. Actors leave, guest stars impress the producer and return. Chemistry between actors is built on, plotlines that aren't going anywhere are quietly put to bed. Going back and watching "Encounter at Farpoint," the first episode of *The Next Generation*, knowing where the show will end up, it's particularly odd what's emphasized in the pilot (the civilian population of the ship, the mission to explore deep into uncharted territory) and what's missing (everything is so very stiff and humorless).

Fans have many and differing opinions about *Star Trek* in all its various forms, but it's fair to say that there's a near-consensus on *The Next Generation*: it took a while to get going; some of the early episodes were terrible; it only really started to come into its own in the second season; the introduction of a powerful new enemy, the Borg, in "Q Who" (the sixteenth episode of season two, broadcast May 8, 1989) marked a turning point; the third season was a very strong one, and the last episode of that season, "The Best of Both Worlds," which ends with the shock cliffhanger of Picard stepping into shot converted into a Borg, and acting-captain Riker immediately giving the order to kill him, is one of the finest episodes of *Star Trek* ever made, possibly even one of the finest episodes of television ever made.

This arc of improvement, from "It's *Star Trek*, so I'll keep watching and hope it improves" to "Wow! This may even be better than the original!" was not a case of Gene Roddenberry and his original team steadily building on what worked and steering the show to reach its potential. Instead, there's an almost complete turnover of writing staff, and the incremental improvements coincide almost entirely with Roddenberry being prized away from the show. Writer walkouts and firings, disruptive events like a lengthy writers' strike that affected the whole industry, and interventions from actors forced the show to try new things that worked far better than Roddenberry's initial plans. As with the original show, as with the movies, things improved despite of Gene Roddenberry, not because of him.

Star Trek: The Next Generation had the time to fix its problems. The first-run syndication deal meant only an utter catastrophe would have seen it canceled mid-season, and in fact the ratings were very strong. To the intense relief of Paramount, more people tuned in than watched many network shows, and there were weeks where it would have been a top ten drama. The show only grew in popularity. Seven years later, the last episode would earn the highest ratings *Star Trek* had ever achieved or ever would again, a Nielsen rating of 17.4.

The first half of the season suffers with some very clunky "message" stories, the second half with the fact that a lot of the money had already been spent. It's striking how so many of the stories are driven by the issues, rather than the characters—the *Enterprise* arrives at a planet, the crew gets a tour of the planet, there's some form of moral dilemma, the crew react to events rather than instigate them.

Roddenberry passed an edict that frustrated the writers: the main characters were professional people from a mature civilization, and so they would never let their passions overwhelm them. No one would go rogue, come to blows, or even raise their voice. Instead of a captain barking orders from his command chair, the crew would gather around a conference table and agree on the best course of action, and then they would follow the plan. It's a warming prospect to think that in the future, there might be great advances in human psychology as well as technology, that there will be an organization of highly skilled scientists with great empathy, dedicated to assessing the needs of others, and non-violent conflict resolution. It didn't, in this case at least, make for compelling action-adventure stories. As so many times in his career, Roddenberry came up with an interesting idea, but one more subtle and delicate than he was able to articulate. It translated into characters telling each other that they were above such petty things as jealousy, rather than showing how that might work in practice.

The older writers who'd worked on the original series felt it was weak beer compared to the infighting and gentle putdowns that marked out the Kirk–Spock–McCoy relationship, and the younger writers felt it hemmed in their attempts to disrupt and challenge the characters. It also left the actors with very little to work with. They were playing perfect people who all agreed with everything their colleagues said, and kept making little speeches about how great humanity was. As one writer, Maurice Hurley, put it: "it takes away everything you need for drama, in Gene's wacky doodle vision of the future."

Roddenberry found it immensely frustrating that his writers needed what he saw as cheap tricks to create false drama. The writers found it frustrating that he would rewrite their scripts without telling them. Everyone, Roddenberry included, struggled with the format. The Writers' Guidelines stressed that these were fast-moving action adventure stories, but what made it to screen was frequently predictable, formulaic stuff. The writers found it hard to come up with stories about the families onboard the ship, and could only think of two ways to involve young Wesley Crusher—he accidentally put the ship in danger, or his genius saved it.

One huge early misfire was the Ferengi. The plan was that they would be the recurring villains, arch capitalists, whip-wielding slavers, a culture that devoured planets in the pursuit of profit. Instead, as Armin Shimerman, who played one of them, said, they ended up looking like "angry gerbils."[18] They only appeared once more in the first season, plans for a Roddenberry-scripted two-part story called "Ferengi Gold" were dropped, and then the Ferengi vanished completely until the end of the second season. It was the third-season episode "The Price" where they found their niche, as comic relief "pests."

A key difference between *The Next Generation* and the original series was that in the Sixties, writers and performers had worked with Roddenberry's material, added to it, adapted it. Much of what worked in the early episodes of the original series came from other people, encouraged by Roddenberry. Now, *Star Trek*'s creator hoarded his control of *The Next Generation*. He made it clear that every decision was to be approved by him, and that he didn't want people coming up with stuff behind his back. It stifled innovation, or indeed the desire to contribute suggestions or improvements.

One of the new writers, Tracy Torme, expressed his surprise at Roddenberry's manner, characterizing him as someone whose "energy level went up and down" and who was "mercurial."[19] Elsewhere, he described the show's behind-the-scenes atmosphere in the early seasons as an "insane asylum."[20] D.C. Fontana and David Gerrold had known Roddenberry for twenty years, had known *both* Gene Roddenberrys: the warm pop philosopher who made you feel great and inspired tremendous loyalty, and the slightly paranoid one who closed the door and railed against the people trying to cheat him, while happily taking credit for others' work. Even as he made self-serving moves against them—for example insisting on a co-credit for Fontana's script for the first episode—they felt very protective of him. It was self-evident that he was in poor health. Fontana says he suffered a series of mini strokes; Gerrold described him as "deteriorating."[21]

But even his old allies found themselves marginalized. Increasingly, Roddenberry would not see people to talk about their scripts, but would issue notes and annotations. Fontana and Gerrold knew Roddenberry's handwriting, and some of the handwritten notes were coming not from Roddenberry but from Leonard Maizlish. The lawyer seems to have taken against Fontana in particular. She had a writing credit on five first-season episodes, but left the staff after the thirteenth. David Gerrold was keen to write a story that was an allegory for AIDS and blood donation, a political issue at the time. Gerrold's script, "Blood and Fire," was a fairly tame—if timely—plea for tolerance. Roddenberry assigned another writer to rework it, and the episode was eventually dropped. Gerrold would leave the series soon afterwards.

"I'll tell you why. Part of the problem on *TNG* was Gene's lawyer [Leonard Maizlish] was making it impossible for anybody to do any real work. He was rewriting scripts. He was committing Guild violations. People were very unhappy. It was one of the worst working environments I'd ever been in. So when my contract came up for renewal, I asked Gene not to [renew it]. Later, I found out that Maizlish was telling people what a troublemaker I was, that I'd been fired because I was mentally ill, that I never did anything useful for the show—real character assassination of the worst sort . . . Maizlish was a disgraceful man."[22]

It was clear Roddenberry's lawyer was rewriting scripts himself and, leaving aside matters like the discourtesy it showed to the original writers or what qualified a lawyer to write television scripts, it was strictly against Writers' Guild rules. Fontana and Gerrold filed separate claims with the Guild, and when Paramount discovered Maizlish was working on scripts, he was banned from the studio lot.

Susan Sackett understood what was happening. "This was Gene Roddenberry's last gasp, he had the need for some support. Maizlish gave him support."[23] She saw the effect the long days and arguments were having on Roddenberry, how it was "exacting an enormous toll of his emotional and physical health. With his reputation on the line, he insisted on writing and rewriting the first eleven episodes (although he only took credit for his original ones)."[24] Roddenberry was living lavishly, had started drinking again. He was diagnosed with diabetes, needed to hire a chauffeur, and was becoming, in Sackett's word, "curmudgeonly."[25]

There was turmoil in the writers' room. Something like twenty-five to thirty writers were hired and fired over the course of the first season. From the eighteenth episode, "Coming of Age," Roddenberry had Maurice Hurley promoted to co-executive producer—essentially making him head writer. Hurley had worked on hit shows *Miami Vice* and *The Equalizer*. He did not consider himself well-versed in *Star Trek* lore, but knew where credit was due: "People get confused about who really is *Star Trek*, and that messes people's heads up. *Star Trek* is Gene Roddenberry and nobody else."[26] Hurley saw his role as preserving Roddenberry's vision for the series, which led to a series of running battles with the other writers. He would remain in the role until the end of the second season.

Many of the actors were unhappy. Patrick Stewart initially found the playfulness of the rest of the cast on set rather irritating, believing that the show would only work if everyone took their roles seriously. The cast began to gel as they compromised on this, Stewart coming to see the value of seeing the lighter side when problems hit filming, and the rest of the cast warming to his sense of commitment to his character.

Three characters in particular were poorly served by the first-season scripts. The show's commitment to non-violent conflict resolution meant that in the early episodes, phasers were rarely drawn, there were no gun battles. This left Tasha Yar, the security chief, with very little to do. Denise Crosby spent most episodes in the Uhura role—reading out to the captain what the computer was telling her.

Many of the writers didn't like Troi's character, and her "empathic skills" were soon downgraded to the mere offer of banal running commentaries that explained that a child who had just been orphaned was lonely, or that the warlord threatening to attack the *Enterprise* was feeling angry and violent. Her relationship with Riker, set up in the first episode as central to the show, was barely ever mentioned, and the idea it would be a model of futuristic sexual partnerships became another example of a potentially interesting idea that Roddenberry was unable to articulate, and which the other writers had no investment in developing.

Rick Berman, supervising producer on the first season, has said that Maurice Hurley "had a real bone to pick" with Gates McFadden because he wasn't satisfied with her performance.[27] Others have said Hurley disliked the actress personally. McFadden's agent was surprised to receive a note from Hurley saying her services wouldn't be needed for the second season, and this decision upset a number of the cast, reportedly including Patrick Stewart. Berman would take over from Hurley at the start of the third season, and he brought McFadden back. Berman would soon become executive producer, assuming the role from Roddenberry, and he steered the whole franchise, television and movies, until 2006.

The show was shifting around, finding its strengths. The first episode spent a lot of time around Picard, Troi, and Beverly/Wesley. With the second season, the writers started concentrating on Picard, Riker, and Data as the core characters. The three most marginalized characters, Yar, Troi, and Beverly, had something obvious in common; the net effect was that, having started with three women in powerful positions, *The Next Generation*'s first season ended with two of the actresses gone, and Troi moved from the heart of the show to become something of a bystander. Was this evidence of sexism among Roddenberry and his team, of institutional gender bias? Or was it just an unfortunate accident?

Roddenberry clearly had good intentions. He had put three strong female characters on the bridge, and had changed the tagline of the series from "Where No Man Has Gone Before" to "Where No One Has Gone Before." Susan Sackett says that one of the things he found irritating about the scripts in later seasons was that gendered language like "four-man landing party" had crept back in, when he'd sought to eliminate it. While there's been some criticism that Troi and Beverly were given feminine, "caring" jobs, they're roles, like Tasha Yar's as security chief/weapons officer, with the potential to be in the middle of the story every week. The writers clearly had more fun writing for Worf than for Troi. LeVar Burton was also given mainly functional lines, but managed to do more with them than Denise Crosby could with hers. There were more interesting things for Picard to do than reminisce with Beverly. The bottom line is that the show was better for the changes.

In 1995 Rick Berman admitted, "The fans never knew that Roddenberry's active involvement in *The Next Generation* diminished greatly after the first season."[28] As with the movies, the studio felt that it was important to present new Star Trek episodes as coming from Roddenberry.

Ironically, a Hollywood writers' strike at the beginning of the second season helped the show. While a number of unused scripts, including material written for the abortive *Star Trek II* television series, had to be dusted off, it also gave the cast and crew a breather, and time to think through fresh approaches to the material. Patrick Stewart introduced a new note to his performance, and started to subtly start playing against the scripts. Rather than sit and nod while someone gives a little speech, he'll make a subtle movement that suggests Picard is secretly more impatient, amused, or angry than he's saying. Gradually, this starts to infect the rest of the cast, who relax a little—start to give each other knowing looks.

Maurice Hurley's big plans to introduce a new enemy, the Borg, who would take a whole season to defeat, were curtailed by the strike. His replacement for McFadden, Diana Muldaur's Dr. Pulaski, proved unpopular. The show, though, was coming together. Geordi was now chief engineer. Data featured more prominently. Picard was involved in the action rather than simply staying on the ship. Whoopi Goldberg was added as the semi-regular guest star Guinan, in charge of a new recreation area, Ten-Forward, where crew members and families socialized.

The emphasis shifted away from the "high concept" of the episode to the featured character. Instead of coming up with worlds that had odd rules or customs ("a planet where every crime is punishable by death," "a planet where men are the weaker sex"), the writers were invited to pitch for "a Data story" or "a Troi story." The approaches weren't mutually exclusive. "The Measure of a Man," a second-season episode Patrick Stewart cites as one of his favorites, is concerned with Data's legal status—is he a man or a machine? Do the rights of a sentient machine trump the rights of scientists who wish to study it? The moral dilemma is the same as the first season's "Home Soil," in which miners have disturbed small crystals and a determination has to be made if they are "alive" enough to suspend drilling, but when it's "a Data story," the audience is more invested in the outcome, the stakes seem higher and more concrete.

By this point, *The Next Generation* was the third highest-rated show in its timeslot. The most successful episodes would get around eleven million viewers, and throughout its run, the show only dropped below nine million for one episode. Roddenberry trusted Hurley enough that he took a break during the production of the second season, heading to the Solomon Islands with Maizlish.[29]

Then the inevitable happened: Roddenberry and Hurley fell out over the direction of the show. The studio had to pick a side, and they sided with Hurley. Roddenberry had fired Fontana and Gerrold, and other people who might have stood up for him. By 1989 and the end of the second season, Gene Roddenberry's day-to-day involvement with *Star Trek: The Next Generation* was all but over. This time, he simply lacked the strength for the fight. He'd had a series of minor strokes in October 1988. He was apparently prescribed amphetamines, and as that meant he was now off the wagon, Roddenberry started using cocaine again. He began having violent mood swings.

He did, though, manage time to start a new love affair, with "a computer programmer and writer from Santa Monica who was an extremely intelligent woman." Maizlish described this as "a delayed mid-life crisis and one last fling as old age set in."[30]

In September 1989, Roddenberry had a more serious stroke, one that left him in a wheelchair. His health had deteriorated to the point he found it difficult to use a pen. Things were slipping away from him.

CHAPTER TEN

OF ALL THE SOULS I HAVE ENCOUNTERED IN MY TRAVELS, HIS WAS THE MOST . . .

Gene Roddenberry had been seriously ill for a long time. Even so, it came as a shock to the cast and crew of *Star Trek: The Next Generation* when people were summoned to Michael Piller's office at three o'clock on the afternoon of October 24, 1991 and the announcement was made that he'd died. He had not been a day-to-day presence on the show for some time, but everyone understood how central he had always been.

Five years before Roddenberry's death, *Star Trek* had been an increasingly creaky-looking Sixties TV show on endless reruns and a movie franchise where the cast weren't far off retirement age. Now, it was a vibrant, highly lucrative property with a bright multimedia future.

Gene Roddenberry had died a rich man, but he also died at a point where it was clear *Star Trek* was going to have a long and lucrative future. *The Next Generation*'s fifth season was just underway, and it had a couple more seasons to go, but plans were already in place to make the seventh *Star Trek* movie a *Next Generation* one. The end of *Star Trek VI* fell over itself to make the point, with Kirk making a final log entry that modified the original series's "Where No Man Has Gone Before" to *The Next Generation*'s more inclusive "Where No One Has Gone Before," and the movie ended with him and his crew literally flying off into the sunset, before the actors signed off—the end credits featured the cast's autographs.

In May 1992 Roddenberry's first wife Eileen went to court to clarify exactly what "*Star Trek*" was. In 1969, when their divorce settlement was reached, the definition had been easy: it was a canceled TV show. She was entitled to half the profits of a series so far in the red that it looked impossible it would ever show a profit. Now, Eileen took the estate to court arguing that "*Star Trek*" meant the whole franchise—movies, *The Next Generation*, all future *Star Trek* projects, and the associated merchandise.

Majel Roddenberry's legal team wanted the court to rule that "*Star Trek*" meant what it would have in 1969, when the settlement was reached—the three seasons of the original TV show. Their argument was that after the divorce Gene and Majel had made a strenuous joint effort to support the show, and that the "unprecedented" revival was a result of that. Having recorded the strenuous circuit of *Star Trek* lectures Roddenberry undertook in the 1970s and the mid-1980s, the documents state that "By 1975 the efforts of Gene, Majel and loyal *Star Trek* fans were beginning to pay off. Paramount wanted to do something based on *Star Trek* and finally decided on a big budget feature film."[1]

The estate argued that Eileen had actually been overpaid, as some of her money had been a share of Gene's payments for work done—consultation fees, writing scripts, advances—rather than "profits."

Susan Sackett—unceremoniously sacked so soon after Roddenberry's death that when she went back to her office from the announcement, she found studio security guards there to prevent her from entering—helped Eileen Roddenberry's team assemble a video montage that was shown in court. It showed parallel scenes of the opening titles, phasers and tricorders, Klingons and Vulcans, and the two captains stressing the importance of the Prime Directive. The aim was to demonstrate that *Star Trek* and *Star Trek: The Next Generation* were "indelibly intertwined." The judge, Macklin Fleming, had never seen *Star Trek* before. The first round went to Eileen, with the court ruling that she was entitled to a 50 percent share of all the profits Gene (and now his estate) earned from *The Next Generation*. Next, a jury decided the level of compensation, and Eileen was awarded $4.5m in overdue residuals and profits, and $900,000 in punitive damages from the estate for withholding them.

Leonard Maizlish had been Roddenberry's lawyer at

the time Norway and Lincoln Enterprises were set up. He'd negotiated the divorce settlement, he'd advised Roddenberry what he should pay Eileen in the eighties. The jury found him liable of conspiracy to commit fraud for his part in withholding earnings from Eileen, although they assessed no damages against him. Maizlish was very ill by this point, and died September 7, 1994.

However, when the jury did not award Eileen any participation profits from the animated series, the movies and merchandising, she eventually appealed to the California Supreme Court, which refused to hear the appeal. This left intact a state appeals court ruling in favor of Gene's estate. Also, the estate appealed the lower court's decision and had Judge Fleming's judgment overturned as well, ruling that Eileen was entitled to a share of the profits from the original series, but nothing else.[2]

The appellate court overturned the jury's decision on April 16, 1996, agreeing with the Roddenberry estate's argument that what was at issue was not whether *Star Trek: The Next Generation* was *Star Trek*, but that payment should be based on language in the settlement that said Eileen was entitled to one-half of all the income from *Star Trek*, "so long as that income was earned on account of services already performed, as distinguished from income for services to be performed." In other words, Eileen was entitled to profits from the original series, but nothing after that. The court ruled that the estate had withheld some money Eileen was due, but after four years of legal action, it was a big win for Majel Barrett.[3] Two months later, the estate successfully argued to disinherit Dawn, Gene's younger daughter.

The will left $300,000 to Gene's sister and his mother (who survived her son), and $175,000 to Susan Sackett. Nothing was left to his brother, Bob. Roddenberry bequeathed $500,000 to each of his three children and set up a trust fund which would share the estate between them on Majel Barrett's death—half to his son, the other half split between his two daughters. The vast majority of the rest of the estate, estimated to be worth a little over $30m, went to his widow.

As executor of the estate, Majel Barrett had considerable power. Engel states, "the terms of the will enable the executor to pay down the costs of the will's administration using these cash gifts . . . even if the costs reduce the value of the gifts to zero."[4] Dawn began a legal action against the estate early in 1993, claiming that her father had always told her he would split things equally between his three children. Suggesting that he had been in no fit state to understand the consequences of revisions to his will made in August 1990, she succeeded in an early hearing in having Majel Barrett temporarily removed as executor of the estate. In November 1993, though, Dawn withdrew the case when her husband was diagnosed with terminal lung cancer (he died in May 1994). Susan Sackett reports that she had also become wary of newspaper coverage of the case: "One of the tabloids had printed a sleazy, misinformed story that claimed Gene's daughter was branding him a drunken sot. Dawn cried for weeks over this one-sided defamation of his character, she was determined not to let it happen again."[5] The Roddenberry estate's lawyers then successfully argued that by disputing the case, Dawn had fallen foul of a clause that stipulated "if any beneficiary under this will in any manner, directly or indirectly, contests or attacks this will or any of its provisions, any share or interest in my estate given to that contesting beneficiary is revoked," and she was cut out of the inheritance.[6]

With lawsuits settled, Majel Barrett-Roddenberry was now in firm control of Gene's estate, including the intellectual property, the Norway Corporation and Lincoln Enterprises. *Star Trek* was at a peak of popularity. Other shows were starting to emulate *The Next Generation*'s "first run syndication" model, and home video could be very lucrative, so there were a variety of new ways to get a television series on air. It was well known in fan circles that Gene Roddenberry had plenty of unfinished projects and ideas for shows that hadn't seen the light of day. Barrett-Roddenberry took a leaf from other family managed literary estates, such as Arthur Conan Doyle's and particularly J.R.R. Tolkien's. She would cooperate with existing business partners (Paramount on *Star Trek*, in her case), while touting Gene's "lost" work to other studios and publishers. She would seek to ensure her late husband's "values" were preserved in work bearing his name, and she would make very sure that name appeared prominently. Central to this was making clear that, for what it was worth, Gene's power to give the Roddenberry seal of approval had passed exclusively to his widow.

Paramount owned *Star Trek*, and however optimistic Barrett-Roddenberry was about the prospects for other projects, she understood that *Star Trek* would remain her bread and butter. There was an abundance of *Star Trek* in the decade after Gene Roddenberry's death: the *Next Generation* movies were made; *Deep Space Nine* was joined on television by *Voyager*, both running for seven seasons; and soon after *Voyager* ended, *Enterprise* started its run. All appeared with the credit "Based on *Star Trek* created by Gene Roddenberry," and the estate was paid fees and a share of the profits. These were substantial. Unlike the original series, *Star Trek: The Next Generation* was in profit by the time it ended. The studio confirmed this a few months later, in January 1993, and an initial payment of $6.8m was made to Roddenberry's estate, followed by multimillion-dollar payments every six months since.

At some point in the last twenty-five years, it's likely that the Roddenberry estate's accountants and the studio's bookkeepers have quibbled over definitions or line items of royalty statements, but if so, they've done it in private. The Roddenberry estate never seems to have sued the studio, although that's an almost routine part of doing business in Hollywood. Both parties seem happy with the deal.

The artistic direction of the *Star Trek* franchise was firmly in the hands of Rick Berman. Having been executive producer—what's known informally now as the "show-runner"—since the third season of *The Next Generation*, he would remain in place until the end of *Star Trek: Enterprise* in 2005. The sequel shows were all credited as co-created by Berman and one other person: Michael Piller for *Deep Space Nine*, Jeri Taylor for *Voyager*, and Brannon Braga for *Enterprise*. He was producer and got a "story" credit for all four *Next Generation* movies.

It had long been rumored among fans that Gene Roddenberry didn't like Berman, and David Gerrold stated categorically that was the case:

> "Yeah, now Rick Berman was not . . . Gene didn't like Rick, at all. But Rick was installed on the show by the studio as a way to keep a control on the show. To keep it from getting out of hand . . . And so they put Rick in place to try and make things work. To work around Gene, to make it work. Well, Rick was busy playing studio politics, and he and the lawyer would work together to get rid of everybody who was a threat to their power. And nobody knew from one day to the next who Gene was friends with, because Gene didn't even remember who he was friends with from one day to the next."[7]

When *Deep Space Nine* was announced in January 1992, some fans were suspicious about the timing. It came mere weeks after Roddenberry's death, and the way Berman described it to *Entertainment Weekly*—"It's going to be darker and grittier than *The Next Generation*, these characters won't be squeaky clean"[8]—didn't sound at all like something Gene Roddenberry would have approved of. Ten years later, Susan Sackett still "wondered if it was just a coincidence that Paramount decided to go with a new *Star Trek* project less than one week after Gene's death. To my knowledge, Gene had never given his blessing to the spin-off."[9] *Star Trek* fans were early adopters of new technology, and *Deep Space Nine* led to a "flame war" on the internet, five years before most people even knew there was an internet. Berman and his team found themselves on the defensive, insisting that they'd started work on the show before Roddenberry's death, that he'd known about it and had been fine with it, and that fans should rest assured that while the situation the Federation characters were in on *Deep Space Nine* would be grim, they still personified the utopian values *Star Trek* fans had come to expect, and that they wouldn't be breaking the rule that Starfleet officers didn't argue with each other:

> "we compromised by not having conflict among the *Starfleet* characters. That's why we created a first officer, Major Kira Nerys who is a Bajoran, and populated the cast with a Trill, a shapeshifter and a Ferengi, and put them all in a sometimes very inhospitable environment filled with everything from bar drunks to temple priests. The combustible mixture allows for conflict, but the solidarity of the *Starfleet* officers is always maintained. So everybody was happy."[10]

The controversy proved that the studio had been right to think for all those years that *Star Trek* needed Gene Roddenberry's imprimatur to be fully accepted by many fans. It also showed that *Star Trek* fandom was not some monolithic bloc. Those in favor of a "grittier" approach felt it was possible to be a *Star Trek* fan and tell *Star Trek* stories without slavishly following Roddenberry's thoughts on what *Star Trek* was and wasn't. Indeed a section of *Star Trek* fandom had emerged that was openly hostile to Roddenberry. The irony was that while Roddenberry purists felt Rick Berman had strayed too far from the original, Berman's opinion was very clear, and far more favouable to Roddenberry than, say, fan favorite Nicholas Meyer's movie version:

> "*Star Trek* is not my vision of the future, it's Gene's, and it is my responsibility to keep it that way . . . you can not fight this vision. You must embrace it. Melinda Snodgrass, a second and third season writer on *ST: TNG* went off and wrote [about her experiences] what a ridiculous vision this was and that [*TNG*] would never work. Well, guess what? That vision happens to be the reason the *Star Trek* shows do work. . . . Gene wanted it to be light. He wanted Earth to be a paradise. As far as I'm concerned, the commitment to honour his vision also forces us to be more creative, to find new ways to tell stories."[11]

Berman understood the formula. *Deep Space Nine* and *Voyager* may have looked away from Starfleet's flagship, and a crew who were the *crème de la crème*, to slightly seedier corners of the *Star Trek* galaxy. Even so, the ensemble of characters didn't stray very often from the "types" established by Gene Roddenberry. There was always an outsider fascinated by the human condition, the sterling commanding officer and the irascible doctor. The casts were diverse, the stories tended to be self-contained moral dilemmas.

For his part, Roddenberry told Yvonne Fern, "My people are all good people. Rick Berman in particular. I trust him to produce my show. And he does. But I still look at everything. I make my evaluations and put my stamp of approval on everything."[12]

As for what Berman thought . . . in *First Contact*, the eighth *Star Trek* movie, he, Brannon Braga, and Ronald D. Moore came up with a story about the *Next Generation* cast accidentally going back in time to meet the inventor of the warp drive, Zefram Cochrane. Cochrane had appeared in one episode of the original series, as a handsome young man in the 1967 episode "Metamorphosis." The man Picard's crew find is old, drunk, with wandering hands, and can't get his brilliant idea to work. The *Next Generation* crew idolize him and love the future he'll bring about. They're disappointed he's not the mythical figure they've read about, but they fix his creation, make it fly, and Cochrane gets all the credit.

COCHRANE:	I've heard enough about the great Zefram Cochrane. I don't know who writes your history books or where you get your information from, but you people got some pretty funny ideas about me. You all look at me as if I'm some kind of . . . saint, or visionary or something.
RIKER:	I don't think you're a saint, Doc. But you did have a vision. And now we're sitting in it.

COCHRANE: You want to know what my vision is? Dollar signs! Money! I didn't build this ship to usher in a new era for humanity. You think I want to see the stars? I don't even like to fly! I take trains. I built this ship so I could retire to some tropical island filled with naked women. *That's* Zefram Cochrane. *That's* his vision. This other guy you keep talking about, this historical figure? I never met him. I can't imagine I ever will.

Even by *Star Trek* standards, the message is hidden in plain sight. For the record, while Gene Roddenberry had been a pilot, he didn't like to fly.

Majel Barrett had no say in the artistic direction of *Star Trek*, and consistently had no pretensions towards one. Just before her husband died, she had been asked if she would be interested in directing a *Star Trek* movie. "Are you out of your mind?" was her reply. And what about writing? She declined that idea also, saying, "I can barely sign my name to the bottom of a check."[13] She remained a frequent guest at *Star Trek* conventions and was, naturally enough, frequently asked about her own thoughts on the current *Star Trek* shows, as well as whether she thought her late husband would have approved. She usually batted such questions away, but when she offered a strong or constructive comment, she occasionally gave an answer expressing the wish that the shows had stronger female characters. Ten years later, she was able to say: "I have absolutely nothing to do with the *Star Trek* franchise. I haven't had for many, many years. Gene sold out all of his rights to *Star Trek* way back fifteen, almost twenty years ago. So, they ask nothing. I volunteer nothing. They invite me to a few of their shindigs. I'll bet you I haven't been on that lot in two years."[14]

She did have a way of making her presence known in new *Star Trek* projects. Barrett had played, uncredited, the voice of the *Enterprise*'s computer since "Mudd's Women" in the original series—an episode filmed before her debut as Christine Chapel, but broadcast later. She did not play any computer voices in the original-cast movies (although she made two brief appearances as Chapel). For *The Next Generation*, though, she was used in well over half of the episodes and all of the movies, and she played the voice of other Starfleet computers in all of the *Star Trek* shows and movies that followed. This was up to and including the first of the "reboot" movies, J.J. Abrams's 2009 *Star Trek*, for which she recorded her lines ten days before she died. She felt that this gave the projects a sense of legitimacy.

Barrett took on an almost ambassadorial role. When *Deep Space Nine* launched, it was in competition with another show, *Babylon 5*, that was also about human officers trying to keep the peace on a space station packed with a weird collection of scheming aliens. Fans of both shows accused their rival of copying them. It was, of course, possible to like both shows, and behind the scenes, there were plenty of links. Walter Koenig had a major recurring guest role in *Babylon 5*, Andreas Katsulas played a recurring Romulan admiral in *The Next Generation* and an alien ambassador in *Babylon 5*. Peter David, one of the more prominent *Star Trek* novelists, wrote *Babylon 5* scripts and novels, too. Majel

Barrett herself appeared in the third-season episode "Point of No Return" (1996), rather pointedly as the widow of an alien emperor. The press release *Babylon 5* put out was titled "The First Lady of *Star Trek* Makes A Royal Visit to BABYLON 5 The Week of February 26, 1996," and quoted the show's creator, J. Michael Straczynski:

> "We're very pleased to have Majel appearing on *Babylon 5*. Because as the wife of *Star Trek* creator Gene Roddenberry, her appearance on our show will help dispel the notion—held by some—that one cannot be a fan of both series. Majel and I discussed this between us, and we both view this rivalry as unproductive. We are both extending our hands across our respective fictional universes in a show of solidarity. So we're very happy that she has chosen to endorse *Babylon 5* in this way, and hope that science fiction viewers of all stripes will check out the series."

Most of Barrett's *Star Trek*-related activity, though, involved the running of Lincoln Enterprises. In the early Nineties, this still consisted of herself and "two or three" assistants. After something of a lull in the Eighties, with retailers remembering that tie-ins to *The Motion Picture* hadn't done well, the Nineties saw a massive surge in the quantity and range of *Star Trek* products. The market was flooded with items, from magazines that cost a few dollars to upscale replicas of the three-dimensional chess set, and limited edition plates. Pocket Books were issuing a *Star Trek* novel a month, and over twenty-six million were sold in total.[15]

There were multiple comics titles, the movies were reissued in different editions and as boxsets, there was plenty of apparel like hats and T-shirts. Toys and models of virtually every starship seen in the shows and movies appeared in a range of scales. The market sustained all of this, and if the release of new lines of action figures slowed down, it was simply because only the most obscure character variants—La Forge as Tarchannen III Alien, Sheriff Worf, Cadet Beverly Crusher—remained to be made.

Lincoln Enterprises had been the only game in town at the dawn of the *Star Trek* phenomenon, but now it was being left behind. Its boss was keen to expand. Asked in 1993 what role her company played, she said:

> "Since we have the only legal place in the world to buy *Trek* scripts I would say that they do want a lot of scripts. But everything varies. There's a lot of jewelry and the pins and the communicators and stuff that is worn; there's a lot of interest in patterns, for example. We sell patterns to the costumes so fans can make their own. There are places that make them, but they're terribly expensive and we've always kept our prices down way, way, way low because Gene felt as though he wanted everyone to be able to have them. So we've kept it way down. We really haven't geared ourselves in all these twenty-seven years toward a profit and we'd like to change that."[16]

The company had tended to produce its own items, now it began offering licensed *Star Trek* products bought from wholesalers. Aware it would be undercut by more traditional retailers on common items like books and action figures, the company began endorsing high-end prop and costume replicas. Their niche was, and remains, exclusive items, generally the sort of things that sell well at conventions, such as limited edition badges and posters, high-quality Starfleet uniforms, and screen-accurate Starfleet badges and other insignia. These days, products are carefully coordinated with Paramount, and the Roddenberry.com website offers everything from $5 Starfleet logo patches to a $500 replica tricorder made from the same mold as the ones from the TV show. The latter comes in a presentation box embossed with a replica of Gene Roddenberry's signature, rather than the *Star Trek* logo. The prime directive of the Roddenberry estate has been to protect the family name—it's trademarked, and Roddenberry.com is registered to them.

David Alexander's authorized biography of Gene Roddenberry, many years in the making, came out in 1994 but had to share a shelf with Joel Engel's far more salacious unauthorized biography. After Roddenberry's death, and as part of the general merchandising boom, virtually every member of the original series regular cast and a number of members of the production team wrote or co-wrote books about their time on the show. Some produced more than one, with William Shatner responsible for eight or nine titles examining aspects of the *Star Trek* phenomenon, including his own life story, but also *Get a Life!* (1999), a book about the business and culture of *Star Trek* conventions, and *I'm Working on That* (2002), about how scientists and engineers have been inspired by the show's technology. There have been a plethora of guidebooks and histories of the show, magazine interviews, and so on. A very common angle for this material has been to examine the truth of the Roddenberry myth. During his lifetime, the majority of *Star Trek* fans saw criticism of Roddenberry as ingratitude or sour grapes, but it's now widely accepted that there are places where Roddenberry's own account of events is guilty of error, oversimplification, and telling omissions. Three common threads run through what the cast and crew have to say when it comes to Gene Roddenberry, with a different emphasis depending on which particular ax they have to grind. The first is a level of thanks to Roddenberry for employing them and coming up with a format that has endured, and which was a smart show. The second is to note that *Star Trek* was a team effort, and Roddenberry doesn't deserve all the credit. The final thread is to note that the man himself could be rather troubled. The books all tend to set Roddenberry up as vitally important to *Star Trek*, but serve to "set the record straight."

Majel Barrett was one of only two major cast members who never wrote an autobiography or authorized someone else to write her life story. The other was DeForest Kelley, who played "Bones" McCoy, and who died in 1999. Majel had a firm opinion on the genre:

> On the emergence of "tell-all" biographies by members of the original series cast and crew, Roddenberry states, "I think they're awful." She points out that they contradict one another, and adds, "I was there!" . . . While she

doesn't believe that any of the books have tarnished Gene Roddenberry's reputation, she wants to know why the actors didn't voice any complaints while he was alive. "I just despise actors who think they've done it all themselves," she notes. "I don't have any bad experiences with any of them, but I really despise the way some of them have taken out after Gene. I'm not going to be doing that kind of thing—I think our private lives in the first place are our private lives, and I don't want to slam into anybody else because while I can refute things, I don't like to be negative. The accolades have already been there, and I'm busy going into the future myself right now with this project of Gene's."[17]

And what would Gene Roddenberry have thought?

"Gene would never have got mad at the naysayers. He never acted strongly to anything. He probably would have said 'let 'em go ahead and say what they want.' Of course, were he alive he would be able to get back at them with his own statements. But, then, most of the inaccuracies would never have been written or said because no one would have ever done it to his face. They all waited to attack until he was gone. I'm sure Gene would have said 'consider the source'."[18]

In 2006, Paramount's parent company Viacom split its movie and television divisions into two separate companies: Viacom (which owns Paramount Pictures) and CBS Corporation. *Star Trek*, referred to internally as "the

Franchise," was a major Viacom asset—and now Paramount Pictures have the rights to make *Star Trek* movies and, independently, CBS Television Studios have the rights to make *Star Trek* television shows. Paramount Pictures moved quickly to produce new *Star Trek* movies under the aegis of J.J. Abrams, and there have already been three: *Star Trek* (2009), *Star Trek Into Darkness* (2013), and *Star Trek Beyond* (2016). CBS are making *Star Trek: Discovery*. Initially, Bryan Fuller—known for the shows *Hannibal*, *Wonderfalls*, and *Dead Like Me*, but who wrote twenty-two episodes of *Deep Space Nine* and *Voyager* at the start of his career—was to serve as executive producer, but he stepped aside before filming started. CBS soon announced that Nicholas Meyer would be involved with the series again for the first time since *Star Trek VI*, a quarter of a century ago. History repeats itself: the plan is for this *Star Trek* to be the centerpiece of a new channel, this time on streaming video.

Gene Roddenberry's only substantial claim to fame is that he created *Star Trek*. Add to that the fact that the studio became so concerned with the way Roddenberry was running the show that they took it away from him, and handed it to a new executive producer, no less than three times—the original series, the movies, and *The Next Generation*—and the drumbeat from the various autobiographies and tell-alls builds until it sounds like a lot of the creative decisions were not made by Roddenberry, were even bitterly opposed by him. Much of the success of the show is the result of investment in their roles by William Shatner and Leonard Nimoy, Patrick Stewart, and other actors. Roddenberry didn't write the theme music, design the USS *Enterprise* or the costumes. He didn't invent the Borg or the Klingons. He never even wrote the line "Beam me up, Scotty," and when he attempted to come up with wording for the opening voiceover, his attempt was missing something: "This is the story of the United Space Ship *Enterprise*. Assigned a five-year patrol of our galaxy, the giant starship visits Earth colonies, regulates commerce and explores strange new worlds and civilizations. These are its voyages . . . and its adventures."[19]

In some ways Roddenberry is hoist by his own petard. Fans tend to love the idea that television has showrunners, that J. Michael Straczynski, Chris Carter, Joss Whedon, Aaron Sorkin, J.J. Abrams, David Simon, Nic Pizzolatto, or Russell T. Davies and Steven Moffat are bringing their personal vision to the screen by sheer force of their individual will, that anyone else with input in the process is an obstacle and compromises the final product. The core of the case Gene Roddenberry made for himself was that he was keenly and consistently a visionary, in a constant battle with "network executives" and "naysayers," and most imperfections in *Star Trek* are their fault.

At the heart of the case *against* Roddenberry is the idea he's a one-hit wonder, that he only ever came up with one show that worked, and that most of the best things about *Star Trek* are demonstrably the work of people who aren't Gene Roddenberry.

The obvious way to counter that would be to prove that Roddenberry had a wealth of other ideas and his problem was that he was ahead of his time, that *Star Trek* is merely one part of a "Roddenberry universe." Majel Barrett seems to have taken that literally—that *Questor*, *Genesis II*, and *Star Trek* were all part of what fans would call the same "continuity" or "canon"—saying, "everything is within Gene Roddenberry's universe . . . within *Star Trek*'s universe, like Questor was, like Planet Earth."[20] The phrasing is a little ambiguous, but in terms of the fiction, this could all fit together. In the twentieth century, operatives like Gary Seven (from *Assignment: Earth*), and Questor were working for advanced alien races invested in guiding the human race to the next level. In the twenty-first century, humanity was threatened by "genetically superior" humans like Khan from *Star Trek* and the Tyranians from *Genesis II*, and civilization fell. Organizations like PAX ensured that the best of humanity would survive and emerge from this dark, lawless time in the twenty-second century into a beautiful, garden-like Earth. Humanity had shed its old ways, and was primed to take to the stars and form a utopian United Federation of Planets, as seen in *Star Trek*'s twenty-third and twenty-fourth centuries.

Legally, the idea that all the Roddenberry shows are part of the same project was a minefield—the pilots for *Questor*, *Genesis II*, and *Planet Earth* were picked up and paid for by three different networks, and if any of them had an explicit story link with *Star Trek*, it would give grounds to Paramount to declare it just another *Star Trek* prequel. The Roddenberry estate wanted to be able to tout original Roddenberry intellectual property, say that there was a lot more to him than *Star Trek*, and they wanted to be able to sell things to lots of different media companies. Roddenberry's projects would share values like diversity, a commitment to a better future, an optimistic, humanist approach.

The Nineties saw an attempt to revive Roddenberry's project "The God Thing," with Michael Jan Friedman completing it. The book was advertised and a cover designed, but it has still not been published. The first product actually to appear was a comic book. *Gene Roddenberry's Lost Universe* ran for sixteen issues from 1995 to 1997. The eighth issue continued the story, but changed the title to *Gene Roddenberry's Xander in Lost Universe* and started with a new #1, a common tactic in the comics industry, as first issues tend to attract new readers, and collectors who treat comics as speculative investments. No one got rich investing in *Lost Universe*—twenty years on, it's easy to pick up a complete set for less than cover price. The publishers, Tekno-Comix, were a new venture seeking to make money from the comics boom of the early Nineties, and to take advantage of new computer technology in a way that seems quaintly incoherent these days:

> These comics, hand drawn and computer-colored will be available in print, on interactive CD-ROMs and comic videos. Fans will be able to communicate with the developers, see extracts from upcoming issues of the range (which includes Leonard Nimoy's PriMortals and Neil Gaiman's Mr Hero), and read their letters to the editors on the CD-ROMs.[21]

Their range consisted of titles that included famous names: as well as Roddenberry, Nimoy and Gaiman, those names included Isaac Asimov, Mickey Spillane, and Anne McCaffrey. The comics themselves were written by other people, so *Lost Universe* was written by Ron Fortier. Tekno-Comix arrived on the scene just in time for a crash in the comics market. It served the Roddenberry estate's purpose of getting a Gene Roddenberry property out into the world, but any hope that it would spark interest in a *Lost Universe* TV show or movie was quickly dashed. A novel of *Xander in Lost Universe* by John Peel (who'd written *Doctor Who* and *Star Trek* novels, among many others), was advertised, complete with cover image, but the book itself was never released.

Lost Universe starts with the *Deliverance*, a spaceship that looks somewhat like the USS *Enterprise*, arriving at the planet Malay, a large world settled by humans and by billions of alien refugees who have fled a galactic war in Andromeda. The ship has been sent by Plan*Net, an organization that is basically the Federation from *Star Trek*, but with an inverted Prime Directive—their First Command compels them to improve individuals, civilizations, and environments they encounter, strictly with the consent of the other party. Contact with Malay has been lost, and the *Deliverance* is to investigate. Our hero is Alexander Grange, a human native of Malay, who is shocked to learn that a great deal of time has mysteriously passed, and the once advanced world has degraded into isolated settlements menaced by weird creatures. Within a few issues, he discovers a body in a cave filled with alien machinery—and a capsule containing Alexander Grange, stored in suspended animation. The person we've been following is a clone, an artificial being with Grange's memories (the clone becomes known as Xander).

That certainly sounds like Gene Roddenberry had his hand in it. Various short interviews and features in the issues of *Lost Universe* explain some of the thinking behind the series, though they're a little reticent about exactly what Roddenberry created, when he developed the project, and how far he got with it. There looks to be a clue in the credits: initially, *Lost Universe* states it's "based on a concept created by Gene Roddenberry with additional character creation and development by Majel Barrett Roddenberry and story development by D.C. Fontana," but with #6 this switches to "Featuring Xander created by Gene Roddenberry." An interesting insight came from an interview with Majel Barrett right at the start of the process, when *Lost Universe* was called "Ranger":

> Gene thought up a bunch of characters for a television show . . . Ranger is the character . . . The character has been shifted around an awful lot since he put it together. [Dorothy Fontana] and I were in at the beginning of this phenomenon called *Star Trek*. If anybody in the world can write Gene Roddenberry she can.[22]

Lost Universe feels "Roddenberryesque," in the sense that elements of it are very similar to his work. The Black

Ghosts who show up are hooded figures like the Archons from the *Star Trek* episode "Return of the Archons," and there are secret immortals and ancient alien energy beings. There's a dash of Virtual Reality, in the form of a holographic recreation of memories, and the *Deliverance*'s computer can create a hologram to talk to the crew. It is, in other words, a mashup of various other Roddenberry projects—Questor as part of an Away Team from *Star Trek* exploring the world of *Genesis II*.

All the "lost" Roddenberry projects have a similar feel. One reason is that Roddenberry worked mainly in television, and television is episodic and formulaic. Another is that he returned to many of his ideas in different projects: before long, there's always going to be some wry outsider commenting on the human condition, some emergent artificial intelligence, savage mutants who are either bestial or superhumanly beautiful, and a confrontation with a godlike being that turns out to be a computer, conman, or child.

Mainly, though, the reason these "lost projects" feel a little like they're Roddenberry magnetic fridge poetry is that he left very few complete, honed television and movie treatments. There are no banks of unused pilot scripts.

Roddenberry had worked on ideas for TV shows and movies his whole career, coming up with most of them in the decade between the cancelation of the original *Star Trek* and the start of production of *Star Trek II*. He clearly oversaw substantial development work for *The Questor Tapes*, *Genesis II*, and the *Star Trek II* TV series. Those projects were commissioned by television networks; time and money was spent developing treatments and scripts (not all of which were written by Roddenberry). Pilot episodes were shot; documents laid out where Roddenberry saw the show going from there.

Elsewhere, though, when Roddenberry wrote down his ideas for series, they weren't much more than single-page summaries. The "pitch" for "Battleground Earth" was a single, half-page paragraph that outlined the setting and briefly explained the dynamic at the heart of the show. Aliens have arrived, and seized control by "taking over the minds" of the world's leaders. The show would have followed a group who resisted the state of docile slavery accepted by the rest of the human race. When it came to the characters, all Roddenberry said was that he wanted

> a group of mixed type story characters, not too unlike our seven *Star Trek* roles, perhaps each one a specialist and led by an unusual man. While being able to root for our characters as "good guys," we get the full dramatic spectrum of them being hunted as criminals, saboteurs, spies, revolutionaries, etc. etc. The series should see them begin to slowly, but very slowly, begin to win.

There was no substantial interest when Roddenberry came up with "Battleground Earth" in the Seventies, but it was picked up by the Canadian production company Tribune and ran for five seasons in first-run syndication from 1997. Renamed to avoid confusion with L. Ron Hubbard's 1982 novel *Battlefield Earth* (a movie version of which was in pre-production at the time), it was pitched as *Gene Roddenberry's Earth*, but was retitled *Gene Roddenberry's Earth: Final Conflict*.

Paul Gertz, one of the writers on the show, says Roddenberry's contribution was "written on a napkin in a lockbox full of obscure notes written on things like receipts, scraps of paper." The names of the characters, and the key idea that the aliens had saved humanity from hunger and disease, but at the cost of some basic freedoms, were added as the show was developed in the Nineties.

A list of nineteen questions has also been published that are said to be topics Roddenberry wanted to tackle in "Battleground Earth." None of them are specific to the project, and he asked many of them elsewhere (and, frankly, a few of them are so banal they have one-word, even yes/no answers). He, apparently carelessly, repeats one of the questions. If we're in a generous mood, these are the vital components of the human equation that Data tried to resolve. If we're feeling more cynical, then this is a list of what we might call Generic Roddenberry. Either way, the list is worth reprinting, as they are the core questions that Roddenberry dealt with, sooner or later, in all his projects:

How can we overcome prejudices? What is Death? Should we orchestrate war? Is patriotism a disease? What is the difference between sexuality and love? When does duty end and morality begin? Should there be government? Who's ethics pre-dominate in a relationship mine or yours? [sic] What does it mean to be human? Do machines live?

What use is religion? Is love the exclusive property of heterosexuals? Just because we can do something, should we? What is the difference between dreams and reality? What is consciences? [sic] Is there a case for drug dependency? What is the difference between male and female power? Are ethics the same as morals? What does it mean to be human?

In May 1999, Tribune announced that they were developing two more series based on Roddenberry's work, intended for first-run syndication: *Andromeda* and *Starship*. The latter was originally a novel, one that Roddenberry wrote "a few chapters" of around 1974.[23] The show itself was never produced, but was described in the original press release as follows:

A futuristic action hour in which a peaceful Earth is run by an organization of artists, scientists, and teachers working to bring harmony throughout the universe, *Gene Roddenberry's Starship* chronicles the exploration space vessel *Starship* that serves as home to a team of Galactic trouble-shooters led by Captain Dylan Hunt. After leaving Earth to study the far reaches of the universe, where a long and brutal territorial war between aliens takes place, Hunt and his crew discover worlds that are vastly different from the humanistic and civilized society they left behind.

Somewhere along the way, a lot of these ideas were folded into *Andromeda*, a series with a premise perhaps best summed up by the season two opening voiceover: "He is the last guardian of a fallen civilization, a hero from another time. Faced with a universe in chaos, Dylan Hunt recruits an unlikely crew and sets out to reunite the galaxies. On the starship *Andromeda* hope lives again."

The show was developed by Robert Hewitt Wolfe, who'd written for five seasons of *Star Trek: Deep Space Nine*. Dylan Hunt was of course the name of the protagonist of *Genesis II/Planet Earth*, and the show is essentially *Genesis II in Space*. The Tyranians are now the Nietzscheans, but still proud of their "genetic superiority." Hunt still has a teammate called Harper. Robert Hewitt Wolfe wasn't working from a pilot script or series bible written by Roddenberry, he was pulling together concepts from a number of undeveloped pitches, combining them into something new.

Majel Barrett was never dishonest with fans about how the process worked. She spelled it out: "We stole parts of *Starship* deliberately for *Andromeda*. We stole names, we stole titles. They were all Gene's, so it didn't matter. We'll be doing that probably until my deathbed. If something works with a particular story, let's use it here, and save this other element for another place."[24]

The star of *Andromeda* was Kevin Sorbo, who'd played Hercules in the very popular first-run syndicated show *Hercules: The Legendary Journeys* (1994–9). *Andromeda* was built around him, and he requested a show set in space. Wolfe obliged, even though that effectively ruled out Tribune making *Starship*. *Andromeda* ran for 110 episodes over five seasons (2000–5), and was the top-rated syndicated show of its time.

A year after Tribune's announcement, another company, Stan Lee Media, announced that *they* would make *Starship*, "based on a lost collection of Roddenberry's original notes and drawings recently discovered by his widow."[25] The project never materialized. The plan had been to produce "innovative interactive storytelling" (images and text features on a website) that would spark demand for an animated movie. When Majel Barrett was asked how this version of *Starship* was going, she conceded there had been substantial changes:

"The original idea was about a bunch of scientists, but that was when they were people—they're no longer people! We always end up with a captain and a crew, there will be in this case. But remember this: we only have one or two humanoids in it. We've got a bug for a lead! I really can't tell you a Starship plot summary because that particular part of it is changing daily. The last time I went to a meeting, Stan said, this is not really going to work with what we have in mind for over here, so the story hasn't been turned in yet."[26]

Majel Barrett died at home, at the age of seventy-six, on December 18, 2008, having been diagnosed with leukemia a few months before. She'd scaled back her convention appearances a little, but had attended an event in Las Vegas that August. Leonard Nimoy's tribute to her was not exactly overflowing with personal warmth: "She worked hard, she was straightforward, she was dedicated to *Star Trek* and Gene, and a lot of people thought very highly of her." Elsewhere, the loss of the "First Lady of *Star Trek*" was marked by many of the thousands of fans she'd met during thirty-five years on the *Star Trek* convention circuit sharing stories online of her generosity, and the time she'd taken to make them feel special. Her death was marked by reports and obituaries in all the major national newspapers.

Gene Roddenberry's elder daughter, Darleen Roddenberry-Bacha, was killed in a car crash in Las Vegas, almost four years to the day after her father died, on October 29, 1995. She was forty-seven, and had been married four times. The Roddenberry estate therefore went to Gene and Majel's only child, Eugene Wesley Roddenberry Jnr.

TMZ reported that Rod Roddenberry, as he prefers to be known, would inherit the Bel Air mansion, along with $6m, to be followed by additional payments of $10m at the ages of thirty-five, forty and forty-five (an age he will reach in February 2019). His total net worth is "over $100m" according to one estimate,[27] meaning the estate has more than trebled in value since his father's death, when Roddenberry was reported to have left $30m.[28] The most eyecatching headline, though, was that Majel Barrett left a $4m residential trust for her dogs, and $1m to "a domestic employee named Reinelda Estupinian" to look after them.[29]

Rod Roddenberry had been CEO of Roddenberry Entertainment since 2001.

The Roddenberry.com site continues, and pushes new projects like *Rod and Barry*, a running three-panel strip about a pair of aliens who are sent to Earth to scout it for invasion, but who fall in love with science fiction television and constantly delay their boss, Hu'Dec (after Majel Barrett's birth name). There's also the graphic novel series *Days Missing*, written by Phil Hester, about the Steward:

> Since the dawn of time, a being has existed whose inter-action and interference with mankind has shaped human development. His powers of time and intellect have allowed him to secretly remove certain critical days from the his-torical record. Their stories have never been told. Their details have never been documented. Their existence is not remembered. But the occurrences of these days have for-ever changed the course of humanity's evolution. These are the DAYS MISSING from our existence, and they are about to be revealed . . .[30]

In 2010, the *Hollywood Reporter* announced that Rod Roddenberry was working with Ron Howard and Imagine Television to develop *The Questor Tapes*, with Tim Minear, who had worked on *The X Files* and *Dollhouse*, as producer. Little has been heard since about this project.[31]

In January 2016, it was reported that data recovery spe-cialists DriveSavers had successfully read two hundred 5.25-inch floppy disks full of documents written by Gene Roddenberry using an early, customized word processing program. When Roddenberry died in 1991, the capacity of data storage was minuscule by today's standards. Added together, those disks only account for "two or three mega-bytes" of data. In the Eighties, Roddenberry had been aware how computer capacity was improving exponentially. *Star Trek: The Next Generation* futureproofed itself by expressing computer memory in terms of "gigaquads," without explaining how much data a "quad" was. Roddenberry's disks could contain the equivalent of about five hundred pages of text. As yet, we have no idea what was on those disks, and how much of it is previously unknown or unpublished material.[32]

Gene Roddenberry's son has ambitions to use the family name as more than a selling point for a few new television formats. His epiphany came when, in the course of making a documentary, *Trek Nation* (2011), he spoke to a number of people associated with *Star Trek* in its various incarnations. Rod was seventeen when his father died, and as he admitted, he never knew him all that well:

"[My father] was on such a pedestal that it was hard for me as his son to identify and connect with him. In fact, I never really got into and understood *Star Trek* until after he passed away in 1991, and as I witnessed the power of his thoughts and ideas as they lived on, I began to crave a deeper connection with him. I spent the years following his death slowly coming to understand not just *Star Trek*, but how far its ideologies had penetrated into society. All over the world, I spoke to fans, from politicians to religious leaders, doctors to teachers, astronauts to athletes, and everyone in between. They all believed in the *Star Trek* ideal of a future where humanity works together for the greater good."[33]

He found himself converting to the cause, and established the Roddenberry Foundation in 2010. The foundation

"honors Gene Roddenberry's legacy by funding game-changing discoveries that will make the world a better place. We genuinely want to work for the greater good of humanity and celebrate (not just tolerate) its full diversity. We want to support institutions doing cutting-edge work that will solve problems, not simply put Band-Aids on them. Our support focuses on four pillars: science/tech, environment, education, and humanitarianism . . . In the end, the Roddenberry name gives me access that I wouldn't otherwise have, and I'm using it to look for ways to further our foundation's mission. I've got a lot of learning, growing and evolving to do myself, but I'm doing what I can to bring about the world my dad envisioned."[34]

The foundation donated $5m to establish the Roddenberry Center for Stem Biology and Medicine at the J. David Gladstone Institutes in San Francisco. It supports a $10m prize to the first person or team to develop a real-life tricorder, defined as "a mobile platform that most accurately diagnoses a set of fifteen conditions across thirty consumers in three days. Teams must also deliver this information in a way that provides a compelling consumer experience while capturing real time, critical health metrics such as blood pressure, respiratory rate and temperature."[35]

On January 3, 2013, William Shatner received the following tweet from astronaut Chris Hadfield on the International Space Station: "Standard Orbit, Captain. And we're detecting signs of life on the surface." And when Leonard Nimoy died in 2015, the occasion was marked by a Vulcan salute from an astronaut on the space station, not to mention a personal statement from President Obama. The President was an acknowledged *Star Trek* fan who three years earlier had been pictured in the Oval Office sharing a Vulcan salute of his own with Lieutenant Uhura, Nichelle Nichols.

These are moments that speak to the cultural footprint of *Star Trek*, and any fair account of Gene Roddenberry's life has to embrace his role in establishing its iconic status. It is generally easy to be cynical about the world, and Roddenberry made cynicism about himself very easy. He wrote memos about Ferengi sex positions, popped a lot of pills and flopped around a paddling pool covered in baby oil with his secretary trying to simulate sex in zero gravity. Roddenberry also created something that has had a genuine, measurable inspirational effect on generations of people who strive to make the future a better place. As Majel Barrett put it, "I'm looking forward to a Gene Roddenberry world, a better, kinder, more gentle world. I don't think he believed that's the way it was going to be either, but suddenly we have enough people who are trying desperately to live in a world like that. And sooner or later maybe we'll all evolve into that."[36]

Roddenberry told Susan Sackett in the late Seventies, "I would like to write and create other things. I would hate to have just *Star Trek* on my tombstone." But—of course—very few people reading this book are doing so because they are fans of *The Lieutenant* or *Questor* and are wondering what else the creator of those shows got up to.

"Creator of *Star Trek*" is not a bad epitaph. A quarter of a century after Gene Roddenberry's death, we can say with confidence that *Star Trek* will still be running when the first astronauts set foot on Mars, and when we build a computer brain so advanced we'll need to establish whether it's alive.

About that tombstone, though . . .

The space shuttle *Columbia* took a portion of Gene Roddenberry's ashes into space in 1992 for the first ever space funeral (a short humanist service was performed and the remains were returned to Earth). A gram of his ashes was sent into orbit by the private company Celestis on April 12, 1997. A third sample, this time alongside a gram of Majel Barrett's ashes, was sent up in early 2009. Roddenberry's public social security records spell out the remarkable journey his life took:

Born: 19 August 1921, El Paso, Texas;

Died: 24 October 1991, Santa Monica, California;

Buried: 1997, outer space.

FURTHER READING

This is a not a comprehensive list of books about *Star Trek*. There have been hundreds of those, many of them excellent general accounts or guides. Nor is this a list of every source referred to in the book—please see the endnotes for that. The following are books that offer a particular insight into Roddenberry personally, usually by people who met and worked with him in some capacity.

Books by Gene Roddenberry

GENE RODDENBERRY never wrote an autobiography. He is credited as co-writer of *The Making of Star Trek* (1968, with Stephen E. Whitfield, Ballantine), the first *Star Trek* behind-the-scenes book, made while the second season was being produced. An essential source for early fandom, it was hugely influential on perceptions of the series and who made it.

Roddenberry wrote the novelization of *Star Trek: The Motion Picture* (1979, Pocket), his only published *Star Trek* prose fiction. It's an important book for offering a number of Roddenberry's insights into Earth society, and—because so many scenes are from his viewpoint—Kirk's psychology.

Roddenberry worked on a number of other novels, but only got a few chapters into each of them. In the mid-1970s he was working on *Starship*. There was the *Star Trek* novel *The God Thing* (based on an earlier idea for a movie). In the 1980s, he worked sporadically on *Report from Earth*. None of these have ever been published.

Biographies of Gene Roddenberry

Just after Roddenberry's death, James Van Hise wrote *Roddenberry: The Man Who Created Star Trek* (1992, Movie Publisher Services), a solid account of a man he characterized as "dedicated and idealistic." Two major biographies of Roddenberry were published in 1994. *Star Trek Creator: The Authorized Biography of Gene Roddenberry* by David Alexander (Roc) is the official version, with an introduction by Majel Barrett and full access to Roddenberry's papers. It is by no means a whitewash, admitting to the problems in his personal life and habit of exaggerating when he told an anecdote. *Gene Roddenberry: The Myth and the Man Behind Star Trek* by Joel Engel (Hyperion) is the same book after a bizarre transporter malfunction. As the cover copy puts it, "A man who dreamed up a utopian universe free of human frailties, Roddenberry himself was beset by many." This was the first systematic challenge to the "Roddenberry Myth" to appear in print, and Engel extensively interviewed people who were keen to redress the balance.

Yvonne Fern's *Gene Roddenberry: The Last Conversation* (1994, University of California) transcribes a long series of conversations between her and Roddenberry, with topics ranging from *Star Trek* minutiae to "big questions" about God and philosophy. Roddenberry was ill, and unguarded, and occasionally a little rambling. But it's an insight into Roddenberry's thinking and domestic arrangements at the end of his life.

Books by the Cast

WILLIAM SHATNER played Captain James T. Kirk in the original series. The 1979 biography *Shatner: Where No Man . . . The Authorized Biography of William Shatner*, by William Shatner, Sondra Marshak, and Myrna Culbreath (Ace Books), suffers from the narrative's constant effusive hero-worship of Shatner, which gets in the way of a neat account of a jobbing actor's life story.

Captain's Log: William Shatner's Personal Account of the Making of Star Trek V: The Final Frontier (1989, Pocket) was "as told by" his daughter Lisabeth Shatner. An account of the making of the *Star Trek* movie Shatner himself directed, it was published to coincide with the movie's release. Posterity has judged *Star Trek V* to be a failure, but the book is brimming with optimism and Shatner's own enthusiasm for the potential of *Star Trek*, ending on the note that a test screening "proved a vindication for all his efforts, hopes and dreams."

Since the 1990s, Shatner has co-written a number of books about aspects of the *Star Trek* phenomenon. *Star Trek Memories* (1993, HarperCollins) and *Star Trek Movie Memories* (1994, HarperCollins) were co-written with Chris Kreski. While inflected to Shatner's own experiences on the show, they're not the self-serving actor's memoirs we might cynically imagine them to be. Instead, there are extensive interviews with the cast and crew, including people who have rarely been interviewed elsewhere, like Ed Milkis. The books strive to be balanced, and people are highly critical of Shatner in places.

In a similar vein, *Get a Life!* (1999, Simon and Schuster), again co-written with Kreski, is a detailed study of *Star Trek* conventions—their history, their business model, who attends and why, and the experiences of actors and other guests.

I'm Working on That (2002, with Chip Walter, Pocket) is a survey of the technological progress made since, and inspired by, *Star Trek*. Discussion ranges from advances in computing and satellite technology to discussions on the likelihood that transporters will ever be invented.

Up Till Now (2008, with David Fisher, Thomas Dunne Books) is Shatner's autobiography, and while it covers his entire career, he obviously has a great deal to say about his time on *Star Trek*. His most recent book, *Leonard* (2016, with David Fisher, Thomas Dunne Books), is a tribute to Leonard Nimoy, a biography of the actor filled with many anecdotes from Shatner.

LEONARD NIMOY (1931–2015) played Mr. Spock. His 1975 autobiography *I Am Not Spock* (Celestial Arts) was followed twenty years later by a sequel, perhaps inevitably called *I Am Spock* (1995, Hyperion). Despite its title, in the first book Nimoy does not renounce the character, merely exploring the odd way he and Spock had become intertwined. The twenty years between the books saw the coming and going of the original series movies, while Nimoy grew to cherish the bond between himself and his character.

JAMES DOOHAN (Scotty, 1920–2005) wrote *Beam Me Up, Scotty: Star Trek's Scotty—In His Own Words* (1996, Pocket) with Peter David. Doohan was a friend of Roddenberry's, and was one of the first of the cast to embrace the *Star Trek* convention scene, but he felt the show left him underpaid and typecast.

WALTER KOENIG (Chekov) started writing *Chekov's Enterprise: A Personal Journal of the Making of Star Trek: The Motion Picture* (1980, Pocket) because he had so little to do on the set of that movie. It's an actor's eye view of production that provides a lot of insight into the process. His autobiography *Warped Factors: A Neurotic's Guide to the Universe* (1997, Taylor Pub) charts his issues with anxiety, and how it affected his life and career.

NICHELLE NICHOLS (Uhura) wrote *Beyond Uhura: Star Trek and Other Memories* (1994, Putnam). A mistress, then lifelong friend of Roddenberry, Nichols has also been one of the main advocates for *Star Trek*'s message of progress and diversity—she has long been involved in public engagement roles with NASA on the subject.

GEORGE TAKEI (Sulu) *To the Stars: The Autobiography of George Takei, Star Trek's Mr Sulu* (1994, Pocket) tells how he was interred in a camp by the US government at the start of World War II, along with tens of thousands of other Americans of Japanese descent. It charts his career in Los Angeles local politics. His role in *Star Trek* constantly promises more than it delivers.

GRACE LEE WHITNEY (Janice Rand, 1930–2015) Her book, *The Longest Trek: My Tour of the Galaxy* (1998, Quill Driver) cataloged a story of an acting career devastated by sexual abuse and substance dependency. In the Eighties, Whitney sobered up, discovered a deep Christian faith and moved to a rural life with her family. She worked for decades counseling other alcoholics and addicts, right until her death in 2015, a month after her eighty-fifth birthday. She remained good friends with Nimoy throughout, and he wrote the introduction to her autobiography.

There are two important cast members who never wrote an autobiography:

DEFOREST KELLEY (1920–99) played Dr. "Bones" McCoy in the original series. Terry Lee Rioux's *From Sawdust to Stardust: The Biography of DeForest Kelley, Star Trek's Dr. McCoy* (2005, Pocket) helps fill that gap.

Gene Roddenberry's second wife, MAJEL BARRETT (1932–2008), is a major figure in *Star Trek*—onscreen she was Number One in the original pilot, Christine Chapel in the original series, Lwaxana Troi in *Star Trek: The Next Generation*, and the voice of the *Enterprise* (and later other Starfleet) computers from the original series until the first "reboot" movie in 2009. She also ran Lincoln Enterprises from when it was set up, and managed the Roddenberry estate after her husband's death.

Crew Biographies

SUSAN SACKETT was Gene Roddenberry's secretary from 1974 until his death. She was also his mistress for almost all of that time. Her book, *Inside Trek: My Secret Life with Star Trek Creator Gene Roddenberry* (2002, Hawk), offers a unique perspective on both Roddenberry at work and the man himself. It is intimate to a fault, a vivid "tell all" that displays deep affection for Roddenberry while exposing some extremely private, and often deeply unflattering, moments. Sackett had previously written *Letters to Star Trek* (1977, Ballantine), which as the name suggests collates examples of fan mail. In many cases, we also see Gene Roddenberry's personal replies, and Sackett provides other examples of Roddenberry addressing the questions by quoting from lectures and articles he wrote.

NICHOLAS MEYER wrote, directed, and otherwise guided the *Star Trek* movies from *The Wrath of Khan* to *The Undiscovered Country*. He has been named as part of the production team in the 2017 *Star Trek* television series. His book *The View from the Bridge* (2009, Viking Adult) concentrates on his *Star Trek* work and offers many insights into the making of his movies—including just how peripheral Gene Roddenberry was to the process.

ROGER VADIM directed *Pretty Maids All in a Row* (1971), a movie written and produced by Roddenberry, based on Francis Pollini's 1969 novel of the same name. Vadim writes briefly about the making of the movie in his 1976 book *Memoirs of the Devil* (Harcourt Brace Jovanovich). He doesn't mention Roddenberry by name, but offers insights into the Hollywood studio culture of the time.

Histories of Star Trek

David Gerrold's *World of Star Trek* (Ballantine) was originally published in 1973. It's an early account of the *Star Trek* phenomenon, and makes an attempt to explain the appeal of the show. Along with *The Making of Star Trek*, it's a book that became a cornerstone of the standard account of the show. Gerrold, writer of the original series episode "The Trouble with Tribbles," has consistently served as a defender of Roddenberry's vision of *Star Trek*, but has also chronicled where he feels Roddenberry and the studio have failed to live up to those ideals.

James Van Hise wrote *The Unauthorized History of Trek* (1991, Movie Publisher Services), a paperback volume that's a good introduction and overview to the series for the time. *The Radio Times Official Collector's Edition Star Trek 30 Years* (1996), a one-off magazine with an impressive array of interviews, was released five years after Roddenberry's death, and within its pages a reassessment of the man and his legacy is clearly underway.

Star Trek: The Complete Unauthorized History (2012, Voyageur) by Robert Greenberger is a comprehensive history of the franchise, and a masterful synthesis of the vast amount of information that's now available. Twenty years after Roddenberry's death, it was accepted that *Star Trek*'s creator was an imperfect individual.

Production Histories

Inside Star Trek: The Real Story (1996, Pocket) is a major work. Written by two key figures on the original series, Herbert F. Solow (executive in charge of production) and Robert H. Justman (co-producer), it's a lavish history of their involvement, complete with reproductions of memos, sketches, and other material from the studio. It's a nuts-and-bolts discussion of the logistics of making the show, but full of personal recollections and discussions of the personalities and politics. Its stated aim is to show that *Star Trek* did not spring fully formed from the head of Gene Roddenberry.

These Are the Voyages (2013–14, Jacobs Brown Press) by Marc Cushman with Susan Osborn is a 2,000-page production history of the original series, split into three volumes, one for each season. It's an immense work, taking in a vast amount of archival resources, interview material, and original research. Other fans have picked away at some of the claims and conclusions of the book (startrekfactcheck. blogspot.com is a good counterbalance), but these books are the current state-of-the-art in *Star Trek* scholarship.

In a similar vein, *Return to Tomorrow: The Filming of Star Trek: The Motion Picture* (2014, Creature Features) by Preston Neal Jones is a 672-page oral history of the making of the first *Star Trek* movie that has a comprehensive set of candid contemporary interviews with almost every conceivable member of the cast and crew (including Gene Roddenberry and director Robert Wise). It's cleverly organized, allowing us a bird's eye view of the production unavailable even to anyone working on the movie at the time.

Star Trek: The Next Generation—The Continuing Mission (1997, Pocket) by Judith and Garfield Reeves-Stevens is an official history of the sequel show, including the decision to make it "first run syndication."

Keys to the Kingdom (2000, William Morrow) by Kim Masters is a book about Michael Eisner, head of Disney and a major Hollywood power player. There's an extensive description of his involvement in the early *Star Trek* movies. This isn't a book "about *Star Trek*" or aimed at *Star Trek* fans, so it offers a perspective that's more hard-headed and businesslike than most accounts.

NBC: America's Network (2007, edited by Michele Hilmes, University of California Press) is an academic work including an article by Maire Messenger Davies and Roberta Pearson that studies the relationship between the NBC network and *Star Trek*.

Conventions and Fan Culture

Star Trek Lives! (1975, Bantam) is a book-length, occasionally rather breathless exploration of the *Star Trek* phenomenon. It was written by three fans, Jacqueline Lichtenberg, Sondra Marshak, and Joan Winston. Two years later, Joan Winston wrote *The Making of the Trek Conventions: Or How to Throw a Party for 12,000 of Your Most Intimate Friends* (1977, Doubleday), a first-hand, richly detailed account of the practicalities and rewards of running a *Star Trek* convention.

BJO TRIMBLE was an important early fan of the show. Her 1982 book *On the Good Ship Enterprise: My 15 Years With Star Trek* (Starblaze) is a detailed anecdotal account of her involvement with *Star Trek*.

Related Works

The Questor Tapes (1974, Ballantine), D.C. Fontana's novelization of the Questor pilot episode, starts with a dedication to Gene L. Coon. The book works in details that weren't seen on screen.

NOTES

Introduction

1 Shatner and Kreski, *Movie Memories*, p394
2 "In Step With … William Shatner", *Parade*, June 2008
3 Hilmes (ed.), *NBC: America's Network*, p219
4 The pilot episode was made under the title "The Menagerie." Halfway through the first season of *Star Trek*, much of the footage of the pilot was used in a two-part flashback episode, also called "The Menagerie." The pilot's title was retroactively changed to "The Cage" to avoid confusion with these episodes.

1 Earning his Stripes

1 Alexander, *Creator*, p55
2 Alexander, *Creator*, p60
3 Alexander, *Creator*, pp77–8
4 http://www.check-six.com/Crash_Sites/ClipperEclipse-NC88845.htm
5 Alexander, *Creator*, p92
6 https://en.wikipedia.org/wiki/Space_Patrol_(1950_TV_series)
7 Fern, *Conversation*, p33: "At one time it was considered that my natural future was to become chief of police."
8 Alexander, *Creator*, p136
9 Alexander, *Creator*, pp186–7
10 Engel, *Myth*, p24
11 Engel, *Myth*, p22
12 Van Hise, *Roddenberry*, p33

13 Cushman, *Voyages* 1, p20

14 Quoted in Cushman, *Voyages* 1, p19

15 Shatner, *Captain's Log*, pp27–8

16 Roddenberry and Whitfield, *Making*, pp21–2

17 Engel, *Myth*, p28. Felton: "it was this story that lost us the cooperation of the Pentagon."

18 Van Hise, *Roddenberry, p33*

19 Van Hise, *Roddenberry, p33*

20 Alexander, *Creator*, p187

21 Koenig, *Warped*, p147

2 Show Me Some More of this Earth Thing Called Kissing

1 Roddenberry and Whitfield, *Making*, p360

2 Roddenberry and Whitfield, *Making*, p360

3 Trimble, *Enterprise*, p16

4 "Vadim's Pretty Maids," *Playboy*, April 1971, p214

5 Whitney, *Longest*, p77

6 Whitney, *Longest*, p133

7 *Inside Star Trek* (LP)

8 Sackett, *Letters*, pp160–1

9 Shatner, *Leonard*, p66

10 http://www.startrek.com/article/grace-lee-whitney-on-trek-life-part-i

11 Cushman, *Voyages* 1, p308

12 Shatner, *Memories*, p209

13 Whitney, *Longest Trek*, p102

14 Whitney, *Longest Trek*, p14

15 Whitney, *Longest Trek*, p15

16 Whitney, *Longest Trek*, p73

17 Whitney, *Longest Trek*, p1

18 Whitney, *Longest Trek*, p9

19 Cushman, *Voyages* 1, p308

20 Shatner, *Memories*, p210

21 www.startrek.com/article/grace-lee-whitney-on-trek-life-2

22 There's been a degree of skepticism from some fans about this anecdote, which seems far too good to be true. http://spinoff.comicbookresources.com/2013/03/20/tv-legends-revealed-mlk-kept-nichols-from-quitting-star-trek/ allays those suspicions by pinning down exactly which event Nichols would have attended.

23 Solow and Justman, *Inside Star Trek*, p75

24 Whitney, *Longest Trek*, p73

25 Sackett, *Inside Trek*, p84

26 Roddenberry and Whitfield, *Making*, p360

27 Cushman, *Voyages 2*, p171

28 Alexander, *Creator*, p114

29 Solow and Justman, *Inside Star Trek*, p75

30 Shatner, *Memories*, p14

31 Nichols, *Beyond Uhura*, p132

32 Nichols, *Beyond Uhura*, p129

33 Nichols, *Beyond Uhura*, p126

34 Fern, *Last Conversation*, p91

35 Fern, *Last Conversation*, p101

36 Sackett, *Inside Trek*, p18

37 Sackett, *Inside Trek*, p143

38 Sackett, *Inside Trek*, p67

39 Sackett, *Inside Trek*, p68

40 Roddenberry, *Motion Picture*, p32

41 *Cinefantastique*, vol. 23, #2/3, pp60–1

42 The story was reworked into *The Way to Eden*, which had the same plot but without any reference to McCoy's daughter.

43 Fern, *Last Conversation*, pp100–1

44 Roddenberry, *Motion Picture*, p22

45 Roddenberry, *Motion Picture*, p32

46 Roddenberry, *Motion Picture*, p5

47 Sackett, *Inside Trek*, p216

48 Fern, *Last Conversation*, p99

3 Created By . . .

1 Roddenberry, *Motion Picture*, first US edition (1979)

2 Fern, *Last Conversation*, dustjacket copy

3 http://peteranthonyholder.com/cjad26.htm. *Star Trek* can be a small world— Solow would marry Yvonne Fern, author of *The Last Conversation*, in the early nineties, and they were interviewed together here.

4 Fern, *Last Conversation*, p50

5 Meyer, *Bridge*, p215

6 Solow and Justman, *Inside Star Trek*, p136

7 Solow and Justman, *Inside Star Trek*, p136

8 Gerrold, *World*, p165 quotes Bjo Trimble as saying, "We made up a mailing list from the fan mail and the letter writing campaign and that was the list we used when we sent out the first catalogs."

9 Solow and Justman, *Inside Star Trek*, p401

10 Court, pp7–8

11 Thomas Vinciguerra, "There Are No Small Parts, Only Long Memories," *New York Times*, October 8, 2006. As the article notes, Winston had recently begun to attend events, and did make an appearance in a fan film.

12 Shatner, *Leonard*, pp140–1

13 Shatner, *Get a Life*, p9. Bjo Trimble sounds a note of caution, saying (*Enterprise*, p18) this went to some guests' heads: "Fan clubs sprang up like dandelions around each of the actors, glorifying them to such a degree that a few of them got rather overblown ideas of their own importance, thereby perpetuating the *Star Trek* hero worship that was starting to grow."

14 http://peteranthonyholder.com/cjad26.htm

15 Shatner, *Memories*, p156

16 Gerrold, *World*, p208

17 For various reasons the episodes weren't always shown in the order they were shot. This was often simply because it took longer to complete episodes with a lot of special effects. The first to be filmed, "The Corbomite Maneuver," was the eighth to be shown, because the script called for a number of complex model shots.

18 Some reports have slight variations on these numbers (it's often cited that Norway has 30 percent and Shatner 15 percent, for example) and some deals were renegotiated over the years.

19 http://peteranthonyholder.com/cjad26.htm

20 You may remember it as the episode that establishes that Vulcans only mate every seven years, but you'd be wrong. "Amok Time" doesn't specify "seven years." That detail of Mr. Spock's sex life was first revealed in Roddenberry and Whitfield's *The Making of Star Trek* (p227), published a year later, but being written while the second season was in production. It took the information from a line in the draft script for "Amok Time" that was edited out. Droxine knows Vulcans only mate every seven years in the third-season episode "The Cloud Minders," but only because writer Margaret Armen gleaned the information from *The Making of Star Trek*.

21 *Inside Star Trek* LP

22 The day of the handover, the *Star Trek* production team were recording the episode "Mirror, Mirror," the one with the parallel universe of evil twins and Mr. Spock with a beard.

23 Solow and Justman, *Inside Star Trek*, p349

24 "How Much Money Has *Star Trek* Franchise Made?", *All Things Considered*, NPR, May 15, 2009. In Hilmes, (p218), Solow asks "Who knew the property would gross near \$3bn?"

25 Trimble, *Enterprise*, p25. One oddity is that Trimble says "When we got home, I wrote up a preliminary contact letter" and the book reprints "an exact copy of that letter." The letter is dated December 1, 1967. "The Deadly Years" was recorded at the beginning of August, and was *broadcast* December 8. *Get A Life!* (pp42–3) restates that it was "The Deadly Years."

26 http://peteranthonyholder.com/cjad26.htm

27 Gerrold, *World*, p167. Gerrold might, of course, be referring to a different issue of *TV Guide*.

28 "Star Trekkers Are Restored," *Hartford Courant*, March 17, 1968

29 Hilmes, *NBC*, p218

30 Trimble, *Enterprise*, p36

31 http://www.startrek.com/article/bjo-trimble-the-woman-who-saved-star-trek-part-1: "So we called Gene Roddenberry to see if he was OK with this idea."

32 http://www.startrek.com/article/bjo-trimble-the-woman-who-saved-star-trek-part-1#sthash.mNE7PZ56.dpuf

33 Trimble, *Enterprise*, p35

34 Trimble, *Enterprise*, p28

35 Gerrold, *World*, p263

36 Trimble, *Enterprise*, p36

37 http://www.gmsr.com/writing/Roddenberry%20v%20Roddenberry%20AOB.pdf. \$1,000 in 1969 would be worth about \$6,700 today, \$1,000 in 1972 about \$5,700.

4 Syndication as Vindication

1 Hilmes, *NBC*, p212

2 Cushman, *Voyages* 1, p614

3 Appellants' Opening Brief, Roddenberry v Roddenberry (1996—Court of Appeal, State of California, 2nd Civil No. B074848), pp4–5

4 http://www.tvobscurities.com/2008/12/star-trek-syndication-advertisements-circa-1969-1970/

5 http://news.google.com/newspapers?id=9y9JAAAAIBAJ&sjid=KYQMAAAAIBAJ&dq=star-trek%20convention%20new-york&pg=861%2C5406685

6 Gerrold, *World*, p187

7 Shatner, *Memories*, p297

8 Appellants' Opening Brief, Roddenberry v Roddenberry (1996—Court of Appeal, State of California, 2nd Civil No. B074848), pp4–5

9   http://startrekfactcheck.blogspot.com/2014/07/the-truth-about-star-trek-and-ratings.html

10   Shatner, *Captain's Log*, p28

11   Shatner, *Captain's Log*, pp41–2. Calculating exactly how many people watched *Star Trek* the first time around, and hence how the show was performing, involves not only a command of the byzantine systems used by various agencies and networks, but also careful interpretation and understanding of context. It was a job for specialists at the time, and anyone using the partial data we can work from now runs a serious risk of failing to take into account a crucial factor, or generalizing from one data point. Harve Bennett's "fifteen, fourteen, ten" cuts the long story short, and indicates the problem *Star Trek* faced: the first season got about fifteen million viewers, the second saw a slight drop to fourteen million, the change in scheduling saw (as everyone knew it would) a dramatic fall, to ten million.

12   Gerrold, *World*, p178

13   Gerrold, *World*, p167, Trimble, *Enterprise*, p32

14   http://www.erbzine.com/mag0/0038.html

15   Appellants' Opening Brief, Roddenberry v Roddenberry (1996—Court of Appeal, State of California, 2nd Civil No. B074848), p1

16   *People*, March 16, 1987

17   Alexander, *Creator*, p372

18   Pollini, *Maids*, p113

19   Alexander, *Creator*, p386

20   "Vadim's Pretty Maids," *Playboy*, April 1971, p214

21   The complete list (in alphabetical order): *Apocalypse Now, The Bad News Bears, Carrie, Dazed and Confused, The Good, The Bad and the Ugly, The Great Escape, His Girl Friday, Jaws, Pretty Maids All in a Row, Rolling Thunder, Sorcerer, Taxi Driver.*

22   Vadim, *Memoirs*, p182

23   Vadim, *Memoirs*, p184

24   Alexander, *Creator*, p381

25   David Bret, *Rock Hudson: The Gentle Giant*

26   Alexander, *Creator*, p389

27   Vadim, *Memoirs*, p185

28   "Vadim's Pretty Maids," *Playboy*, p214

29   Alexander, *Creator*, p389

30   Alexander, *Creator*, pp388–90

5 Gene Roddenberry's Lost Universes

1 Solow and Justman, *Inside Star Trek*, pp416–17
2 Richard K. Shull, "Creator of *Star Trek* comes back to TV," *Des Moines Register*, November 26, 1972
3 Shull, "Creator"
4 Solow and Justman, *Inside Star Trek*, p421
5 Engel, *Myth*, pp150–1
6 "Drawn to the Final Frontier: The Making of *Star Trek: The Animated Series*", documentary feature on the DVD boxset
7 Shatner, *Up Till Now*, p171
8 Koenig, *Warped Factors*, p216
9 Sackett, *Inside Trek*, pp11–12
10 Gerrold, *World*, p270
11 Alexander, *Creator*, p394
12 Gerrold, *World*, p271
13 Fern, *Conversation*, p34
14 Gerrold, *World*, p271
15 Interview with Allen Asherman in the *Star Trek Interview Book* (1986)
16 *Inside Star Trek* LP
17 *Inside Star Trek* LP
18 Address at Florida State University, January 23, 1975
19 *Starlog*, Jan 1980, p24
20 Nimoy, *I Am Spock*, pp136–8
21 Nimoy, *I Am Spock*, p157
22 Alexander, *Creator*, pp397–8
23 *Starlog*, Jan 1980, p24
24 Sackett, *Inside Trek*, p43

6 Fan-Topia

1 Hilmes, *NBC*, p218
2 Gerrold, *World*, p188
3 http://culttvman.com/main/a-history-of-the-amt-enterpise-model-by-jay-chladek-part-1/
4 Lichtenberg, *Lives!*, p3
5 Gerrold, *World*, p195
6 Trimble, *Enterprise*, p63
7 Gerrold, *World*, p160
8 Gerrold, *World*, p174

9   Nimoy, *I Am Not Spock*, p17

10   Nimoy, *I Am Not Spock*, p63

11   Fern, *Conversation*, p63

12   *Late Night America*, September 24, 1985

13   Fern *Conversation*, p69

14   Engel, *Myth*

15   Shatner, *Leonard*, pp120–1

16   Fern, *Conversation*, p106

17   Fern, *Conversation*, p156

18   Fern, *Conversation*, p76

19   Gerrold, *World*, p177

20   Lichtenberg, *Lives!*, p222

21   *New Voyages*, p ix

22   Lichtenberg, *Lives!*, p225

23   Gerrold, *World*, p200

24   Engel, *Myth*, p249

25   Fern, *Conversation*

26   Roddenberry, *Motion Picture*, p22

27   *New Voyages*, Introduction

28   Shatner, *Where No Man*, p12

29   Brin, "Star Wars despots vs. *Star Trek* populists," *Salon*, June 15, 1999

30   Lichtenberg, *Lives!*, pp144–5

31   *Entertainment Weekly*, April 8, 1994

32   Gerrold, *World*

33   Quoted on the NASA website—http://er.jsc.nasa.gov/seh/quotes.html

7 Bigger than *Star Wars*

1   Shatner, *Movie Memories*, p87

2   Roddenberry was so keen on this numbering system that when he pitched a second *Star Trek* movie to Paramount in 1980, he called it *Star Trek IV*—I being the original series, II the revival, III *Star Trek: The Motion Picture*.

3   Nimoy, *I Am Spock*, p157

4   Shatner, *Leonard*, p123

5   Jones, *Return to Tomorrow*, p55

6   Jones, *Return to Tomorrow*, p55

7   Nimoy, *I Am Spock*, p162

8   Shatner, *Movie Memories*, p92

9 Sackett, *Inside Trek*, p71

10 Shatner, *Movie Memories*, p100

11 Jones, *Return to Tomorrow*, p143

12 Jones, *Return to Tomorrow*, p317

13 Doohan, *Beam Me Up*, p189

14 Shatner, *Movie Memories*, p 112

15 Jones, *Return to Tomorrow*, p169

16 Nichols, *Beyond Uhura*, p240

17 *Starlog* 32, p58

18 Jones, *Return to Tomorrow*

19 Sackett, *Inside Trek*, p64

20 Sackett, *Inside Trek*, p75

21 Roddenberry, *Motion Picture*, p8

22 Sackett, *Inside Trek*, p76

23 http://boxofficemojo.com/movies/?id=startrek.htm

24 *Playboy*, January 1980, p310. The presentation was given in spring 1979.

8 The Best of Times, the Worst of Times

1 Engel, *Myth*, p206

2 Engel, *Myth*, p206

3 Meyer, *View from the Bridge*, p82

4 Meyer, *View from the Bridge*, pp90–1

5 Shatner, *Movie Memories*, p150

6 Meyer, *View from the Bridge*, p213

7 Shatner, *Movie Memories*, p140

8 Meyer, *View from the Bridge*, p81

9 Greenberger, p118

10 Aljean Harmetz, "New *Star Trek* Plan Reflects Symbiosis of TV and Movies," *New York Times*, November 2, 1986

11 Shatner, *Leonard*, p216

12 Alexander, *Creator*, p461

13 Appellants' Opening Brief, Roddenberry v Roddenberry (1996—Court of Appeal, State of California, 2nd Civil No. B074848), p45

14 Alexander, *Creator*, p466

15 *Starlog*, Nov 1985, "Inside Gene Roddenberry's Head"

16 *Starlog*, Nov 85, p18

17 *Starlog*, Nov 85, p20

18 *Starlog*, Nov 85, p20

19 Sackett, *Inside Trek*, p95
20 http://monsterkidclassichorrorforum.yuku.com/topic/20784/
    Majel-Barrett-wife-of-Gene-Roddenberry

9 Second Chances

1   Aljean Harmetz, "New *Star Trek* Plan Reflects Symbiosis of TV and Movies,"
    New York Times, November 2, 1986
2   Harmetz, "New *Star Trek* Plan"
3   "Leonard Nimoy—Preparing Star Trek IV," *Starlog* 100, Nov 1985, p55
4   Sackett, *Inside Trek*, p129
5   *Chaos on the Bridge* documentary, 2014
6   Sackett, *Inside Trek*, p139
7   Sackett, *Inside Trek*, p128. La Costa is named in, e.g., *Chaos on the Bridge*
8   *TNG* Guidelines, p3
9   *TNG* Guidelines, p15
10 Gerrold, *World*, p242
11 http://io9.gizmodo.com/a-new-documentary-shows-how-gene-
    roddenberry-almost-kil-1721153875
12 "Star Trek: TNG: An Oral History," Adam By Vary, *Entertainment Weekly*,
    September 25, 2007
13 Sackett, *Inside Trek*, p133
14 *Chaos on the Bridge*
15 *Chaos on the Bridge*
16 Hilmes, *NBC*, p222
17 Sackett, *Inside Trek*, p138
18 *Art of Star Trek*, p94
19 *Chaos on the Bridge*
20 Engel, *Myth*
21 *Chaos on the Bridge*
22 http://www.startrek.com/article/trek-writer-david-gerrold-looks-back-part-2
23 *Chaos on the Bridge*
24 Sackett, *Inside Trek*, p141
25 Sackett, *Inside Trek*, p155
26 *Starlog* 152, p29
27 *Chaos on the Bridge*
28 Tulloch and Jenkins, *Science Fiction Audiences*, 1995
29 Sackett, *Inside Trek*, p154
30 Sackett, *Inside Trek*, pp157–9

10 Of All the Souls I Have Encountered in My Travels, His Was the Most . . .

1 Appellants' Opening Brief, Roddenberry v Roddenberry (1996—Court of Appeal, State of California, 2nd Civil No. B074848)

2 Sackett, *Inside Trek*, p216

3 "California's appellate court has overturned a jury's decision to order the estate of *Star Trek* creator Gene Roddenberry to pay his first wife, Eileen, more than $4 million in damages," *Broadcasting and Cable*, April 22, 1996

4 Engel, *Myth*, p262

5 Sackett, *Inside Trek*, p219

6 "Roddenberry Heir's Losing Enterprise . . .," *Daily News*, June 29, 1996

7 http://www.tvshowsondvd.com/articles/dg3.cfmhow.

8 *Entertainment Weekly*, March 6, 1992

9 Sackett, *Inside Trek*, p212

10 Michael Logan, "Keeping the Flame," *Radio Times Official Collector's Edition Star Trek 30 Years*

11 Logan, "Keeping the Flame"

12 Fern, *Conversation*, p165

13 Interview by Carol Davis in *Imzadi, The Official Marina Sirtis Newsletter*, Jan/Feb 1991

14 Interview with John C. Snider at Sci-Fi Dimensions, June 3, 2000

15 Fern, *Conversation*, p215

16 Jo Davidsmeyer, "Lincoln Enterprises: A Little Piece of *Star Trek*. An interview with the ~First Lady of *Star Trek*,~ Majel Barrett-Roddenberry," *Strange New Worlds* 10, Oct/Nov 1993

17 Michelle Erica Green, *First Lady of* Star Trek: *Majel Barrett Roddenberry's Life Among the Aliens*

18 Michael Logan, "The Great Bird of the Galaxy," *Radio Times Official Collector's Edition Star Trek 30 Years*

19 Reprinted in Solow and Justman, *Inside*, p145. Justman claims (p149) that William Shatner's delivery of the final version sounds breathless because the wording was finalized so late in the day that in order to get it onto the titles of the first episode, he had to run from the soundstage where he was filming the episode "Dagger of the Mind" over to the dubbing studio.

20 "Part of the Legacy: An Interview with Majel Barrett Roddenberry," Ali Kayn, http://www.festivale.info/ffeatures/majel.htm

21 "Part of the Legacy"

22 "Part of the Legacy"

23 Sackett, *Inside Trek*, p13

24 http://www.littlereview.com/getcritical/trektalk/majel3.htm

25 Christian, "Stan Lee Media Developing 'Gene Roddenberry's Starship',"
    http://www.trektoday.com/news/180900_04.shtml, September 18, 2000

26 http://findarticles.com/p/articles/mi_m0EIN/is_1998_Oct_20/ai_53099756/

27 http://www.boldergiving.org/stories.php?story=Rod-Roddenberry

28 Engel, *Myth*, p262

29 http://www.tmz.com/2009/04/22/
    star-trek-widows-trust-for-the-dogs/#ixzz431DfSrD3

30 https://shop.roddenberry.com/collections/bundle-items/products/
    days-missing-volume-1?variant=12725804806

31 James Hibberd, "Gene Roddenberry pilot gets a Deal," *Hollywood Reporter*,
    January 21, 2010

32 http://www.geek.com/news/data-from-200-floppy-discs-containing-
    unpublished-gene-roddenberry-works-recovered-1643990/

33 http://www.boldergiving.org/stories.php?story=Rod-Roddenberry

34 http://tricorder.xprize.org

35 "Brainscan", *Lost Universe* #1

EPISODES QUOTED

The Lieutenant

"To Set It Right" (Writer: Lee Erwin, Director: Vince McEveety)

"Pretty Maids All in a Row" (Screenplay: Gene Roddenberry)

Star Trek

"The Cage" (Written by: Gene Roddenberry, Director: Robert Butler)

"Balance of Terror" (Written by: Paul Schneider, Director: Vincent McEveety)

"Is There In Truth No Beauty?" (Written by: Jean Lisette Arbeste, Director:
    Ralph Senensky)

"The Savage Curtain" (Teleplay by: Arthur Heinemann and Gene
    Roddenberry, Story by: Gene Roddenberry, Director: Herschel Daugherty)

"The Way to Eden" (Teleplay by: Arthur Heinemann, Story by: Michael
    Richards and Arthur Heinemann, Director: David Alexander)

Star Trek: The Next Generation

"Encounter at Farpoint" (Written by: DC Fontana and Gene Roddenberry,
    Director: Corey Allen)

"Manhunt" (Written by 'Terry Devereaux'—pseudonym for Tracy Torme,
    Director: Rob Bowman)

"Star Trek: First Contact" (Screenplay by: Brannon Braga & Ronald D Moore,
    Story by: Rick Berman & Brannon Braga & Ronald D Moore, Director:
    Jonathan Frakes)

Index